THE ESSENCE OF
AFRO-CUBAN PERCUSSION
AND DRUM SET

INCLUDES
THE RHYTHM SECTION
Parts for Bass, Piano, Guitar
Horns & Strings

by ED URIBE

Rhythms
Songstyles
Techniques
Applications

THE ESSENCE OF AFRO-CUBAN PERCUSSION AND DRUM SET

Book design, typesetting, music engraving, and
photo editing by Dancing Planet

Audio CD recorded and produced by Ed Uribe
at Dancing Planet, Cresskill, NJ

Instruments played by Ed Uribe

Photographs by Gildas Bocle

Copyright © MCMCXVI, MMVI Alfred Publishing Co., Inc.
All rights reserved. Printed in USA.

ISBN-10: 1-57623-619-6
ISBN-13: 978-1-57623-619-2

About the Author

In the process of earning his degree from the world-renowned Berklee College of Music, Ed Uribe so impressed his professors that they invited him to join their ranks. In the fifteen years since, he has developed the curriculum for the school's Latin Percussion Program. He now oversees that program and serves as a primary professor in the electronic percussion curriculum. His expertise in these areas has led to constant work as an educator, author, artist, clinician, and composer throughout the world.

Ed has lived in South America and also toured Latin America and the Caribbean extensively, both as a performer and a student of the music and culture, studying local and indigenous rhythms, which he shares with his students. In addition to his busy class schedule at Berklee, Ed is a guest educator at the New England Conservatory of Music and has appeared as an educational clinician at over 50 universities worldwide.

His studies in South America and the Caribbean have resulted in two books and videos on Brazilian and Afro-Cuban Percussion and Drum Set published by Warner Bros. Publications. Ed has also written extensive educational material on Latin percussion and Afro-Cuban drumming.

In addition to teaching classes and writing, Ed pursues an active freelance career performing with major artists throughout the world. These have included Ray Barretto, Paquito D'Rivera, Randy Brecker, Michel Camilo, George Coleman, Tania Maria, Donald Byrd, Dave Samuels, David Friedman, Claudio Roditi, Andy Narell, Gary Burton, and the Toshiko Akiyoshi-Lew Tabakin Orchestra, among others.

His skill and knowledge as a performer have earned him endorsement contracts with Zildjian Cymbals, Pearl Drums, Afro Percussion, and Vic Firth Sticks. These contracts allow him to work on behalf of these companies as a spokesperson, performer, and clinician, sending him around the world for featured performances at every major jazz festival, NAMM, university clinics, and PASIC.

One of the first experts on MIDI and electronic percussion, Ed works as a MIDI clinician and consultant. He performs solo concerts of his own compositions, and does programming and production work for various artists and studios. Ed also composes and produces music for video, television, advertising and film, and creates multimedia works for education and advertising.

Originally from San Francisco, Ed currently makes his home in New York.

ACKNOWLEDGMENTS AND DEDICATION

It is sometimes easy to lose sight of what a wonderful thing it is to be able to play and teach music as my livelihood, and I am indebted and grateful to many people for helping me realize this goal. Most importantly I would like to thank my teachers Ed Valencia, John Rae, Gary Chaffee, Alan Dawson and Dean Anderson for helping me develop the skills necessary for having a happy life in music. This book is dedicated to you. My gratitude also goes to all the other teachers and musicians that I've studied and played with, and from whom I've learned so much about this music.

Thanks to my colleagues in the Berklee College Percussion Department. It is a privilege to be able to work alongside you all in teaching music. Special thanks to Mike Ringquist and John Ramsey for sharing valuable information with me from their personal research and study of Afro-Latin Music.

Thanks to Lennie D. and John King at Zildjian, Scott, and Richie at Pearl Drums, and the Vic Firth family for all their support over the years. Also thanks to Tim Self at Opcode Systems. To Tony, Mike, and all the guys at O. DiBella Music in Bergenfield, NJ, thanks for everything. You guys are the greatest! Thanks to Gerry and Ben James at Interworld Music for helping me get this book started.

Special thanks to Sandy Feldstein at Warner Bros. for making this project possible. Also at Warner, thanks to Joe Testa, Gayle Giese, Jewyl Esthes, Debbie Cavalier, and all the great staff who helped with this project. Last but certainly not least, my deepest thanks to my wife Robin for the long hours spent editing the book and for her endless support of all my endeavors.

Table of Contents

Part I~The Percussion Instruments

Part II~The Rhythm Section and the Songstyles

Part III~The Drum Set

ABOUT THIS PRESENTATION

THIS MATERIAL IS A "FORMAL" ORGANIZATION OF MUSICAL STYLES THAT HAVE SURVIVED AND PROGRESSED FROM GENERATION TO GENERATION THROUGH A VERY "INFORMAL" PROCESS—THAT OF AN oral tradition. This is not music that evolved from or was taught through schools or formal education as we know and perceive it (even though today it is taught that way in Cuba as well as in many other parts of the world). It did not have the orthodox methodologies that the study of European classical instruments—piano, strings, woodwinds and brass—had (even though those methods have now also been developed for teaching these instruments and this music).

Regardless of the fact that this music is now taught in schools and specific methods are in place for learning these styles and instruments, this is primarily and fundamentally the study of a culture and of musical folklore. You are, in essence, learning a language—the language of Afro-Cuban rhythms and songstyles. In learning any language, you study its mechanical components, the alphabet and its pronunciation, how to form words from those letters, how to make sentences from the words and so on. The study of this material is the same. You will practice basic techniques and fundamental rhythms. These are the components. You'll then practice putting them together to develop a vocabulary in this idiom. This will enable you to play specific songstyles and to improvise in this idiom. In the serious study of a language, your goal is to speak, understand and be understood—to "speak like a native." Your final goal in the study of a musical style should be the same. You should strive to play this music as if you had learned it in its purest, handed-down, oral tradition. Then you can truly feel you know how to play a style. The goal of this study is *not* to learn how to play a particular Mambo or Songo or Guaguancó *beat*, but to learn how to *play* Mambo and Songo and Guaguancó, (along with the many other styles presented). There is a big difference between playing a beat and playing a style.

While I've stated that this music hasn't evolved through formal education, this doesn't mean that there are no guidelines for its study. Quite the contrary. There is great order and a very systematic procedure. For example, in certain folkloric styles—such as that of the *Batá* drumming traditions for the *Santeria* rituals—there is a very rigid, demanding, and competitive tradition of study in which a *Santero* (priest of *Santeria* and most likely a master drummer) takes on a student—his disciple—and teaches and indoctrinates him into the practices through a very rigid process of study of the oral tradition. This style of music is not something you just decide to study, and then you get your teacher of choice by making a phone call. You are chosen for this study based on both skill and commitment to the tradition. Santeria and Batá drumming is a sacred tradition, and its study is approached with great respect, dedication, and methodical study and practice.

In the secular/folkloric styles, as well as in the commercial styles of this music, one learns in the same oral tradition—from the masters and other great players that came before. This is how one studies all musical styles, but in these styles it was—up until very recently—the only way to study. It was very difficult to get anyone to teach you anything unless you were innately a great player. Otherwise you were generally left to deal on your own. Today more players are availing themselves to teaching, there is more material being published on this subject and there are even some official degree-granting college programs teaching this music and instruments. Of course if you make your way to Cuba you can study it from the source. There are many people to study with and their conservatories teach their musical folklore. Regardless of which path you end up on, the end result must be that you know how to play your instruments and these songstyles "correctly." (This word itself also opens a can of worms, since there can be several versions of the "correct" way to play certain things in the various Latin cultures). Nonetheless, as musicians we all basically know what playing a style "correctly" means. It means you have the necessary chops on each instrument to be able to play music with the traditional phrasing of an idiom, and to know enough about it that you can improvise meaningfully, and have enough vocabulary and confidence to handle the wide variety of musical situations that may present themselves. To have this ability you must approach this material and your study of this music not as the theoretical study, but as if you were being taught these rhythms by ear and you then had to memorize and practice them until you can play them in your sleep. That's how the oral tradition works. Unfortunately those of us who were not fortunate enough to be handed down the traditions have to work backwards to it by *learning* this written material, and then going back to the source and listening and analyzing with our ears to learn how it really should be played. This is the only way to learn how to truly play "correctly."

Latin American cultures are generally very nationalistic and for lack of a

better word, "macho." This characteristic is certainly prevalent in the music and in the approach to playing the drums. There is no glory, media glitz or peer respect in being a lightweight player—like there often is in American pop culture. In this type of drumming the more prevalent attitude is that there are those who can play and then there's everybody else. You either play or you don't, and if you don't, you have nothing to say. This is not meant to intimidate. It is merely a fact to accept. *Two thoughts on this*: as a musician and a player, a high level of playing should be what you strive for, and though this approach is a little rough, it should inspire you to work towards this. If on the other hand you are not striving for this level of playing and are interested in learning about this music purely out of interest, or maybe just setting out to learn it, don't let this discourage you. You can deal with this music on any level you want, but keep some perspective on the depth of this material and the players out there, and on how much there is to learn.

This book is divided into three parts. *Part I* deals exclusively with the percussion instruments. There is an individual section for each instrument that includes a description of the instrument and its traditional uses, the techniques of playing it and various rhythmic patterns for the more common styles. These include various dance styles such as the *Son, Mambo* and *Cha-Cha* as well as folkloric styles such as the various *Rumbas—Guaguancó, Yambú and Columbia*, the *Conga, Mozambique, Songo, 6/8 styles—Bembé, Guiro* and many others. Applications of these instruments and rhythms in styles such as jazz and funk are also included.

Part II addresses the rhythm section and includes parts for the bass, piano, the tres (a small guitar-like instrument with three sets of strings—two per set—that is the key instrument of the *Son*) and guitar, horns and strings. This section also presents the songstyles and the various ensembles that play them. Various styles and ensembles are presented with brief historical information and the instrumentation used. It is important to understand the makeup of the various ensembles and the function of each player within the ensemble. Although the emphasis and majority of the musical examples deal with the percussion, there are examples of all of the instruments' parts. There is also a description and example of a musical arrangement showing basic arranging practices for a standard Latin piece—what might be called a Salsa chart. It is important to know the basic construction of an arrangement and the function of each instrument and player at each section of an arrangement.

You should practice with the rhythm section examples provided on the audio portion of the book by playing them into a sequencer and cutting and pasting so you have a vamp or tune of your liking to play along with. If you don't have a sequencer or some piano chops, you should ask a friend to record versions of these onto a tape machine and you can practice playing with the tape. *If you don't have anyone to play this music with, playing with commercial recordings is essential.*

Part III addresses the drum set. Before beginning, and as you practice the drum set parts, refer back to Parts I & II until you thoroughly know at least the basic rhythms of each percussion part. Remember, the drum set was not originally a part of this music and each component of any rhythm played on the drum set evolved directly from a percussion part. When you practice the drum set, put yourself in a percussion oriented frame of mind. To capture the essence of these styles in your drum set

playing you must draw from what the percussion plays. The more you can do this, the more authentic you will sound.

The audio recording includes examples from each section. Use it as your guide for how the instruments should sound and how the rhythms should be phrased. The recording follows the order of the book.

The rhythmic patterns and material included in this book are not simply technical exercises. They are the actual patterns played in this style. The approach of this book is for you to learn the techniques of the percussion, drum set and all the instruments, through learning the musical styles; thus really learning the instrument's role in this music. While this compilation of material is by no means exhaustive, it is a reasonably thorough presentation of the role of these instruments in this genre. Combine this material with listening to and studying as many recordings and live performances as possible. Even if you have no intention of actually performing this music, what you can gain by exposure to and assimilation of it is of tremendous value, especially to the drummer/percussionist. Further study of the songstyles and arrangements themselves—separate from the drum set and percussion parts—will only enhance your performance on these instruments, so don't be afraid to spend some time getting totally into the piano or bass or some other instrument, or even learning how to arrange and compose in these styles. This will only open other doors to your playing on the percussion.

Before delving into the musical examples, here is a very brief history of the development of this music and my connection to it.

BACKGROUND INFORMATION

MY COMING TO PLAY AFRO-CUBAN AS WELL AS OTHER LATIN STYLES OF MUSIC DEVELOPED FROM BEING EXPOSED TO AND STUDYING THEM ON DRUM SET. I then worked backwards to the folkloric rhythms and the percussion instruments—pretty much the opposite of the way it's normally done by the traditional players—percussion first, then on to drum set. While growing up I heard a lot of music at home that I'll generically call Latin—Son, Mambo, Rumba, Cumbia, Tango and all the music that later became known as Salsa—though at the time I didn't know specifically what it was and paid no particular attention to it. Some moved me and some didn't and it wasn't until years later that I realized that I had been exposed to music from much of Latin America and began to feel the advantages of having had this exposure.

On the streets I heard Latin music everywhere, but I couldn't identify the styles or playing in any specific way either. At that time—the late sixties to mid-seventies— San Francisco had many musicians that were involved with integrating Latin—particularly Afro-Cuban styles—with rock and funk styles. (Groups like Santana, Malo and Azteca come to mind.) Many younger rock-oriented players were tapping some of the older resident Latin heavies like Armando Peraza and Francisco Aguabella for their sound and this combination was developing a new sound. Everyone was into this stuff and it was a great place to be at that time because Afro-Latin music and the live music scene was thriving there. The melding of the contemporary rock sounds with the Latin stuff is much like the marriage of Jazz and Latin in the '40s with people like Dizzy Gillespie and Chano

Pozo, Machito and the birth of CuBop and Latin jazz, only now the result was Latin rock and Latin funk. Also, leaders of established traditional Latin bands—Tito Puente, Ray Barretto, Mongo Santamaria and Eddie Palmieri were also involved in integrating some of these newer sounds with their styles. The Mozambique appeared in the '60s and these bands were incorporating that and some Rumba styles with their sound and that was all influencing the Latin rock scene. This Latin-influenced music sounded different and I thought some was very hip, but being primarily a drum set player at that time, I was still more into the Funk, R & B, Soul and Rock sounds prevailing at the time. Aside from this, I had no other exposure or connection to this music. My experience was pretty much peripheral.

I mention this because in my involvement with performing and recording Latin-American musics, I've come across some attitudes and philosophies that say you cannot play these styles "correctly"—whatever that means—unless you are "born into it," from a certain country and the like. This tends to sometimes discourage people from even trying to learn. It's true that to some degree you are a product of your culture and your time. If you had been born into the musical family of ensembles like the Muñequitos de Matanzas or Grupo Afro-Cuba you undoubtedly would have a certain familiarity, intrinsic skills and a musical vocabulary that would be hard to match—even with very concentrated study. But this can be said about any style. If you had grown up around Philly Joe and Max and Art instead of around Ginger Baker and Keith Moon your swing would be a whole lot deeper. Nonetheless, you can learn how to play great Jazz and not have come up in that time—there's certainly plenty of evidence of that—and with very committed study, Afro-Latin styles and instruments can also be learned and your playing developed to a very high level. If you can groove you can learn any style. It's just like learning a language. You have to be around it, live it, and speak it enough, and you'll start to sound like a native. There will always be people who will play styles better and more traditionally than you. Accept that as a given and try to learn from these people. In the end, your best lessons will be from people like this who are willing to show you how to play, and help you understand more clearly. If someone discourages you just move on.

When I first began taking drum lessons, I was shown, among other things, Brazilian styles like Bossa Nova, Samba and Baiaó, and Afro-Cuban styles like the Cha-Cha and Mambo. Initially these were presented just as "rhythms every drummer should know," because you need to know them to gig. I was—at first—just shown the basic patterns, but these rhythms were so different from any of the other styles I was practicing on the drums. At first they felt awkward. They didn't feel like they were from the drum set and of course, I later found out they weren't. The syncopations in the rhythms felt so different and so good. I started to check out recordings and to go see this music played live, and as I mentioned earlier, there was plenty around to see. This music made me move my body in such a different way. I kept checking out more music and I kept asking to be shown more of these grooves and it hasn't stopped to this day. While at that time most of these rhythms were merely hip grooves on the drum set, it wasn't long before I got completely immersed in the different styles and percussion instruments. My first musical tour to the Caribbean and then to South America was in 1982. I was to play there six weeks and return home. Instead I

returned almost a year later. I've since had the good fortune to perform in Latin and South America extensively, and every time I go I inevitably come back amazed at some new rhythm or instrument I was exposed to. New York also is, and always has been, a spawning ground for major developments in the Afro-Latin idioms, and being based here for the last few years has allowed me the opportunity to both professionally and informally interact with this musical community as well—a wonderful opportunity for exposure, learning, and performance. This book is the result of my experience with this fascinating world of Afro-Latin music—as a student, performer, educator and fan.

In the course of exploring and performing this music I've discovered an unfortunate fact. Many Americans, and even more unfortunately, many American musicians, perceive everything south of the Texas border to be just plain *Latin*—one big generic category with a singular identity. Not only is this perception grossly imprecise, but for a musician it is extremely limiting. As a musician it is important to be aware of the vast differences that exist between the various cultures in Latin America and the Caribbean, especially if you are a drummer/percussionist. There is an endless pool of musical information to tap into that—at a minimum—can give you many new ideas for your drum set playing and with full exposure completely change the face of your approach to drums and percussion and maybe your whole life.

The music of Latin America shares three common cultural elements: the various African cultures of the slaves (brought there by the Europeans), the folklore of the native Indians, and the European traditions of whatever power dominated a particular region between the fifteenth and eighteenth centuries. Aside from this, there are countless distinctions to be noted and countless musical styles to explore.

Following is a list of musical styles from various Latin American and Caribbean countries:

Argentina: Tango, Milonga, Zamba, Chacarera

Uruguay: Candombe, Zamba

Columbia: Cumbia, Bambuco

Venezuela: Joropo, Valse Venezolano

Ecuador: Pasillo, Taquerari

Chile: Cueca

Peru: Guaino, Vals Peruano, La Marinera

Andean Styles: Baguala, Carnavalito, Vidala

Mexico: Musica Ranchera, Mariachi, Mayan Marimba Styles and forms of Danzón, Joropo Mejicano

Trinidad: Calypso, Soca

Jamaica: Reggae

Brazil: Bossa Nova, Samba, Baiaó, Frevo, Maracatú, Chorinho, Capoeira, Candomble, Afoxé, Xote, Maxixe

Puerto Rico: Bomba, Plena

Dominican Republic: Merengue

Haiti: Merengue, Charanga & Tumba Francesa

Cuba: Son, Mambo, Cha-Cha, Guajira, Bembé, Abakuá, Guiro, Danzón, Rumba Guaguancó, Yambú and Columbia, Batá rhythms, Songo, Conga and Comparsa, Mozambique and countless others.

These are just a few of the many musical styles and cultures to explore. All of these have some very unique percussion instruments or rhythmic vocabulary and looking into them will undoubtedly enhance your musical perspective and certainly expand your rhythmic vocabulary. Next, we'll examine some historical developments of the Afro-Latin cultures and their music.

DEVELOPMENTS IN THE WEST INDIES~THE CARIBBEAN

THROUGHOUT HISTORY CULTURES HAVE MERGED AND FORMED NEW, OR AT THE VERY LEAST, INTEGRATED FOLKLORE. UNFORTUNATELY MUCH OF THIS MERGING WASN'T A willful, cooperative effort between cultures. It was generally forced upon certain peoples by stronger, imperialist powers whose motives were certainly not to develop new cultural traditions, but to capitalize on the resources of other lands. History shows that in many instances this imposition of power has completely annihilated entire native peoples, or has left cultures in conflicts that have lasted generations. The transferring of people from their homeland, (as was done with West Africans made slaves in the fifteenth through seventeenth centuries by European powers), or the drawing of a geographic boundary through the land of a people existing intact, have forced cultures to create new homelands and acclimate to the practices of unfamiliar peoples. Undoubtedly these situations caused much suffering, and while this can hardly be seen as positive, the forced geographical integration (there really was no social integration for quite some time) planted seeds that gave birth to musical styles that have shaped the development and direction of music throughout the world.

In the course of these forced integrations generally a couple of things happened. The empowering culture enslaved and imposed its customs on the native people of a desired land often under the guise of religious education. They then brought other already enslaved people for labor purposes in the exploitation of what they now viewed as their new land. While the ruling powers were working to reorient these enslaved people to their customs, and in many instances forbidding them to continue their own cultural practices, the slaves undertook to continue their traditions in whatever way they could. Each ethnic group carrying on its own practices in the new land, and the exposure of the various cultures to each other, resulted in a tremendous blending of music, religion, languages and social customs that spawned the beginning of one of the richest and most influential musical cultures in the world.

This all began taking place in the early 1500s as Spain, Portugal, France and England began colonizing the "new world"—what is now known as the Caribbean region, the West Indies and Latin America. Of these four great European powers, Portugal had the least influence in the Caribbean, and established its largest colonies and slave trades in Brazil. Spain, England, France (and later the Netherlands) all made strong marks in the Caribbean with Spain making the strongest marks in colonizing Cuba, Puerto Rico and the Dominican Republic. Spain colonized many other lands as well but these three regions are where the most prominent developments have taken place in the evolution of Afro-Latin music. (Another key element was the French presence in Haiti, to be discussed in the following section.)

Upon the European arrival to these new lands, the explorers found an indigenous population of numerous tribes of Indians that had existed in this area for thousands of years. (Historical accounts show two to three million inhabitants, dating their migration towards these regions back 40,000 years.) In a very short time these people were enslaved and many eliminated. The enslaved native Indians did not provide the Europeans with the labor force necessary for their exploitation of these lands and thus began the influx of the African Slaves.

The integration of the Spaniards, French, English (and later the Dutch) with the African slaves and the native Indians gave birth to what has over time come to be known (generically) as Afro-Caribbean, Afro-Antillean or Latin American music—terms which take into account musics from this entire (new world) region and from all ethnic descents. Since the topic of this book is Afro-Latin, and particularly Afro-Cuban music (and its derivatives), we'll now focus more specifically on the developments of this region and culture.

DEVELOPMENTS IN CUBA

CUBA IS THE LARGEST ISLAND IN THE CARIBBEAN. ITS NAME IS DERIVED FROM THE INDIAN WORD *Cubanacan*, MEANING "CENTER PLACE." THE FIRST INHABITANTS OF CUBA WERE THE TAINO, SIBONEY AND CARIB Indians—tribes who were basically annihilated by the Spanish. Under the rule of Spain, Cuba grew to be the largest sugar producing region in the world. Sugar was an extremely valuable commodity in the 1600s and 1700s and the national economies of Spain and other European colonizing nations were reaping tremendous profits from this trade. When the local Indian populations were nearly eliminated and the enslaved Indians that remained did not provide the labor force the Spanish needed to work the vast sugar cane plantations, the influx of thousands of African slaves began. From the early 1500s to the mid-1800s approximately 3.5 million Africans survived the crossing to the "new world" regions. (This is five to six times more than were brought to North America during its period of slavery). This began the merging of the native Indians, Africans from a variety of regions (though mostly from the northwestern and central parts of Africa), and the Spanish settlers.

Cuban music evolved from these three cultures—Indian, African and Spanish—but of the three, the Indian influence is the least pronounced. The minor role Indian music played in the musical evolution was due in part to the Jesuits who, upon their arrival in Cuba, set out to reeducate the Indians, teaching them to practice European customs and teaching them to practice Christianity; thus suppressing their cultural and religious practices. This reeducation was part of the mission of the explorers in the new world. Although the Indians had a long-standing folklore, they were often displaced as lands were colonized and they tended to lose their cultural traditions in their diaspora and in their integration with the whites. The Indian population in Cuba is virtually nonexistent today.

The Spanish also sought to suppress the cultural practices of the Africans by imposing, among other things, Christian practices and the Spanish language. For the Africans, music and drumming was an integral part of daily life. Their religious rituals also involved them extensively. The Africans were more defiant in their struggle to maintain their own cultural practices and secretly continued to worship their own gods by sometimes giving their own deities the names of Christian saints and continuing their musical practices through this obfuscated worship. This form of worship gave rise to the practice of *Santeria* in this region. (*Santeria* is derived from the religion of the *Yoruban* people from Nigeria.) These worship rituals and ceremonies involved extensive drumming and chanting. *Batá* drums were and are used for these rituals to contact the *Orichas*—the deities of the *Santeros*. In this drumming tradition—which continues today in Cuba and other parts of the Caribbean and Latin America —one can hear the essence of this West African influence.

The African people succeeded in maintaining their customs in a form more indigenous to their cultural roots. This is due to several reasons. First, the re-education the explorers were attempting with the native Indians was not such a priority with the Africans. They were enslaved and their education was not part of the agenda. The only effort made was to not allow them to practice their folkloric customs, but they were not as closely observed as the Indians and thus were able to continue some of their rituals. Second, throughout history all European conquerors made an effort to keep their African slaves from practicing their customs (with the northern Protestant Europeans being the most oppressive) and the Spanish were no exception. But although they made efforts to suppress the religious practices of the Africans, they were more tolerant of the African cultural practices than their northern European counterparts. This may in part be due to the fact that the Iberian Peninsula had had interaction with the North Africans—mostly in the form of wars and enslavement between the Moors and the Christians—that dates back to the twelfth century and were thus more accustomed to some integration. Another reason for the tolerance and accelerated integration between the blacks and Hispanics (versus the Protestant whites and enslaved blacks in North America), may have to do with the fact that the Spanish explorers, as well as the Portuguese and French, were mostly male, (versus the migration of entire families of English Protestant backgrounds to North America where integration was virtually nonexistent). Thus their tendency to integrate, (even if only for propagation), was greater than that of the northern Europeans, who, having emigrated with their entire families, generally disdained any type of integration and went through great efforts to suppress and segregate from the African culture. The southern European explorers and settlers, to some degree, had no choice but to mix and the Cuban melting pot began.

The Spanish brought with them the European melodic and harmonic traditions. These included Spanish, Portuguese, French, and some northern European influences. Elements of both sacred and secular music were present in their melodies, harmonies, polyphony in the vocal music, and certain verse-chorus and chant song structures. This was basically the music of the European (Spanish) courts and later these elements directly influenced the development of the Son and the Danza Habanera which led to the Danzón. (Apart from the Rumba styles, the Danzón and the Son are the most significant musical forms in the development of Afro-Latin popular music.) Another form of folkloric European music also made its way to these regions. This was the music of the peasant classes, that of the Spanish workers that came to these regions as laborers. Though a step above the slaves in the social hierarchy, they nonetheless were poor peasants—campesinos—but brought with them their own music, primarily in the form of songs. These songs—*canciones* or *trovas*—also later directly influenced the development of the Son (and later other popular music styles) with their lyric style and verse-chorus structure—the *decima* and *estribillo*—which became the lyric structure of the Son. The accompaniment to the *canciones* of the *campesinos* were played on stringed instruments (early guitars) also brought by the Spanish to these regions. These instruments later directly influenced the development and use of the Tres—a small guitar-like instrument with three sets of strings (two per set) that is the key instrument of the *Son*. These early Spanish guitars also influenced the development of the Cuatro (like the Tres but with four sets of strings and more indigenous to Puerto Rico) and later the six-string guitar styles. Certain percussion instruments such as bass drums and snare drums were brought through the European military and evolved and were integrated with certain folkloric styles. An example of this is in the Comparsa's use of the *bombos* (bass drums) and *cajas* (snare drums) during the Cuban Carnaval parades. These parades initially evolved from the European military parades that took place during festivities. (The Brazilian Carnaval parades evolved from the same source.) Other folkloric European instruments included the *pandereta* (tambourine)—an extremely popular instrument in the Basque regions of Spain as well as in Portugal and France. (This instrument found its way and greatly influenced certain Puerto Rican folkloric styles as well. The Panderetas became the hand drum used in the *Plena*.) Another folkloric Spanish songstyle that greatly influenced the Rumba styles was the Flamenco and the Rumba Flamenca. Last, but certainly not least, the Spanish brought their language, which became and remains the primary language of Latin America except for Brazil.

The African slaves brought with them predominantly vocal and rhythmic elements as well as drums and percussion instruments. (The majority of the instruments were not actually brought, but recreated over time by the displaced slaves. Many were simply improvised or created from whatever was around them to use for performing their music.) These early instruments and those that were recreated over time served as the origin for the majority of the instruments that are now an integral part of Latin-American music. The Spanish initially brought African slaves from their colonies in northwestern regions of Africa. Later, as slave trading to the "new world" increased, many were also brought from central regions, in particular what is now Zaire. This greatly expanded the variety of African cultural practices present in the region, with the Abakuá, Dahomean, Congolese, and Yorubaland cultures all now present in the geographical area. Both sacred and secular elements are also present in the African contributions.

The call-and-response vocal styles and drumming of the Yoruban people (from present-day Nigerian regions) influenced many Cuban song forms—particularly the *Rumba* styles, and the religious music and dance of this culture is still very present in Afro-Cuban folkloric music. Simultaneous duple and triple meter inflections as well as the layering of various rhythms over an ostinato pulse, are some rhythmic characteristics of African music that are very much the structural foundation of many Afro-Cuban rhythms. Many percussion instruments of African origin—various shakers made of weaved baskets, rattles and shakers made from gourds, single headed conga-like drums, some double-headed drums and scraper-type instruments—gave way to the development of the shekeré, cowbells, conga drums, shakers, bass drums, wood sounds, clave and the like. African musical culture was the most influential in the development of the styles of Cuba and Latin America. It has survived more intact, and is more prevalent in these regions than in any other area of the world away from Africa.

Indian influence, as mentioned before, was less apparent. Nonetheless, contributions in the area of flutes, certain vocal styles, and certain percussion instruments such as rattles and shakers made from gourds and some weaved basket shakers can be traced to Indian roots. Although not as prevalent in the Cuban musical styles that are presented in this text, Indian music is quite present in many western (Amazonian) regions of South America, especially in Brazil and in many of the Andean regions of Ecuador and Peru, as well as some Caribbean regions.

All of these cultural elements combined to form the basis of the musical styles presented in this book. The styles presented are the most prevalent styles in Afro-Cuban music, and some of these have also had a large effect on music throughout the world. Their influence and integration into American styles of jazz, funk, R & B and other popular music is so great that it is almost essential that all musicians become familiar with them. It can safely be said that in the present day, Cuba (along with Brazil and American popular music) has had the greatest influence on popular music throughout the world. Cuba and Brazil—along with Africa—have also had the greatest influence on all types of American music.

The cultural integration of the Spanish and the African resulted in many new song forms. These include the religious and ritual song forms of the *Santeros* and *Batá* drummers, many folkloric styles that developed into what are known as *Rumba* styles—the *Rumba Guaguancó, Yambú* and *Columbia*, which are folkloric song and dance styles, the *Conga* which accompanies the Carnaval march and dance called *Comparsa*, the *Mozambique, Pilón, Songo, Bembé, Guiro* and *Abakuá*. While these styles have a tremendous presence in the Cuban culture, are performed and studied regularly by Cuban musicians and ensembles and are present in the minds of any serious musician that has any awareness of Afro-Latin music, they are more eclectic in nature. Although some—like the Mozambique, Songo, Guaguancó and some generic versions of $\frac{6}{8}$ styles—have become quite popular over the years, they have not had the universal exposure that the Son and its derivatives have.

The most influential style in the evolution of Cuban popular (dance) music and its spread throughout the world is the *Son*. It is the root and predecessor of most Afro-Cuban popular dance forms. From it spawned many other styles that later partially comprised the musical category known as *Salsa,* as well as the Latin-Jazz styles of the 1940s, the dance orchestras of the 1950s and the Latin Bands (*Salsa* and *Orquestas Típicas*) of the 1960s, which continue to the present.

The *Son* developed through a marriage of *Musica Campesina*—Spanish peasant music—and the musics of the African slaves. Its origins can be traced back to the second half of the nineteenth century in the eastern Cuban province of Oriente. Slavery in Cuba was nearing its end—at least on paper—and a further integration of the Spanish and the African cultures began taking place. The predecessor or original Son was the *Changui*. Rural street bands performed this vocal music derived from the Spanish *canciones*, accompanying them with the early form of the *tres*, the *marimbula*—an African derived thumb piano similar to a large Kalimba built onto a large wooden box with an open hole for resonance—the clave, guiro, maraca and bongo. These six instruments—with the vocals—played the first *Sons*—*Changui* style—and created what later became the *Sexteto* ensemble. These *Changui* groups initially played their music for audiences comprised primarily of their own people, but during the later part of the 1800s they continued to develop and gain popularity, and from the Changuis came the established Son groups. (Although the Son groups began to develop a new identity at this point, some Changui groups maintained the original traditions and a small number of them exist to this day—most notably the Grupo Changui. They maintain the original instrumentation—including the marimbula and the original approach to the music.) In the Son groups the marimbula was eventually replaced with the string bass (another instrument called the Botija—a clay jug used to transport olive oil—was also used as a bass instrument before the string bass), a regular six-string guitar also came to be used and musicians began to expand and develop the style. Its popularity continued to grow and by the turn of the twentieth century the *Son* was being played in the Cuban capital of Habana. By the 1920's it was an acknowledged national style. The Sexteto Habanero was a premier ensemble of this style and the most notable individual pioneer of the Son was bassist Ignacio Piñeiro. As musicians continued to experiment and

develop the style, the *Corneta China* (later replaced by the trumpet) was added forming the *Septeto* ensemble. The *Septeto Nacional de Ignacio Piñeiro* is another landmark group in the development of the Son.

The Son style is characterized by a verse-refrain (*decima-estribillo*) vocal style in which the verse (the decima which is a ten line and eight-pulsed form) is sung and followed by a refrain. Then it goes back to the verse and back to the refrain (creating a simple ABAB form), but now the refrain is repeated in a call-and-response fashion. This approach and form led to the *montuno section* of later arrangements of the Son styles. Other distinguishing characteristics are the instrumentation (primarily that of the sexteto and septeto ensembles), the clave and layering of the rhythmic patterns of the clave, percussion and tres and the bass.

During this period another significant musical event took place—the spawning of the Danzón. The slave rebellion in Haiti took place in 1791, and with slavery eliminated in Cuba earlier in this same period, a large number of Haitian slaves and working-class poor migrated to the eastern Cuban province of Oriente. Haiti had been colonized by the French and the same developments that have been described thus far pertaining to the Spanish and African integrations in Cuba, were practically paralleled in Haiti by the African and French. These Haitian slaves brought with them their music and cultural practices which were now a result of the merging of the French and African cultures (some Africans from different regions of Africa than those brought to Cuba by the Spanish), and a new level of integration began taking place. Musical styles brought by these people included the *Contredanse, Merengue, Tumba Francesa, Vodu* and *Gagá*. These were all to influence the development of Cuban styles. (There are groups in this region that still maintain the initial traditions that were born in this period, most notably the Grupo Locosia.)

19

The (French) *Contredanse* (developed in Haiti during the eighteenth century and then brought to Cuba during the slave rebellion of 1792) was first developed in Cuba as the Danza, Danza Habanera (or Habanera) and finally the Danzón. Early groups interpreting the contradanzas consisted of woodwind and brass instruments, strings and a percussion section with a *Guiro* and the *Timbales Criollos—Creole Tympani*—which were European concert tympani. These were the predecessors of the *timbales*. (Note that except for the guiro the instrumentation is basically comprised of European instruments.) While the *Son* was developing and becoming very popular among the lower and middle classes of Cuba, these *danzas* were gaining popularity among the Cuban upper class. By the late nineteenth and early twentieth centuries, these styles were being played in the ballrooms and dance halls of the high society. Groups which became known as *Orquestas Tipicas* performed the *Habanera, Ritmo de Tango* and the *Contradanza* and continued to develop the instrumentation and compositional style. The early 1900s gave birth to the Charanga Francesa. These were smaller versions of the *Orquestas Tipicas*. They made significant contributions and developments in establishing the compositional and arranging approach and in standardizing the instrumentation of this style. They incorporated wooden flutes (and later the standard flute), string section (violins & cellos), string bass, guiro, and *pailitas* (a smaller version of the European tympani then making their way to becoming the timbales). (The addition of the piano took place in the late 1930s and early '40s.) These ensembles and instrumentation became known as *Orquestas Tipicas* (now called *Charangas)* and were the traditional interpreters of these styles. Between 1900 and 1925 these groups gained extreme popularity in the ballrooms of the aristocracy and paved the way for another most significant development in Afro-Latin music. (A most notable and "must-check-out" group of this tradition is Orquesta Aragón.)

The basic form of the Danzón is an ABAC form with the A section (called the *Paseo),* the B section (the principal flute melody), a repeat of the *Paseo*—another A, and the C section (the trio, a soli of sorts for the strings). In the late 1930s and early '40s a bassist by the name of Israel "Cacháo" Lopez, while playing with a group called *Arcaño y sus Maravillas,* (a group led by flutist Antonio Arcaño), developed a D section to the Danzón called the *Nuevo Ritmo,* creating an ABACD form. This section was a vamp or improvisational section. A cowbell was added to the timbales and a conga drum was added to the ensemble. These instruments initially were played only during this section. This *Nuevo Ritmo* helped spawn the *Montuno* section of present day Salsa arranging, as well as the *Mambo* and *Cha-Cha* styles.

The Son and Danzón, while certainly having common threads of cultural influence in their evolution, developed in separate worlds (although they did have some chronologically parallel developments in that both became established and recognized forms in the early twentieth century). The Son evolved in the streets and rural areas, and the Danzón in the ballrooms of the high society. Now there was to be another integration of cultures. Not only were elements of these two styles to merge, but a third culture and musical style had entered the picture—Jazz and Swing and the scene in New York. This led to the birth of a new type of Cuban or Afro-Latin group that was not only a product of its own culture but was being greatly influenced by the swing and big band orchestras of Duke Ellington, Count Basie, Chick Webb, and the like. The new *Conjuntos* and *Orquestas* that resulted from this influence created the Mambo dance craze of the 1940s that took over New York and elsewhere. BeBop was developing at a rapid pace and gaining popularity—especially among musicians. This too melded with Afro-Cuban music in New York to form

CuBop. All the while the folkloric song forms—the Conga, Rumba and religious/folkloric styles—continued to evolve and influence developments in Cuba, but these had yet to gain the widespread popularity of the Son and Danzón. But before continuing with these developments in New York let's introduce another significant element into this picture.

DEVELOPMENTS IN PUERTO RICO

PUERTO RICO WAS A COLONY OF SPAIN UNTIL 1898 WHEN IT BECAME INDEPENDENT. ONE YEAR LATER IT WAS MADE A COLONY OF THE UNITED STATES. ON THE WHOLE Puerto Rican folkloric styles have not had as great an influence in the development of specific Afro-Latin song forms as the Cuban songstyles. This is due in part to a lack of African and Hispanic integration in the early forms of this Puerto Rican music. A clear line can almost always be drawn between the upper and lower economic classes of any society, and Puerto Rico, being no exception, has always maintained a wide gap between its *haves* and *have-nots*—with the *haves* being mostly whites of Spanish decent and the *have-nots* being mostly blacks of African descent. This kept a wide gap between the early forms of Puerto Rican music, which tended to be either heavily Spanish-influenced forms—varieties of the *danza, ritmo tango, aquinaldo*—or heavily African-influenced forms such as the *Bomba* and *Plena*. Though the upper classes referred to all African-derived songstyles generically as "bomba," there is a specific musical style called *Bomba* with very strong African roots, and it is a mainstay of Afro-Puerto Rican folklore, along with the *Plena*. In the '40s and '50s both styles were adapted for dance bands and gained wider appeal. They also became more influential in other styles of Afro-Latin music.

Puerto Rico has been tremendously influential in its contribution of many great composers, instrumentalists and bandleaders, who became some of the greatest interpreters of the Cuban styles—many of them first-generation New Yorkers. In the 1920s the United States granted Puerto Rico citizenship status, and thus began a tremendous influx of Puerto Ricans to the New York area. Most settled in or near Harlem, and in turn began another integration of musical cultures. These communities continued to grow and provide one of the largest audiences for Afro-Latin music. Later, after the Cuban missile crisis and the resulting embargo against Cuba, when all the movement between Cuba and New York ceased, these Puerto Rican musicians and bandleaders were almost solely responsible for the continued flourishing of Afro-Latin music in New York, and what eventually became known as Salsa.

DEVELOPMENTS IN THE DOMINICAN REPUBLIC

THE DOMINICAN REPUBLIC LIES ON THE EASTERN HALF OF THE ISLAND CALLED HISPAÑOLA, WITH HAITI COMPRISING THE WESTERN HALF OF THE ISLAND. Haiti was colonized by the French, while the Dominican Republic by the Spanish. The proximity of this region to Haiti accounts for the French/Haitian influence in the development of the music of the Dominican

Republic—particularly the *Merengue*—its most popular songstyle. This quick $\frac{2}{4}$ dance style exhibits influences from the French *Contredanse* and *Polka*. The original *Merengue* groups used the accordion, guiro, and a drum called the *tambora*. Today's groups include horn sections and sometimes feature theatrics and dance by the performers. Not only is the merengue one of the most popular dance forms in the Caribbean, but, due to the large population of Dominican immigrants, it is also extremely popular in New York's Latin communities, as well as throughout the world. While this style has not been influential in the development of the other styles addressed in this book, it is derived from many of the same sources and is an integral part of the Latin music scene today.

DEVELOPMENTS IN NEW YORK

IN NEW YORK CITY THE CARIBBEAN IMMIGRANT POPULATION—PARTICULARLY THE CUBAN AND PUERTO-RICAN—CREATED A HAVEN FOR TRADITIONAL AFRO-LATIN MUSICAL FORMS. Not only was New York a spawning ground for significant musical developments in Jazz, but it was also the center where the integration of the Afro-Cuban and American Jazz forms took place. In the 1920s many Cuban and Puerto Rican people migrated to New York and settled in New York City's East Harlem, which came to be known as *El Barrio* and *Spanish Harlem*. This area played a vital role in the thriving developments of Afro-Latin music, its integration with Jazz, and its reaching the large audiences it has enjoyed since the early part of this century. It wasn't long before the music these people brought to New York began to gain widespread attention.

In the 1930s a Cuban song called *El Manisero* (The Peanut Vendor), written by Moisés Simons and performed by Don Azpiazu, (the leader of the *Havana Casino Orchestra*), brought widespread attention to Cuban music. Many new Latin bands began to appear, and with the concurrent fascination with a popular dance hall dance called *Rumba* (*not to be confused with the folkloric Rumba styles*), a Latin music movement had begun. With this music being predominantly music of the blacks and Latins but now also being devoured by the high society of New York, the issue of social class entered the picture and created a division between the musical styles. While the uptown bands were playing a more traditional version of the Latin styles, bands like the *Xavier Cougat Orchestra* were catering to the downtown, upper-class, non-Hispanic crowds. (This same scenario was mirrored in the Jazz big band scene, with the white groups playing for the upper-class white audiences and the black groups playing the black clubs.)

During this same period many Latin and Jazz musicians began crossing over into each other's musical territories. Significant collaborations took place between Latin composer Juan Tizol—composer of *Caravan*—and Duke Ellington, as well as between Cab Calloway, Chick Webb and the innovative Cuban arranger Mario Bauza. In the 1940s, the group *Machito and his Afro-Cubans* surfaced with Bauza as musical director. This group had a tremendous impact on the Latin musical community with it's powerful rhythm section, horn section and Jazz influences brought to the group primarily by Bauza's arrangements. This group paved the way for the *Mambo* and what came to be known as *Latin Jazz*—the two major musical innovations of the 1940s.

The *Mambo,* which was originally the montuno or vamp section of the Son style—the *Estribillo*—and the D section—*Nuevo Ritmo*—of the *Danzón,* became a songstyle itself. This created the Mambo *dance,* and this fast became the new Latin music craze. This remained so through the '50s when two of the most influential bands of that period were formed—the bands of timbalero Tito Puente and vocalist Tito Rodriguez. These bands set a precedent for what the new Latin orchestras would be. This began a period where the leaders of bands modeled after these bands were great instrumentalists, or the groups would feature great soloists, and the music, although it would always feature vocals and songs that appealed to the general public, always featured instrumental solos in the forefront.

While these events were taking place, another landmark integration of styles was happening in New York—the merging of Afro-Latin styles and BeBop music. The resulting style was called *CuBop,* with its biggest and most significant exponent being Dizzy Gillespie. His Carnegie Hall concert in 1947 introducing Cuban conguero *Chano Pozo* marked the birth of a new style that has remained a major musical force to this day. This movement continued into the 1950s with new Latin Jazz bands forming under the direction of instrumentalist-leaders like Mongo Santamaria and Cal Tjader. These bands always featured outstanding drummers like Armando Peraza and maintained the precedent for high level instrumental performance. The popularity of the *Mambo* continued through the 1950s but a new style was soon to come to the forefront.

In Cuba the *Charanga* group *Orquesta Aragón* popularized the *Cha-Cha* (also from the Nuevo Ritmo of the Danzón), which quickly became another one of the most popular Latin dance styles for both the Latin and non-Latin public. While many of the estab-lished Latin orchestras in New York played this as a serious new style, it also had many watered down commercial offshoots which diluted the style and spawned stereotypical Hollywood imitations and the like. Aware of this situation, many Latin musicians began looking to other musical forms to work with. (During this period the *Merengue* style also began to gain popularity.) While Afro-Latin musical styles were certainly well established at this point, they weren't resting on their wide-spread popularity, and new developments were just around the corner.

As the sixties rolled in so did another dance craze—the *Charanga* and *Pachanga.* Charlie Palmieri's *Charanga Duboney* is informally credited with setting off this movement. It wasn't long before other prominent leaders like Mongo Santamaria and Ray Barretto created *Charangas* (also playing a faster *Pachanga* dance style) and dozens of other bands followed. With the excitement that this new style generated one would have thought it would last longer than it did, but as with the previous crazes created by the *Mambo* and *Cha-Cha,* the momentum died. With the gaining popularity of each new movement, so came a certain diluting of the styles and this led to a resurgence—or really a return to—the *Tipico* style. (*Tipico* is a term used for the typical or traditional sound.) The early 1960s marked the beginning of the embargo against Cuba, and the interaction of musicians that had lived so freely for almost fifty years all but died. The mid-sixties found many new bands as well as the already established bands modelling themselves after the old *Son* groups and trying to recapture the feel of an earlier time. While this was a step back to a previous era, the music was not without modern elements and the influences of the integrations it had gone through since the turn of the century. These new "traditional" styles paved the way for what would in the 1970s become the music called *Salsa.* Unfortunately these events would take place without the influx from Cuba for some years.

Salsa itself is not a rhythm or a songstyle but a term used to describe the hybrid of styles that had come to exist. (The term is the Spanish word for sauce and is typically used to describe a hot or spicy sauce.) This became the generic term by which the general population of the world came to know Latin music. To a non-musician and a non-Latin, (and even to many Latins), this term encompasses the total scope of this music. But within the musical community, and to any true aficionado of the style, it is too generic a label, and there quickly came to exist several musical derivations within the category. These essentially amounted to different approaches to playing the various *Salsa* styles. One approach was more traditional, more reminiscent of the early bands of the movement, with the instrumental performance having more of an edge, solo instrumental features, and the lyric content dealing more with the scene on the streets and everyday life. Another approach was more commercial and with no solo features in the instrumental performance. The band only played an accompanying role to the vocals. The focus was on the singing and the persona of the singer, with the lyric content being more romantic and pop-oriented. Still another is a more progressive, jazz-oriented approach, where there is a prevalent role of instrumental performance and improvisation, and the blending of the styles is more far-reaching (although this approach straddles the Salsa and Latin-Jazz labels). Salsa lived particularly well in the 1970s and '80s, and continues to enjoy a very large and culturally varied audience.

Another significant movement that took place in the instrumental arena and runs parallel with both the rumba styles and the Jazz-oriented jam session are the *descargas*. The term translates into the word "unload," and essentially the soloist in a *descarga* is doing just that with their musical ideas. These descargas were vehicles for experimental and improvisational performance, as well as for experimentation with different instrumentations and combinations of musicians. They were often impromptu and unrehearsed, though many great recordings were made, and took the form of both full band as well as exclusively percussion jams in the Cuban *Rumba* tradition. Bassist Israel "Cacháo" Lopez is a must to check out, as are any recordings of percussion groups.

Another level of integration took place in the late sixties and seventies with the merging of the Latin styles and the rock and funk styles prevailing at the time. This integration created the Latin-Rock and Latin-Funk styles of groups like Santana, Malo, Azteca and the like. All the while, Cuban musicians continued to develop their styles and approaches separate from all of this.

FURTHER DEVELOPMENTS IN CUBA

OVER THE LAST THREE TO FOUR CENTURIES THE DEVELOPMENTS OF THIS MUSIC HAVE TAKEN US FROM EUROPE WEST TO THE NEW WORLD, BACK TO AFRICA, AND THEN WEST AGAIN, to the Caribbean and South and Central American regions, then north to New York and to other urban Latin music centers such as San Francisco and Miami. The developments that took place in the 1940s and '50s in New York, Cuba, and elsewhere happened with the direct and active contributions of Cuban musicians, American Jazz musicians and Puerto Rican and other Latin musicians in New York. Unfortunately, the United States severed all interaction and exchange with Cuba back in the early sixties and this led to two separate tracks of development in Afro-Latin music—what was taking place in New York and the Caribbean with Salsa and other related styles, and what was continuing in Cuba. For the last thirty years the paths didn't really meet except for the few musicians that were already in the United States, or those who chose to leave Cuba, and who were steeped in the Cuban folkloric styles. While significant developments continued in the United States during this period, many very significant ones took place in Cuba over the last thirty years. This brings us full circle back to the point of origin of most of these musical styles.

The further development of the dance (Son) styles described earlier continued in Cuba, but what happened there that didn't happen here in the U.S. was that many of the folkloric styles that were earlier described as eclectic have been incorporated into much of the mainstream music. This has led to new approaches to those older styles as well as the birth of many new ones. It has also led to new approaches on the traditional percussion instruments as well as adaptations of many of the rhythms and percussion styles on the drum set. Furthermore, many Cuban musicians have managed to keep abreast of many of the significant developments, musicians, and composers of Jazz, Rock, Funk and Fusion styles, and integrated some of those elements with the folkloric Cuban styles. It seems that many Cuban musicians are much more familiar with our musical vocabulary than we are with theirs. This has led to many innovative

and unique approaches to the drum set, percussion, and really all instruments, as well as composition and arranging styles. Fortunately, through touring in other nations and a committed following of this music, many American as well as European musicians have kept abreast of the further evolution of these styles and the musicians and ensembles responsible for them. A new awareness and interest in this folkloric Cuban music is very much alive. As the influence of Afro-Latin music and the current interest in the culture and traditions of the folkloric styles continues to grow, we can safely expect to see the continuing trend of this music as one of the most evolving and influential musics in the world. Along with the present-day global embracing of music from other regions of Africa, the world's entire musical community will undoubtedly hear styles continue to evolve and develop.

In summary, it would be impossible to list all of the musical styles of Cuba and the Caribbean and present their precise origins and development, as many are even unknown. To present in detail those that are known would require a multi-volume work and a lifetime of study. While I encourage the in-depth research and study of the culture and its many different musical styles, the purpose of this presentation is to learn the most popular and influential of the rhythms, songstyles and percussion instruments, and how to apply them in your musical situations; so we move ahead to the musical examples. For those interested in further study and research there is a list of reading material and other resources at the end of the book.

Maps of Cuba, the West Indies, Africa, The Caribbean, and Related Regions

The following maps show Cuba, the Caribbean, and other regions of Latin America and Africa that are relevant to the material presented in this book. If you were to do further research on these musical styles and cultures, you could pick any of the highlighted regions in Africa and work towards the regions in Latin America and the Caribbean or start in Latin America and work backwards. Either way you look, you'll find that all of the regions shown here—and many others not shown, (since Europe should be included here, particularly Spain and Portugal)—have common threads running through much of their musical cultures.

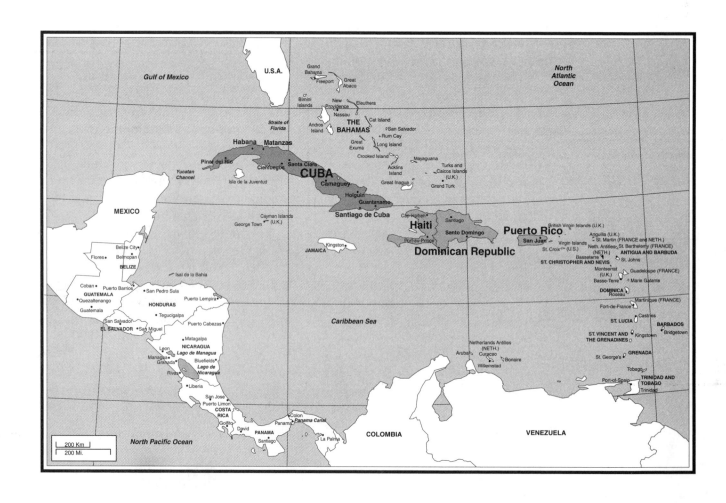

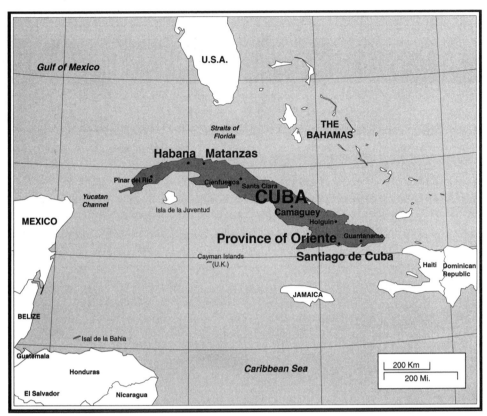

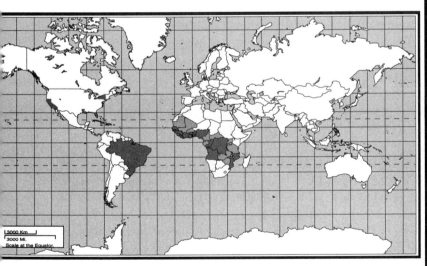

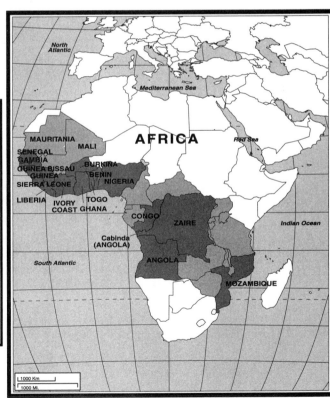

HOW TO LEARN AND PRACTICE THIS MATERIAL

HOW YOU SHOULD APPROACH LEARNING THIS MATERIAL DEPENDS LARGELY ON YOUR TECHNICAL PROFICIENCY ON THE PERCUSSION INSTRUMENTS AND DRUM SET, and on whether or not you have any prior exposure to these styles. It should go without saying, but I'll say this anyway: You have to have your basics down before you can make this material sound right. Learn your basic hand and stick techniques, coordination, foot technique, reading, counting in various time signatures, and more than anything, work on your time. Without the time you have nothing!

If you are primarily a drum set player, you should focus on learning the percussion instruments and rhythms first. As mentioned earlier, the more you can incorporate and draw from the percussion and traditional rhythms, the more you will play the style with an authentic sound. When you're actually playing, the choice becomes yours, but having this knowledge under your belt will enable you to play this way if you want or need to. If you are primarily a percussionist, then you may already know some or all of the material in the first part. You should review it and then work on the drum set. If you don't have basic drum set skills, you may need to do some other technical studies since some of this material requires a considerable degree of hand–foot coordination and stick technique.

If you already play on an intermediate to advanced level, you should get familiar with this material from a more traditional perspective. Practice it, memorize the patterns, and practice improvising with it. Get recordings— there is suggested listening throughout the text—and learn how this material works in the actual music. Your next priority should be to find playing situations where you can apply this material.

If you are more of a beginner or are coming to this music for the first time, my advice is to get a good teacher to guide you. If you don't know how this material is supposed to sound, you need someone to hear you play and tell you if you're on the right track. It is also very important that you listen to recordings of these styles. The recording provided with this book should be your primary guide for how these examples should sound. Next, listen to how these rhythms take place in actual recordings and live performance.

A few things to keep in mind: The music itself will almost always tell you what can and should be played. Hence, patterns, variations, and articulations— other than those in this book—will enter into the picture. In an improvisational idiom, other factors—particularly those of interplay between the musicians—will also dictate what to play. However, many situations will accommodate and may even require the types of rhythms presented here so these should be memorized as the basics. Listen to the recording provided and as many recordings and live performances as you can, and find performance situations in which you can apply this material. Your actual playing and experimentation will be your best learning experience. When you do get an opportunity to play this music with people who really know it, keep your eyes and ears wide open. These will be your most valuable lessons. Pick their brains whenever the situation allows. When practicing, think music not exercises. What you're striving for primarily is a good authentic feel.

PART I

AFRO-CUBAN PERCUSSION

THE PERCUSSION INSTRUMENTS

The following is a list of the more common percussion instruments from Cuba. You must be completely familiar with these instruments to function in ensembles that play Cuban styles. Some of these instruments are also referred to by other names. Some of these alternate names are listed in the glossary.

Clave _____ *Pair of polished wooden sticks used to play the rhythm called Clave.*

Guiro _____ *Scratcher made from a gourd and played (scraped) with a stick to produce rhythm. The Dominican (Merengue) version, the Guira, is made of metal and scraped with a metal Afro-comb.*

Maracas _____ *Pair of dried hide or gourd rattles filled with pebbles, seeds, or rice used to produce rhythm.*

Cowbells

    1. Guataca _____ *The predecessor of the cowbell, it is a hoe blade struck with a large nail or spike.*

    2. Campana/Cencerro _ *Also called the Bongo Bell or Hand Bell, it is the bell played by the Bongo player during the Montuno section of an arrangement and mounted and played by the Palito player during some Rumbas.*

    3. Mambo Bell _____ *The large mounted bell on the Timbales played for the Mambo style and during the Montuno section of arrangements.*

    4. Cha-Cha Bell _____ *The small bell mounted on the timbales and used for the Cha-Cha, Guajira, and similar styles.*

    5. Charanga Bell _____ *The smallest of the mounted timbale bells, it is used for the "Tipico" Charanga style.*

    6. Sartenes _____ *A pair of metal pans (frying pans) welded together and used as bells by the Comparsas during the Cuban Carnaval.*

    7. Brake Drums _____ *Auto brake drums used as metal percussion sounds by the Comparsas in the Cuban Carnival.*

    7. Agogo Bell _____ *Small bells welded together on a flexible metal rod traditionally used by the Comparsas during the Cuban Carnaval.*

Congas~Tumbadoras _____ *Note: The names of each individual drum sometimes varies within different styles.*

    1. Quinto _____ *The highest-pitched and smallest of the set of three drums. The solo drum in Rumba and other folkloric ensembles.*

    2. Segundo _____ *The middle-size and middle-pitched drum of the set of three congas. It is called the Tres Golpes in the Rumba.*

    3. Tumba _____ *The largest and lowest-pitched of the set of three drums.*

Bongos _____ *Pair of small high-pitched drums emanating from the Changui and Son tradition as the original drum of these styles.*

Timbales _____ *Pair of tunable drums mounted on a stand and played with thin dowels and some hand (finger) strokes, developed in Cuba but emanating from the European tympani and Timbales Criollos brought to Cuba after the Haitian revolution of 1791. The set almost always includes* *cowbells, woodblocks, and a cymbal.*

Timbalitos _____ Like the timbales but smaller and higher pitched. Usually added to the larger pair of timbales to make a set of four and used mostly for soloing and improvised variations.

Timbalones _____ Like the timbales but larger in diameter and with a deeper shell. They can be tuned much lower and added to a regular pair for a set of four or tuned on the higher side and will provide a much bigger sound than the regular pair. Used mostly in larger orchestras.

Bombo _____ The bass drum. Also the name of the second note of 3-2 Rumba clave—the "and" of beat two.

Cucharas _____ Literally a pair of spoons originally used to play Rumba and other folkloric styles.

Palitos _____ Pair of sticks as well as the rhythm played by the sticks. The sticks are used to play the GuaGua.

Gua-Gua _____ A thick bamboo log mounted on a stand and played with the Palitos. Used to accompany the Rumba and other folkloric styles.

Quijada _____ The jawbone of a donkey or mule played by hitting the lower part of the jawbone against the top and producing the clattering sound. Used for percussive effect and punctuating passages. Predecessor of the present-day Vibra-Slap.

Tambora _____ Two-headed barrel-shaped drum of the Merengue style of the Dominican Republic. Either hung around the player's neck or placed on the lap and played with one stick and the hand.

Cajones _____ Wooden boxes originally used to play the Rumba and other folkloric styles.

Cascara _____ Name of the shell of the timbales, the term used to describe playing on the shell, as well as the name of the rhythm played on the shell. Also referred to as Paila.

Batá Drums _____ Two-headed hourglass-shaped Sacred drums originating from the Yoruban people of Nigeria and used for Santeria ceremonies.

1. Iyá _____ The largest and lowest-pitched of the three Batá drums and the lead drum of the ensemble.

2. Itótele _____ The middle-size and middle-pitched drum of the three Batá drums.

3. Okónkolo _____ The smallest and highest pitched of the three Batá drums.

Shekeré _____ Large gourds (calabash) with beads wrapped around them and played by shaking, rattling, and striking the base of the gourd. In the Yoruba tradition also called Agbé. Originally also called Guiros, they were instruments used in the rhythm called Guiro.

Tres _____ Form of the guitar with a smaller body and three sets of two strings. The original Tres had three sets of three strings. The tuning is G below middle C, middle C and the G above.

Cuatro _____ Similar to the Tres but having four sets of two strings. More indigenous to Puerto Rico.

Botija _____ Clay jug used to import olive oil to the "New World" regions by the Spanish. It became one of the early bass instruments of the Son traditions.

Marimbula _____ Large wooden box with a hole and a kalimba-like thumb piano placed over the hole. The original bass instrument of the Changui and Son, and currently still used by the traditional Changui ensembles.

TIPS FOR GETTING THE RIGHT SOUND AND FEEL ON THE PERCUSSION INSTRUMENTS

YOU MAY HAVE TO ACQUAINT YOUR-SELF WITH SOME CONCEPTS THAT MAY BE UNFAMILIAR IN ORDER TO GET THE RIGHT SOUND. SOME ARE OF A TECHNICAL NATURE, others are more interpretive.

When you strike a drum, or any part of a drum set or percussion instrument, you have at least three considerations that will affect the type of sound you'll get. One is what part of the stick you are playing with—the tip, the shoulder, or the butt end. The second is what type of stroke you use—an upstroke, downstroke, open stroke, dead-sticking stroke, accented, unaccented, loud, soft, or ghosted. Third is what part of the surface you strike. Virtually any part of the instrument can be played—not just the usual parts. Try experimenting with this. You may hear yourself playing sounds you've never played before. Getting the right sound and feel in these styles requires the use of these various stroke types—particularly dead-sticking, use of the shoulder of the stick on the ride cymbal or hihat, and rim shots and buzz strokes.

The same myriad of sounds are available on instruments that you play with your bare hands. The shape of your hand, what part of the hand strikes the surface, and what part of the surface you play all create different sounds. It is necessary to develop control of all the various sounds in order to make the patterns you play feel right and to have a broad variety of sounds at your disposal.

In terms of musical concepts, the way you feel and play each particular style will be different, but there are some general things common to many Afro-Cuban styles—or at least to styles of a given region. Styles played with the *Son* Clave (i.e. *Salsa* styles), while they may be different song forms, share certain characteristics between them, as do folkloric styles played with the *Rumba* clave (i.e. *Rumba* styles). This holds true for styles played with the two $\frac{6}{8}$ Claves as well. There will be more specific details on each style in its respective chapter, but here are some general feel factors to keep in mind.

It is important to feel the *pulse* correctly before actually playing any-thing. Duple meter styles are either felt *in four*: c| ♩ ♩ ♩ ♩ || (Cha-Cha, Guajira, Bolero); *in two*: ¢| ♩ ♩ || (Mambo, Son); or *in one*: ¢| o || (some Rumba styles, even though the pulse is in two, are actually felt in one). This is also the case for most styles played with two $\frac{6}{8}$ Claves. Additionally, styles in com-pound (most commonly triple) meter must be felt in a way that you can feel as well as project both the duple and triple phrasing—feeling this: $\frac{6}{8}$| ♫♪ ♫♪ || and this: $\frac{2}{4}$| ♫ ♫ || simultaneously. This also holds true for some styles in duple meter because the simultaneous articulation of the duple and triple meter is one of the fundamental rhythmic elements in many of these songstyles—both in the "writ-ten" parts as well as in improvisation.

There is another primary rhythm to learn to feel both *in four* and *in two*. Following is the same rhythmic inflection written in both in duple and triple meter: *Duple Meter:* c or ¢| ♩. ♩. ♩ | ♩. ♩. ♩ ||; *Triple Meter:* $\frac{6}{8}$| ♩ ♪♩. | ♩ ♪♩. ||. Practice feeling a basic pulse and sort of "falling" into this note. Once the pulse is firmly established inside your body, you must focus on the feel of each style. Phrasing certain parts in a very "laid back" or very "on top" way, or slurring a group of notes in the playing of a rhythm, are all integral to the correct interpretation of each style. It is also very important to develop the ability to hear all parts, as well as their variations and improvisations, while playing yours and interacting with the ensemble.

The clave rhythm also presents a set of notes to bear in mind for phrasing. In the *Son* clave there are three combinations to be particularly aware of. *These same concepts also apply to the $\frac{6}{8}$ counterpart of this clave.*

The first is the *Bombo Note*: ¢| ♩. (♪)♩ ♩ | ‡ ♩ ♩ ‡ ||. This is the note emphasized by the bass drum in the *Rumba* styles. This note is also sometimes played on each of the two bars of the clave phrase as follows: ¢| ‡. ♩ ‡ | ‡. ♩ ‡ ||. Whether it is actually stated or not, it is always felt.

The second is the *Ponche Note*: ¢| ♩. ♪♩ (♩) | ‡ ♩ ♩ ‡ ||. This note is a strong target point used both as a cadence or a beginning or takeoff point for phrases. It is also a prevalent accent point.

The last is the following combination: ¢| ♩. (♩. ♪) | ‡ ♩ ♩ ‡ ||. It is sometimes called the "conga" or "tumbaó." This functions like the *Ponche Note* does alone, but now with a lead-in from the "and" of beat two. It is also a prevalent rhythmic combination in the general phrasing.

The *Rumba* clave also has several combinations to be particularly aware of, some identical to the Son clave. *These same concepts apply to the $\frac{6}{8}$ counterpart of this clave as well.* The first is the *Bombo Note*: ¢| ♩. (♪)♩. ♪ | ‡ ♩ ♩ ‡ ||, the note emphasized by the bass drum and sometimes played on each of the two bars of the phrase depending on the style being played. *Whether actually stated or not, it is always felt.*

The second is the *last note of the first bar*: ¢| ♩. ♪♩. (♪) | ‡ ♩ ♩ ‡ ||. This note is a strong target point used both as a cadence for phrases, a beginning or takeoff point, and a prevalent accent. It also must "lay just right" for the rhythm to swing correctly.

The last is the combination: ¢| ♩. (♪♩. ♪) | ‡ ♩ ♩ ‡ ||. This functions the same as the "tumbaó" in the *Son* clave, and is also a prevalent rhythm in the general phrasing.

Keep in mind that the *Son* clave: ¢| ♩. (♪)♩ ♩ | ‡ ♩ ♩ ‡ | evolved from this clave variation: $\frac{6}{8}$| ♩ ♪ ⁊ ♩ | ⁊ ♩ ♩. ||, and in like fashion, the *Rumba* clave: ¢| ♩. ♪♩. ♪ | ‡ ♩ ♩ ‡ || evolved from this clave variation: $\frac{6}{8}$| ♩ ♪‡ ♪|⁊♩ ♩. ||. This is a very important relationship. The real phrasing of these clave rhythms is not a strict interpretation of either of these notations. It actually *falls in the cracks* between the two, with the duple and triple rhythm happening simultaneously as mentioned earlier.

When playing any pattern, be aware of how each note is supposed to sound, both in terms of how it is struck—and its resulting tonal quality—as well as its placement in the time. *No pattern consists of notes which are all struck the same.* It is a combination of different stroke types— some accented, some ghosted, some dead strokes, and the like. There is also a certain slur to some groups of notes, a way of *stretching the time* that you must become completely familiar with.

One of the easiest ways to immediately start phrasing traditionally in any style is to learn its *cliches*. These are typical patterns that you hear played constantly in a given style. Memorize these, learn how and where they are used, and work them until you've personalized them. Through the listening you'll do to learn the *cliches*, you'll gradually begin building your own stylistic vocabulary.

CLAVE~THE INSTRUMENT AND THE RHYTHM

figure 1

figure 2

"LA CLAVE ES LA LLAVE, LA LLAVE ES LA CLAVE." THE CLAVE IS THE KEY, THE KEY IS THE CLAVE. THIS STATEMENT BASICALLY SUMS UP THE ROLE OF THE RHYTHM CALLED CLAVE in Afro-Latin music. The word clave literally means "key" in Spanish and this is precisely what the *clave rhythm* is—the rhythmic key and fundamental building block of all of the Afro-Cuban songstyles. The various clave rhythms are played on the instrument also called clave. This is a pair of sticks (*figure 1*) made from a wide variety of woods—sometimes very carefully crafted and polished and sometimes just thrown together to serve the purpose of playing the rhythm. To "play clave" means to play the rhythm as well as the instrument. If the instrument is not available, then the rhythm is played on virtually any wood sound.

One stick is held in one hand with the hand cupped (*figure 2*). The cupping of the hand acts as a resonance chamber. By not grasping the clave with the fingers, the sound will not be choked. The natural sound of the wood should echo. The other hand holds the other stick and strikes the rhythm against the first.

To many students of this music the clave rhythm is the great enigma. There is so much terminology and information that has come to be associated with it—much of it erroneous or at best unclear—that it seems to confuse rather than to aid in understanding it. To further compound matters, it is also a topic of contention between cultures or schools of playing certain styles, each maintaining that theirs is the "right" way and that others simply don't know how to "play in clave." This makes it even more difficult to get clear information.

The concept of Clave (both the rhythm and the instrument) has descended from generation to generation through various African cultures, and its influences can be found in all music where African culture has had a presence. It is present in the Spanish rhythms of the *flamenco* styles, (predating any New World explorations by the Spanish), and in practically all of Central and South American and Caribbean musical styles. Because the development of styles in the Caribbean and Latin America developed through the integration of the African and the Spanish, the clave's significant presence is a given.

In Afro-Cuban music, as we know it today and have known it for several decades, there are four clave rhythms, two in duple meter, $\frac{4}{4}$ or ¢, and two in $\frac{6}{8}$ meter. The two variations in duple meter are called the *Clave de Son* and the *Clave de Rumba*. Each of these has a parallel version in $\frac{6}{8}$ making up the four clave rhythms. *The two $\frac{6}{8}$ variations are the predecessors of the Son and Rumba claves.* The *Clave de Son* and the *Clave de Rumba* emanated from the two $\frac{6}{8}$ patterns. In this text we'll be dealing with these four clave patterns and examining how they function in musical styles—in ensemble performance as well as in composition and arranging—and how to "play in them." To better understand this, it is first necessary to look at some theory, as well as examine the origins and developments of these rhythms into the forms and applications that exist today. Hopefully, through this methodical breakdown, any mysteries about the clave and its functions will be cleared up.

We'll begin with the two $\frac{6}{8}$ claves. Starting with a string of eighth notes (in

$\frac{6}{8}$) along with some accents, we'll derive a specific rhythmic pattern (commonly known as the Afro $\frac{6}{8}$ bell pattern) and the two $\frac{6}{8}$ variations. (**Note**: This is not to say that these two clave patterns definitively came from this bell pattern nor vice-versa—although this is probably the case. This is also not to say that this is the definitive origin of clave—although some version of this scenario led to its inception. Since this pattern is a familiar one to many musicians and correlates so fully with the clave patterns, it provides a solid starting point to illustrate specific concepts and fundamentals of the four claves we'll be working with.) This bell pattern is present in many African rhythm styles. In Cuba it is used in *Batá* drumming traditions as well as in many other $\frac{6}{8}$ rhythm styles, and was originally played on the *Guataca*—a hoe blade—struck with a large nail or metal spike in styles such as the *Bembé, Rumba Columbia* and many others. (More on all of this later.) Now look at the following examples:

Afro $\frac{6}{8}$ Basic Bell Pattern with Eighth Note Accents

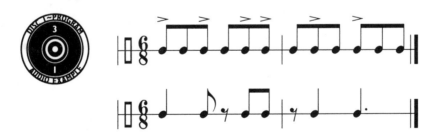

Afro $\frac{6}{8}$ Clave Variations with Basic Bell Pattern

The accent pattern in the string of eighths above spelled out the basic bell pattern. Notice that the notes in this basic pattern are the notes of the two clave patterns. The difference between the two claves is in the notes on beats 5 and 6—one clave uses the first of the two notes and the other the second. (*Note: Even though we are looking at this

"in six," it is not felt or played this way. We'll get to the pulse shortly. For now just make sure you understand how the notes lay. The rest of the notes are exactly the same.*) Play the bell pattern in one hand and each of the clave patterns in the other. Make sure you understand the relationship between these two parts and can play them together smoothly.

⅜ Bell Pattern

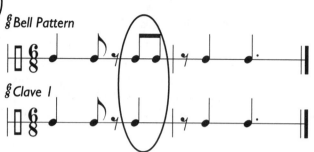

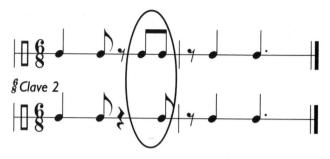

⅜ Clave 1

⅜ Clave 2

Next we move to the Son and Rumba Claves. We'll use the same approach to arrive at these. In the following examples notice how the duple meter eighth notes have the same accent relationship as the ones in ⅜. The same is the case with the Afro ⅜ bell pattern and the duple meter pattern. This relationship between the triple and duple rhythms is very significant so make sure you understand this clearly. Although we are now looking at this "in theory," in actual performance the simultaneous coexistence of these two rhythms (three and two, or three and four) forms the fundamental compound meter relationship that is part of the essence of this music.

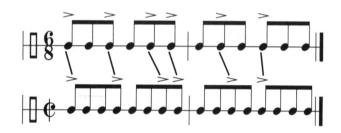

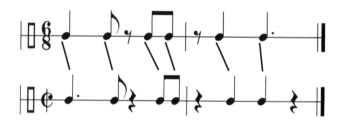

¢ Bell Pattern with Eighth Note Accents

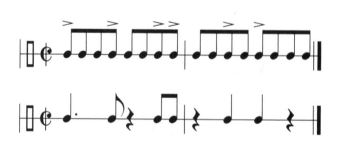

Son and Rumba Clave with ¢ Bell Pattern

As with the ⅜ clave examples, all of the notes are in the bell pattern and the only difference between the two clave rhythms is one note. The first example is the Son clave and the second the Rumba clave.

¢ Bell Pattern

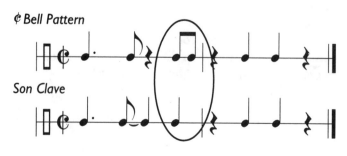

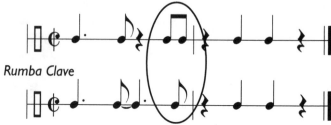

Son Clave

Rumba Clave

Relationship Between the ⁶⁄₈ and the Corresponding Son and Rumba Claves

With all of these rhythms now established, let's look at one final but very important relationship—that of the ⁶⁄₈ claves with the corresponding Son and Rumba variations. After studying the previous examples, and when you take note of how the rhythms line up, it is easy to see how one pattern relates to, and evolved from,

the other. Again, there is the compound meter relationship shown on the previous page (with the eighth notes and the bell patterns). Also keep in mind that though this looks one way when notated, in actual playing the interpretation of the rhythms falls somewhere "in the cracks" between the two meters.

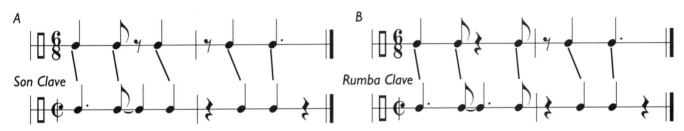

The Basic Pulse

With all four clave patterns now established, let's look at how they are felt and played. This is the next important element to grasp—the pulse. There are two basic pulses to practice playing these rhythms with: "in one" and "in two." To play these patterns "in one" means to play one pulse, or beat, per bar. The following example shows one of the two ⁶⁄₈ claves and the rumba clave

with a pulse "in one". Notice that regardless of which clave you play, the pulse stays the same and the feel of the pulse stays the same. The only difference between the two is that in the first set you have six subdivisions (notes) for each pulse, and in the second you have eight. The eighths are shown underneath each set of examples to make this more clear.

1. Basic Pulse—"in one"—one pulse (beat) per bar.

Practice playing the clave as well as the eighth notes while tapping a strong single pulse per bar. Practice the following: Play the clave or eighths with one hand and tap the pulse with the other. Next, play the rhythms with the

hands and play the pulse with your feet. Work on making this groove then practice going from one clave to the other and back without disrupting the groove. Do the same thing with the other two clave patterns.

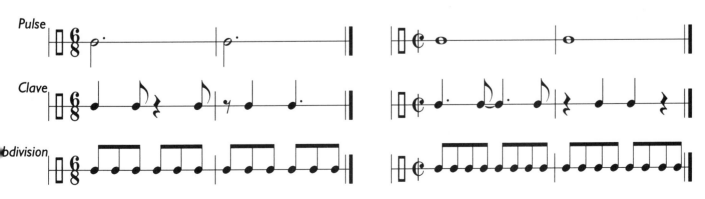

2. Basic Pulse—"in two"—two pulses (beats) per bar.

The following examples show the pulse "in two"—two beats per bar. Again, keep in mind that the pulse doesn't change as you move from triple to duple meter and back. Practice these in the same way as the last set of examples.

Pulse

Clave

Subdivision

The Compound Pulse

The previous two examples show the fundamental pulses of this music. The only remaining *basic* pulse would be "in four." This is used for the slower Son styles like Cha-Cha and Guajira, but once the first two are grasped playing "in four" is relatively simple. All other more complex (compound) structures—two against three, three against four, eight against three—are derived from these basic rhythms and the first two basic pulses.

The following examples illustrate the most fundamental compound pulses—that of two and three and three and four. Note that they are actually present in the patterns already. These examples show a written compound pulse or polyrhythm which can be played verbatim. But keep in mind that this duple and triple meter relationship exists in all aspects of this music, both in the specific instrumental parts as well as in the variations and improvisation.

In the first example we have the first of the two 6/8 claves (along with one note added at the end, creating another common 6/8 bell pattern which is based on a subdivision of three even notes per measure). It is shown with the pulse "in two." This establishes a "three over two" compound pulse. In the second example the "two" pulse is subdivided in half. This establishes a "three over four" compound pulse. Both of these are extremely common in this music. Practice playing these between your hands as well as between your hands and feet. Start by repeating only one measure and then work towards playing the two-measure phrase.

A

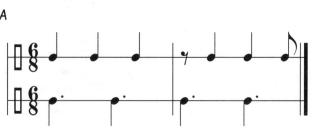

B

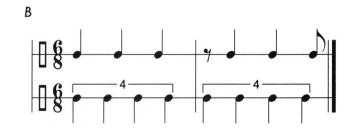

With the foundation of the four clave rhythms now established, we'll introduce more specifics about each and examine how they are applied in actual musical situations. But before doing so let's look at some important aspects common to all four types. The clave is a two bar phrase with three notes in one bar and two in the other. The bar with the three notes is referred to as *fuerte*—strong—and the bar with the two notes is referred to as *debil*—weak. The two bar patterns maintain two conceptual qualities to be aware of. First, the strong and weak bars establish a pattern of tension and resolution— the three side creates an "up" and the two side "brings it down." Second, the three side and the two side set up a pattern of call and response—the three side calls, the two responds. This in itself is a tension-resolve pattern. Before moving further, go back and play each pattern bearing this in mind and feel this effect in the rhythms. Keep in mind that this isn't rhythmic theory. If you had never been specifically told this, but just played the pattern and maintained an awareness for how it *feels* to play it, you would *feel* this—maybe not in these terms, but you'd know it by feel and that's all that matters. Remember to establish a strong pulse in your body before playing the pattern.

Continuing with the two-bar phrase idea, most of the instrumental patterns played in this style are two-bar phrases repeated as timekeeping patterns. (If they're one-bar phrases then there is some rhythmic turnaround that puts them with the clave somewhere along the line.) As I'm sure you've heard, each pattern must sync with the clave. How do you do this? No problem! There is something specific in each instrument's pattern that not only makes it sync with the respective clave rhythm, but each instrument's pattern maintains the same call-and-response tension-resolve characteristics in and of itself, as described in the previous paragraph . Consequently, there is a key element in each instrument's rhythm that *tells you* how it syncs with the clave—melodies included. Therefore, in learning any pattern it's important to know not only the pattern and its correct interpretation, but what element in the pattern creates this sync with the clave. While you'll learn this through studying, also try to develop—and then rely on—your most basic instinct of *feel* when you play. Chances are you'll be much closer with this than with analysis. Let's look at one final and important topic before getting specific about each clave rhythm. This is probably the grayest area for most people.

3-2 VERSUS 2-3 CLAVE

In the course of teaching these styles I consistently hear the following questions:
  1. What is 3–2 and 2–3 clave?
  2. How is one or the other established?
  3. What determines the direction to begin with?
  4. Does it always stay the same once a direction is established?
  5. Why does it sound like one section of a piece is in 3–2 and another in 2–3?
  6. Are the Son and Rumba claves interchangeable?
  7. How do I know which one to use?
  8. Can I really get lots of hot dates playing the clave?
  9. So how do I look playing these things?

The answers to all of these questions are really quite simple:
1. The same rhythm played starting on either the first or second bar.
2. By the arrangement of a piece.
3. The melody.
4. Yes, in traditional arrangements.
5. Because you're not familiar with it.
6. Sometimes.
7. The particular style and ensemble determine this.
8. Yes but the lead singer will always get more.
9. Very cool but your steps could use some work.

Now that that's all cleared up we'll get into a little more detail. The topic of 3–2 versus 2–3 clave requires explanation from a couple of different perspectives. Working from the traditional to the contemporary we'll examine the concept thoroughly.

Traditionally speaking there is really no such thing as 3–2 or 2–3 clave. The clave rhythm is the clave rhythm and starts from the beginning, (the bar with the note on beat one), continues this way throughout, and the music is played with all the parts corresponding in the way they should. So one can safely assume that the clave exists in only one direction and never changes and if you were dealing exclusively with folkloric songstyles this would be true and correct.

For example, a traditional *Rumba* or *Batá* ensemble is never going to say, "…lets play this tune. Should we do it in 3-2 or 2-3?" for the simple reason that *the tune only works one way*—with the clave, and the tune, and the rhythmic parts all starting at the beginning, and everything syncing with the clave. The thing that becomes confusing for the unfamiliar ear is that even though every part has a beginning, *it doesn't always start **playing** at its beginning,* and so if there are staggered entrances of the instruments or vocal or melody and harmony parts, or a player comes in halfway through the first or second bar of a pattern, or enters with an improvised variation, the unfamiliar ear sometimes interprets this as a new downbeat, or a pulse not being where it

really is. This then is believed to be 2-3 instead of 3-2 or something of the sort. This is simply not the case and through assimilation of these styles this will (or should) no longer happen. There is nothing wrong with being at this stage when you are first learning a style. Just keep in mind how critical it is to have this information straight and try to develop the right concepts and use the correct terminology.

However, once commercial arranging—especially for popular dance—of these folkloric and other styles came about with the *Son* and *Charanga* groups, and also mixed with jazz and other idioms, the concept of 3–2 and 2–3 began defining itself.

Let's continue with the traditional area and examine another question: Does the music determine the position of the clave or the clave of the music?

This is really a variation of the old "which came first, the chicken or the egg?" question, and I really hate this question since it requires some philosophical speculation, and nothing serves the purpose of creating confusion more than philosophical speculation, but here goes. I'll give a *four part* answer with three of the four parts being pretty easy—meaning they won't subject me to the wrath of an angered Inspector Clave from the Clave Police—and the third being the philosophical (i.e. confusing) one; up for as many interpretations as there are musicians.

Part I: When traditional, folkloric ensembles develop or create new material it is based on traditions and these traditions are strictly adhered to—whether consciously or not. These traditions are ingrained in these musicians and in this case it can be said that the clave (and the tradition) is determining the music (melody) and hence all of the other parts. Let's look at a couple of examples of folkloric-type melodies to illustrate this. Note that *example 1* is written with *Son* clave and *example 2* with *Rumba* clave. In the case of both of these melodies, either one could be played with either clave, but that's not always so and which one to use has to do with the ensemble that's playing, the style being played and the composition itself. Notice how the rhythm of the melody syncs with the rhythm of the clave.

Example 1

Example 2

Notice that each of the two previous examples is a four bar phrase repeated, and note how everything begins and continues completely aligned. Now, this is not to be interpreted as a musical style in which the rules of clave create a strict and inflexible scenario and that everything is always in two-bar phrases and completely square. Quite the contrary, this music is steeped in improvisation and personal interpretation. It's just done within the context of the clave and the resulting vocabulary. Let's take the second example from the previous page and assume that this is the beginning of the tune (the melody), and let's assume that the ensemble (in this case percussion) was playing for eight bars before the melody entered. Let's also say that the singer would take the melody and rephrase the rhythm so that he enters before the downbeat shown in the previous example. There are no pickup notes added (though this could also be the case); only the melody notes are rephrased. Let's say he starts on the eighth bar—one bar before what's written in the previous example. Then his melody would look like the following. The rhythms are phrased to sync with the clave.

Example 3

Notice that the tune remains in the original clave position. Also notice that in bar six the rhythm is varied again. (These variations take place in all the instruments within the confines of a given songstyle.) Now, just because the melody entered in the second bar of the two-bar clave phrase, that doesn't now make it the first bar of the phrase of the tune. Let's say that now this eight-bar melody is repeated again. The second time it repeats, the singer could choose to sing the rhythms of the example from the previous page or any other interpretation as long as it lines up with the clave. So the conclusion:

This is what I mean by the clave (and the tradition) dictating the music. The clave rhythm existed long before these melodies came to be, since it has existed for generations, and I wrote these melodies two minutes ago, but I was writing in the *Rumba* tradition so the melodies had to work a certain way. Again, any one of a number of rhythmic interpretations of this melody would work. As in any style, if you know it well, you have a lot of room to interpret.

Part II: When a composer or player decides to write, arrange or perform a new piece in the Latin *commercial/dance* tradition (as in *Salsa*), then those traditions are adhered to. But the composer may well create a piece that, *by virtue of the rhythm of the melody,* dictates that the clave be played in 3–2 or 2–3, whichever the case may be. Let's look at a couple of examples to illustrate this. The rhythm of the melody of *example 4,* in and of itself, without any arrangement for an ensemble, specifically outlines 3–2 clave. *Example 5,* a short excerpt from a popular Cuban folk song, a Son called "El Manisero"—"The Peanut Vendor"—specifically outlines and implies 2–3 clave. Look at these and the previous examples and take note of how the rhythms of the melody and the clave rhythm line up.

Example 4

Example 5 El Manisero (The Peanut Vendor) in 2–3 Clave

THE PEANUT VENDOR
(El Manisero)
Music by MOISES SIMONS
© 1928 Edward B. Marks Music Co. (Renewed)
All Rights Reserved   Used by Permission

It has already been established that the rhythm of these two melodies by themselves spell out 3–2 and 2–3 clave respectively, but this is rarely how you would hear these tunes played. There would almost certainly be an arrangement. In creating an arrangement, an arranger has the liberty—within the confines of the tradition and the idiom—to create the music he hears. Let's take the example of "The Peanut Vendor" and give it a simple intro, and now look at how you may be playing in two different clave positions in different parts of the arrangement. (*We'll be looking at the arranging aspect of these idioms in detail in the Songstyles section. For now we'll just look at how it relates to the clave.*) Once again, the rhythm of the melody calls for 2–3 clave so we'll just say that the song is in 2-3. Even though we've determined this, it's very possible that the addition of arranged material

may have you starting the piece, or a section of the arrangement, in 3–2 clave because *the rhythm of the arranged material*—which in essence is a composition itself—calls for it. If that's the case then that's how you play it, and if the arranger were to write everything to work in 2–3, then that's how you play it. What will not change—no matter what—is that when you actually state the eight bars of the tune's melody written above you will play 2–3 clave—period. That part is not an option. If you don't, then you may get a visit from the Clave Police. Look at *example 6*. (Keep in mind that these are condensed examples to illustrate a point and not an actual arrangement.) In example 6 the introduction calls for 3–2 clave and happens to be three bars long. Notice how bar three sets up the entrance of the melody in 2–3 clave even though you started the piece in 3–2.

Example 6 *El Manisero (The Peanut Vendor) in 3–2 Clave with 3-bar intro*

THE PEANUT VENDOR
(El Manisero)
Music by MOISES SIMONS
© 1928 Edward B. Marks Music Co. (Renewed)
All Rights Reserved   Used by Permission

In an actual arrangement, the rhythm section might play a rhythmic unison with the three bars of introductory melody and then play time when the melody starts. Or it may play time from the beginning for two bars, and then play the rhythm of the third bar of the intro, and then play time again at the fourth bar with the melody. Or it may lay out for the intro and make staggered entrances, or whatever. A real arrangement would be considerably more involved but regardless, the clave would work like this. In *example 7*, we take a four-bar rhythmic cliche and use it as the introduction. This rhythm happens to imply 2–3 so the whole thing starts and continues in 2–3 when the melody enters.

Example 7 El Manisero (The Peanut Vendor) in 2–3 Clave with 4-bar intro

THE PEANUT VENDOR
(El Manisero)
Music by MOISES SIMONS
© 1928 Edward B. Marks Music Co. (Renewed)
All Rights Reserved   Used by Permission

So here's the conclusion to Part II. In this scenario the tradition is dictating the creation of the material, and this in turn is dictating the direction of the clave, and consequently of the entire ensemble.

Part III: When an arranger or an ensemble decides to arrange or perform or in some way adapt a piece that did not emanate from the Latin tradition into one of the traditional styles, then the piece has to be molded to fit the clave and the tradition, but there is still the liberty—as in the examples in *Part II*—to decide which clave and which clave direction to work with along with all of the other creative decisions.

A very common practice among both Latin and Jazz musicians is to adapt Jazz standards to Latin idioms. Let's follow along this path with a couple of examples. Say you're in a Jazz group that wants to play some tunes in a traditional Latin groove. You're going to take the tune "On Green Dolphin Street" and arrange it so you can play it like a Mambo or a Songo. The melody rhythms of the tune "Green Dolphin Street" are not in and of themselves in any clave, so you have to adjust the rhythms of the melody—part of the arranging process—to put it in clave, along with whatever introductions, interludes, and endings you arrange. The resulting arrangement can be very elaborate or it can be a quick throw-together. Here are two examples of "On Green Dolphin Street." The first in 3–2 and the second in 2–3 clave. Once you know the idiom, this is something you would do naturally—just simply improvise. Anyone in a band could start playing a rhythm or the melody and everyone would know how to play their respective parts. Or one person in the ensemble might say "...let's play such and such a tune in 2–3," knowing that it works well in that clave, or it just may be a preference, since it might work either way if handled correctly, and everyone knows what that means and how to make it happen in that particular clave.

Example 8 *On Green Dolphin Street in 3–2 Clave*

ON GREEN DOLPHIN STREET
Music by BRONISLAU KAPER
©1947 (Renewed 1975) METRO-GOLDWYN MEYER INC.
All Rights Controlled by EMI FEIST CATALOG INC. (Publishing)
and WARNER BROS. PUBLICATIONS INC. (Print)
All Rights Reserved

Example 9 *On Green Dolphin Street in 2–3 Clave*

ON GREEN DOLPHIN STREET
Music by BRONISLAU KAPER

So here's the conclusion to Part III: In this type of scenario, you basically have the choice of not only the clave direction but which clave—*Son, Rumba* or $\frac{6}{8}$—and which of the many rhythm styles you want to play the tune in. The key here is that once you have established what you are going to do, you then must do it with all the elements of that particular tradition intact. In practical terms it is perfectly all right to say "…let's play "Footprints" as a Songo in 3–2." But if

you say this just make sure you know how to play Footprints, a Songo, and in 3–2 Clave. What you would *not* say is "let's play a *Rumba Guaguancó* in 3-2." This would be incorrect terminology, and worse yet an incorrect perception, since Guaguancó and all its parts correspond with the clave in a very specific way and it's not referred to as 3-2 or 2-3. So unless you're referring to some nontraditional adaptation, this would definitely get you a visit from Inspector Clave.

Part IV: As you should see from the previous examples, it's pretty clear what the role of the clave is in these varied scenarios. Nonetheless, there still seems to be lots of room for discrepancies about clave and the approach to playing and writing in it. There is one major topic that we didn't touch upon here but will address in detail throughout later parts of the book: improvisation. When you improvise in any of these songstyles, your improvisation must also be in clave—meaning your phrases, articulations, and cadences must sync with the clave. This is an area where big stances have been taken—probably because improvisation is such an interpretive and subjective thing that can be influenced by so many elements. Furthermore, even though I've defined very specifically the function of the clave in these examples, the first question was still not really answered. Did the melody come from the clave or the clave from the melody? I guess to really answer this you'd have to think about generations-old Africans (or whatever they were at that time in the related regions) going about their days and try to determine whether they sang first or clapped first, or did they kind of slide into both simultaneously, and when was the rhythm they were clapping or tapping actually identified as clave. The voice was really the first instrument and percussion followed—by virtue of striking things in the environment. That is a fact. So it's logical to say the melody came first, but I don't think anyone can really answer this definitively nor do I think it happened like this. A safer speculation is that it was more of an evolutionary process.

Dr. Fernando Ortiz, the foremost author, musicologist, and historian of the Afro-Cuban culture, says in his authoritative multi-volume work, *La Africania de La Musica Cubana,* that the concept of clave actually developed in Cuba. One could certainly concur that the concept of clave *as it exists in Afro-Latin music* developed in Cuba. But there are many African cultures whose music

contains some form of clave rhythm and instrument, and they are not playing Afro-Latin music. They're playing their music and they were an original source of the Afro-Latin developments ages ago, so it might be safe to assume that this element was intact prior to their arrival in the New World regions. This is certainly not to disagree with Dr. Ortiz but only to point out the many views that can be taken on this subject and how unanswerable this part of the question really is. Fortunately, what you do need to know to play this music is very answerable and is in this book, and it's waiting to be gotten to, so let's move forward.

On the more practical side, continue with the following section to further help you get this clave business inside you. Also practice playing all of the preceding clave patterns while tapping the suggested pulses. It is essential that you can project a strong pulse. If you don't have a strong pulse and sense of time fixed inside you, don't even start playing—even if you can play in clave. There is one thing that supersedes the clave and that is the pulse. This must happen before anything else. Focus on this first and then start to work on the specific rhythms. Play all of the rhythms as written and then play them all again starting on the second bar. This way you're covering practicing the clave in both directions.

Also practice tapping the rhythms of the tunes with one hand while tapping the clave with the other hand or your foot. Then play these tunes on some melody instrument—piano, guitar, horn, marimba—while tapping the clave with your foot or free hand, or program the clave on your drum machine, or record it somehow and play to it if you don't yet have the coordination to do both parts at once. While it's relatively easy to see the rhythms line up on paper, its another to *hear it* and respond to it immediately in a musical situation. Now let's look at some specifics of each of the four claves and some terminology.

The *Son* Clave came to exist with the music of the *Changui* and *Son* groups. Since—as mentioned in the *Background Information* section—the *Son* style is one of the most influential in the development of Afro-Cuban music, it only follows that all of the styles that were derived from the *Son* (and *Charanga*) styles use the *Son* Clave. Consequently the Guajira, Cha-Cha, Bolero, Son Montuno, Mambo and many others are all played with the *Son* Clave, although depending on the arrangement and the ensemble they might also be played with the *Rumba* Clave.

Here is the *Son* Clave pattern written in $\frac{2}{2}$ time and in the 3–2 position. It can also be written in $\frac{2}{4}$ time or $\frac{4}{4}$ time. You must be able to feel and play it at tempos from very slow to very fast and with both the $\frac{4}{4}$ and $\frac{2}{2}$ pulses—the slower styles being in four and the faster in two.

There are several key points about this clave that are important to know.

Beat *two-and* on the three side of the clave is called the *Bombo* (bass drum) *note,* as this is the note the bass drum of the *Rumba* styles emphasizes. (This *Bombo note* element applies to all four clave variations.)

Beat *four* of the three side of the clave is called the *Ponche* (punch), as this note is a strong accent point, take-off point, target point, and cadence point. These are both illustrated in *example 1.* (This also applies to all four claves but functions differently in the other three. It is in this clave that the *Ponche* was defined.)

Example 2 shows another key point to be aware of. This is referred to as the *Conga* rhythm (by Dr. Fernando Ortiz), and it is also referred to as a *tumbaó*—although the term tumbaó is also used as a name for a conga drum pattern as well as a generic term for a repetitive pattern played by any rhythm section instrument. Irrespective of the names, you must be aware of these aspects of the clave.

Example 1

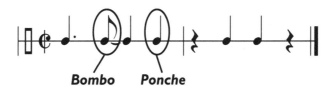

Bombo   Ponche

Example 2

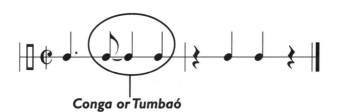

Conga or Tumbaó

These notes maintain their function regardless of which position the clave is in. Here it is shown with the clave written in the 2-3 position.

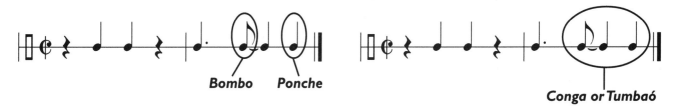

Bombo   Ponche

Conga or Tumbaó

The *Rumba* Clave developed with both the secular and sacred styles of Cuban drumming but did not have a presence in popular dance music until the 1960s. Today it is the prevalent clave rhythm in most *Rumba* styles as well as in many commercial and Latin Jazz instrumental styles. It has one major rhythmic difference from the *Son* clave in its delay of the last note of the three side of the clave. But, while this looks like a simple and subtle difference notationally, it creates an entirely new feel and swing to the clave rhythm itself, as well as the styles played with it. *Rumba* Clave (and the styles played with it) not only maintains many rhythmic connections with its African ⅛ predecessors, but due to its unique swing, it has also been a takeoff point for many funk and related styles. Both the Son and Rumba clave also have a strong presence in the music of New Orleans

though not specifically treated as clave rhythms. While in some commercial or hybrid styles the Son and Rumba clave rhythms may be interchangeable, in their most traditional uses they are not.

Following is the *Rumba* Clave notated in both the 3–2 and 2–3 positions (*examples 1 & 2*). The *Bombo note* is the same—the *and of two* of the three side—but the *ponche* note is now delayed to the *and of four*. This gives you the target point at the *four and* but the *ponche* of the *Son* clave is the more traditional *ponche*. The *Conga* or *Tumbaó* rhythm mentioned earlier also takes on another light in the *Rumba* clave. While the *Conga* rhythm from the *Son* clave is also used while in this clave, the use of the *four and* instead of the *four* has brought about a number of variations. Further points about this last note of the three side as well as other clave concepts will follow.

Example 1

Example 2

In conclusion here are the two African ⅛ clave variations. They are each listed in both the 3–2 and 2–3 positions. As mentioned previously, the function of the *Bombo note* and other key points is

essentially the same in these patterns. *Example 3* is the ⅛ parallel and predecessor of the *Son* clave and *example 4* is the ⅛ parallel and predecessor of the *Rumba* clave .

Example 3

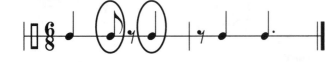

Example 4

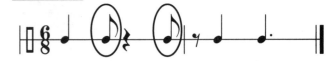

FURTHER CLAVE CONCEPTS AND TERMINOLOGY

Here we look at some other essential areas related to the clave. First let's finish up on a couple of topics already presented. With regard to the *Bombo Note*, while we've already identified this specific note in each clave rhythm, keep in mind that the *Bombo* is an instrument itself—the bass drum—and plays many variations in its patterns in the various songstyles. These will be addressed at length in the chapter on this instrument. The *Bombo* note in the clave pattern is just one essential note that is not only played by the bass drum *but is an inflection that can be articulated and/or emphasized by any instrument, and it clearly identifies the three side of the clave.* Here are the *Son* and *Rumba* claves with the *Bombo* note. The exact same thing applies to the $\frac{6}{8}$ claves.

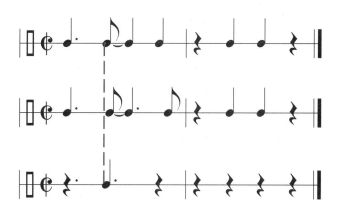

With regard to the *Ponche Note*, let's look at three very common varieties—the first two were already presented with their respective claves. The third is kind of a result of the first two and a very common rhythmic inflection. All three are used with the Son clave. Theoretically only the second and third are used with the Rumba clave but all really work with either clave if they're played correctly. They occur with beat four of the three side of the clave regardless of the position the clave is notated or played in. Here they happen to be notated in the 2–3 position. The same applies to the two $\frac{6}{8}$ claves.

Son *Clave with Ponche Notes:*

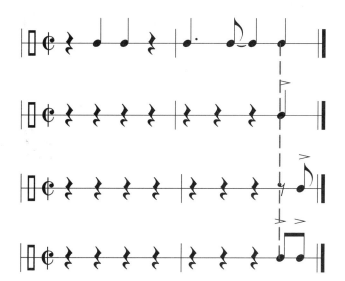

Rumba *Clave with Ponche Notes:*

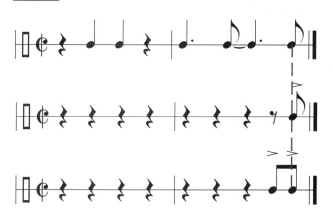

Let's look at one final set of rhythmic relationships to close this section. Looking once again at the basic Son clave, we'll look at an alternate notation to arrive at another rhythm style and rhythmic articulation, and cover some terminology at the same time. The following example is the Son clave notated in $\frac{2}{4}$ meter with the use of beams all the way through the three side. The first bar of this clave is known as the *tresillo*—the triplet. When written in $\frac{2}{4}$ time it is not literally a triplet, but remember this clave's evolution from the $\frac{6}{8}$ clave. The first three notes (first bar) of that $\frac{6}{8}$ rhythm literally spell a triplet. A very common phrasing or articulation in both the interpretation of written rhythms as well as in improvisation is to play between these two written rhythms so that the interpretations are sometimes literal and sometimes stretched or pulled so they're in the cracks between the two.

Example 1 ~The Tresillo

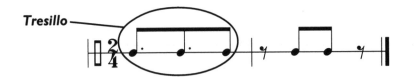

Example 2 ~The Cinquillo

Now let's take the bar line away and examine another important phrasing to be aware of. This is still the exact same clave rhythm, but now let's stretch and pull things out a little. If you stretch and try to place the notes in an equally spaced fashion you transition to this quintuplet.

Continuing with this transition, let's take the same clave rhythm—again without the bar line—and stretch the notes so they line up to create this next rhythm. This $\frac{2}{4}$ example has the bar line missing and is really two bars long, so let's make it a one bar rhythm in $\frac{4}{4}$. This rhythm is called the *Cinquillo*—the quintuplet—and if you stretch it when you play it, it may sound like a quintuplet or it may be phrased somewhere in between the even and odd groupings.

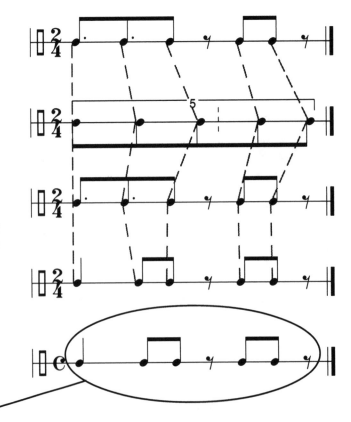

Cinquillo

Since everything in this style must work in clave and the clave is a two bar rhythm, let's put this back into a two bar phrase. Here are two notations. The rhythm is still referred to as the *Cinquillo,* but it also clearly outlines the three side of the clave. Listen for it in the rhythmic phrases of all instruments and melodies. You'll hear it constantly.

This *Cinquillo* is part of the *Baqueteo* that the *Timbalero* plays in the songstyle called *Danzón* (to be discussed in its own section). Here is the basic pattern.

This concludes the section on the clave. A tremendous amount of information was presented here and this section is the key to your understanding and playing this music correctly. Study it and practice it carefully. ***May the clave be with you*** and more importantly, ***may you be with the clave.***

THE PALITOS AND THE GUA-GUA

figure 1

figure 2

THE WORD PALITOS LITERALLY MEANS "LITTLE STICKS" AND THE PALITOS ARE JUST THAT—TWO STICKS USED TO PLAY VARIOUS RHYTHMIC PATTERNS—MOST COMMONLY USED in the Rumba styles Yambú, Guaguancó, and Columbia. When the term is applied in these styles it refers to both playing the *palitos*—the instrument—as well as playing the *palitos rhythm*—whatever specific pattern is called for in the particular piece that is being played. This is identical to saying "play clave," in that the term encompasses both the instrument and the rhythmic pattern. The Palitos are traditionally played on an instrument called the *Gua-Gua*—a piece of bamboo mounted on a stand that produces a hollow wooden sound. (Gua-Gua is the name of a bus or van in Cuba—and Puerto Rico and other Latin American Islands—and this instrument sort of *drives* the ensemble, hence the adaptation of the name.) It is also played on any wood sound such as

a woodblock, shell of a conga drum, shell or rim of the bombo or large tom-tom, jam block, or anything that produces a round, hollow, wooden tone. In certain pieces or in sections of certain pieces the palitos are also played on a cowbell which is either mounted or strapped to the side of a bombo or tumbadora (conga drum). This often happens in a section that has built-in rhythmic activity and intensity. Sometimes the rhythmic pattern is also changed to a more active or rhythmically complex one. The switch from wood to metal along with the change in pattern increases the volume as well as creates more intensity.

The patterns of the palitos are closely tied to the clave. Generally, once a pattern is begun it is kept constant except for perhaps an arranged change at a specific section. In traditional styles the palitos player does not improvise within a piece, but may introduce some variations of the pattern. In nontraditional styles these patterns are excellent as improvisational motifs, especially when used in Latin Jazz styles on the drum set or percussion and in soloing in these styles.

The palitos rhythms can be played with either the Son or Rumba clave, but are most used in the Rumba styles and consequently heard with the rumba clave.

Following is the Rumba clave with the basic palito rhythm (with no accents for now). All of the two-handed palito combinations are derived from this rhythm. Play this rhythm in one hand and the clave rhythm in the other. Also keep in mind that you should be able to start these on either bar to accommodate both the 3–2 and 2–3 clave positions.

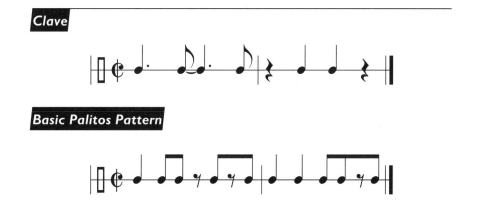

Clave

Basic Palitos Pattern

The following are two-handed combinations based on the basic pattern above. There are a couple of things to notice and practice. There is an accent pattern (usually in the right hand) that outlines a specific rhythm. Which accent pattern is used depends on the musical style being played and the rhythmic effect desired by the player. The first three examples contain the most common accent patterns. The first accents the rhythm of the clave, the second accents the basic Rumba rhythm of the bombo. The third is the most common for comping in the Son styles. The remaining patterns all contain common variations.

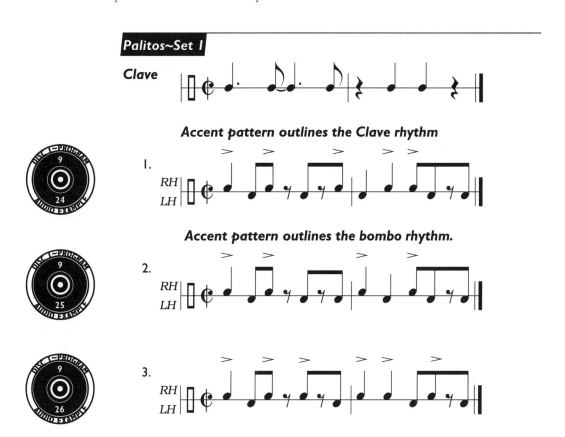

Palitos~Set 1

Clave

Accent pattern outlines the Clave rhythm

1.
RH
LH

Accent pattern outlines the bombo rhythm.

2.
RH
LH

3.
RH
LH

The following are another variety of two-handed patterns. Patterns two and three are extensions of pattern one. Notice how they line up with the clave. Each of the three patterns create different degrees of rhythmic intensity with #1 creating the least and #3 the most. The slur markings in #3 mean just that. Each group of four notes is slurred together. Refer to the audio recording for the correct interpretation.

Palitos~Set 2

Clave

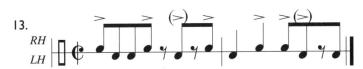

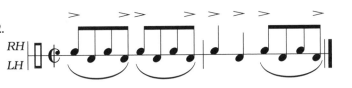

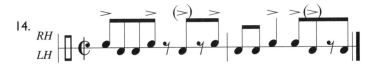

The following are yet another variety of two-handed patterns. These patterns are for one player playing both the palitos and the bombo (bass drum, discussed in the next chapter). There are many possibilities when combining parts of different instruments. The following are some common ones for this combination. In each of the patterns the bombo note of the clave (the accented and open-tone *and* of two on

the bass drum) is struck by reaching and playing the note on the head of the drum. The rest of the pattern is played on the wood sound. This type of combination can be done with a gua-gua and a bombo but is more commonly done by playing the entire pattern on a bombo or large tom-tom. The wood sound is played on the side or the rim and you reach in and hit the head for the bombo note.

The following are palito rhythms played on the gua-gua in many ⁶⁄₈ feels. Depending on the setting, arrangement and ensemble it might be used in a Rumba Columbia, Abakuá or any of a

number of styles. Pattern #1 is the basic pattern, pattern #2 shows a different inflection of the same pattern. Patterns 3 and 4 add some grace notes (flams) to the pattern.

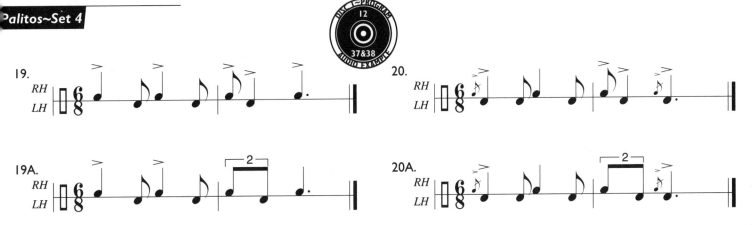

THE BOMBO~BASS DRUM

The bombo is the bass drum of these Cuban styles and there are a couple of different types used for different styles. For our purposes we'll focus on the specific patterns of each style rather than the different drums, but there are a couple of specific drums to be aware of.

The bombo used by the Comparsas for the Conga rhythms of the Cuban Carnaval is a flat and wide two-sided drum that is hung around the player's neck and played with a mallet or thick dowel and the hand. The bombo used in Rumba can vary. The original bombo was the large *Cajon*—large wooden box from the sets of three wooden boxes, Cajones—originally used to play the

Rumba. The Rumba Yambú is still very often played on the cajones and still uses the traditional bombo. The cajones are played with the hands. For the Rumba Guaguancó the drum can be a large bass drum mounted on a stand or a large bass drum turned on its side and sitting on the floor with the player sitting on top of it and playing by reaching down to the head on one side—much like how the drums of the Tumba Francesa are played. This is played with a mallet or dowel and the hand. Today many groups use a large floor tom from a drum set and that seems to work quite well for virtually all styles.

The first group of patterns are the fundamental patterns for the Rumba Guaguancó. There are also improvised variations played as the energy and intensity of the Rumba progresses. These examples are written in the 3-2 clave position. The "+" indicates closed/muted tones played by muting the head with the hand and playing closed tones into the head with the mallet. The "o" is for open tones.

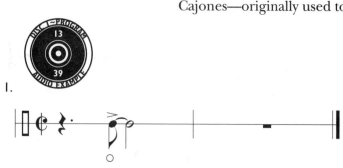

1.

2.

This next example is played for the Rumba Yambú. Again there are variations that are improvised by the player. This is traditionally played on the Cajon.

3.

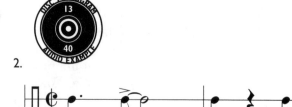

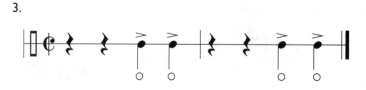

These patterns are for the Conga de Comparsa and are also used for the Mozambique. (More on this later.) Which of these patterns is used and when depends on the musical setting—the ensemble, instrumentation, geographical region of origin of the piece being played, and musical arrangement. Again there are the basic time-keeping patterns and the variations improvised by the player. The first pattern is the most fundamental and the second the most common variation. The last five are sometimes played as patterns themselves but usually for a section of a piece or more often used as variations to the more basic patterns. (Written in 3–2 clave.)

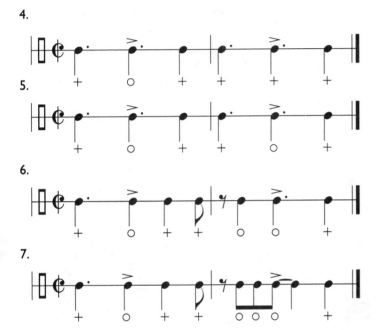

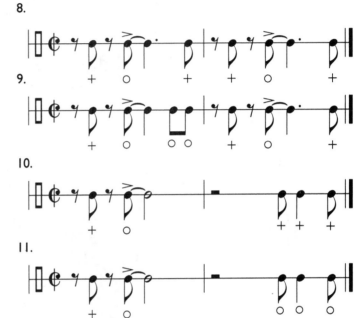

Following are two patterns for the Mozambique. This rhythm evolved from the Conga de Comparsa and was developed primarily by Pello El Afro-kan. There are now many variations of this style. It very often has these two different Bombo patterns playing simultaneously.

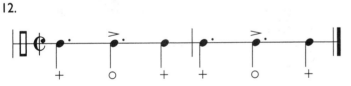

The following is another combination from some Mozambique arrangements of Pello El Afrokan. These create a much more syncopated feel. These two and the two above could be arranged as the Bombo parts for two different sections of one piece. Also, all of the Conga/Comparsa patterns above could be combined with any of these four Mozambique patterns.

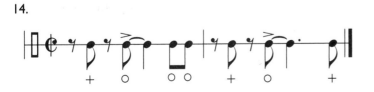

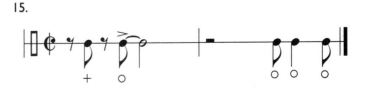

THE COWBELLS AND THE HOE BLADE ~THE GUATACA

figure 1

figure 3

figure 2

figure 4

THE COWBELLS OF THE AFRO-CUBAN STYLES COME IN A WIDE VARIETY OF SHAPES AND SIZES AND A WIDE VARIETY OF BELLS ARE USED—SOMETIMES SIMULTANEOUSLY—FOR THE VARIOUS STYLES. While many bells exist, we will concern ourselves with only the following bells and their respective patterns.

- *Guataca~Hoe Blade*
- *Campana~Cencerro*
- *Mambo~Timbale Bells*
- *Cha-Cha Bells*
- *Charanga Bells*
- *Comparsa Bells~Sartenes*

Pictured at the top left, *figure 1* shows the Guataca—literally a hoe blade that is struck with a nail or a spike. This was the first cowbell or metal sound used in Afro-Cuban music and is still used today in folkloric ensembles. Also pictured are four varieties of the Guataca's descendents, the large cowbell commonly referred to as the Cencerro or the Campana (grande) or—in Salsa Orchestra terminology—the Bongo Bell—since it is the bell that the *Bongocero* (bongo player) plays during the Montuno section of an arrangement. This hand-held bell is also used in the Cuban Carnaval's *Conga de Comparsa* rhythm as well as in *Mozambique* style.

Figure 2 shows several varieties of the *Mambo Bell*—also called the *Timbale Bell*. This bell is usually mounted on the timbales and is played by the *Timbalero* during the *Montuno* sections (and sometimes other sections) of an arrangement. This is one of the timbale's three *ride* sounds—the other two being the sides of the drums (called *Paila* or *Cascara*) and the cymbal.

Figure 3 shows three varieties of the *Cha-Cha Bell*. This is the second-to-smallest bell and is used almost exclusively in the *Cha-Cha* and other slower styles like the *Guajira*. The quarter note pulse played on this high-pitched bell is

one of the signature sounds of these styles.

Figure 4 shows the *Charanga Bell*. This is the smallest and highest pitched bell we'll deal with and is used almost exclusively in the *Charanga* style.

Now let's move on to how they are played and what's played on each one.

The *Guataca* (pictured at right) can be said to be the father of the present day Afro-Cuban cowbell and its rhythmic functions. It is literally a garden hoe blade played with a large nail or spike. It began as an impromptu instrument created by slaves working the fields and adapting to maintain their musical traditions. While not common in popular music settings, many traditional folkloric ensembles still use it for its very distinct sound.

The most common patterns played on it are those we know today as the basic Afro ⁶⁄₈ bell patterns. The two most common patterns are shown below in both the 3–2 and 2–3 clave directions. (A wealth of these patterns are presented later in this section.) Today these patterns are more commonly played on the *Cencerro*.

Example 1 *Afro ⁶⁄₈ Bell Pattern Variation 1 in 3–2 and 2–3*

Example 2 *Afro ⁶⁄₈ Bell Pattern Variation 2 in 3–2 and 2–3*

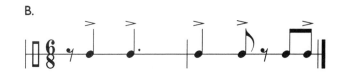
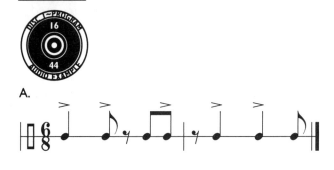

The *Cencerro* (pictured below) is the descendant of the *Guataca* and all of the Afro $\frac{6}{8}$ patterns that were played on the Guataca are now generally played on this bell—along with many other patterns and styles. Originally the Cencerro was exclusively a hand-held bell and continues to be used as such, but today it is also often mounted for use in percussion setups and on the drum set. Our primary discussion and practice with this bell will be with the hand-held method. The bell is held in one hand and struck with a large stick with the other hand. The hand holding the bell also does some damping on the backside of the bell to produce open and closed tones (see *figures 1* and *2*). The index finger of the hand holding the bell is used. When it is held against the bell it muffles the tone, and when held away it allows the bell to ring producing the open tone. The open and closed tones correspond with certain strokes in certain parts of the bell as well certain notes of the patterns.

figure 1: Index finger muting the bell

figure 2: Index finger not muting the bell

There are three basic strokes necessary to play the bell's patterns correctly. They are illustrated in figures 3, 4, and 5 on the next page. The first (*figure 3*) is a stroke on the mouth of the bell with the side of the stick. This stroke is generally open—the finger unmutes the back of the bell and the tone rings. This stroke can also be muffled or semi-muffled. The second (*figure 4*) is a stroke almost in the center of the neck—the base area approximately two to four inches from the bottom end of the bell. This tone is generally muted. The index finger presses against the backside and the ringing of the tone is dampened. The third (*figure 5*) is a stroke in the same base area as stroke two but on the right edge of the bell. This tone is generally also muffled or sometimes half-muffled, meaning the index finger lets the tone ring a little more than the muffled tone. This third tone is the least essential of the three. Most patterns can be and are played with only the first two, but when a pattern calls for two notes to be played consecutively as muffled tones in the neck of the bell, playing them as two separate tones—one in the center and one on the edge—gives the pattern a nice flavor and a different swing. In addition to the two Afro $\frac{6}{8}$ patterns listed with the Guataca on the previous page, the most common patterns played on this bell are *examples 1, 2 and 3* on the following page. Many other patterns are presented later in this chapter as well as later in the book, but you have to have these basic ones down first.

We'll use the following notation code: *1a, 1b, 2,* and *3* to identify the stroke types. *Note: This notation puts the lower pitch above the line and the higher pitch below it, but it mirrors your holding of the bell as you play.*

1a–Open stroke on mouth of bell. (figures 3&2).
1b–Muffled stroke on mouth of bell. (figures 3&1).
2–Muffled stroke on neck of bell. (figures 4&1).
3–Semi-muffled stroke on edge of bell. (figures 3&1).

figure 3

3.
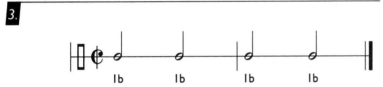

1b   1b   1b   1b

4.
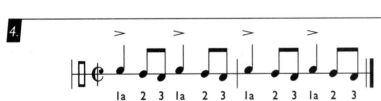

1a 2 3 1a 2 3 1a 2 3 1a 2 3

figure 4

5.

1a 2 3 1a 2 3 1a 2 1a 2 3

figure 5

Keep in mind that these patterns have many variations and subtleties which are an integral part of the correct sound and feel. Also keep in mind that cowbells are like cymbals in that no two are alike. Each has its own sound and personality, which is also a consideration in selecting bells for a particular songstyle and ensemble.

Following are several variations for each of the basic patterns presented thus far. Remember that each variation is based on the basic pattern *and* the clave, so stay aware of this as you practice them. Also remember that once a pattern is started it is pretty much kept constant until a change in section or rhythm within a piece calls for it. Whichever it is, there must be a musical reason for a change. These patterns are usually not played *ad lib.* They are a very strong and present texture and are generally responsible for a strong groove achieved through repetition of the same pattern.

First we'll start with the $\frac{6}{8}$ patterns and then we'll move on to the duple meter combinations.

CENCERRO PATTERNS IN 6/8

These patterns can and are also played on other bells like the timbale bells or the African Agogo bells and can be played on any bell if the musical situation warrants. Also depending on the musical situation, these patterns can be played on the mouth of the bell, on the neck, or any combination of the two.

3–2 Clave Position

2-3 Clave Position

1a.

1b.
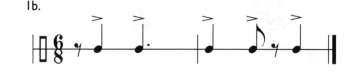

2a.

2b.
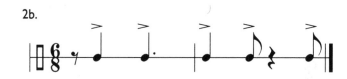

3a.

3b.
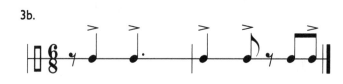

4a.

4b.

5a.

5b.
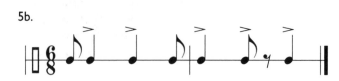

6a.

6b.

7a.

7b.

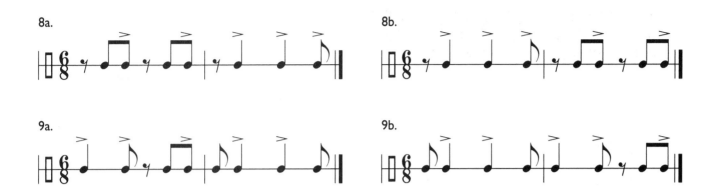

8a.

8b.

9a.

9b.

CENCERRO PATTERNS IN ¢

The first group of patterns are commonly referred to as *Bongo Bell* patterns since they are the most common patterns played by the *Bongocero* during the *Montuno* section of an arrangement and during the high dynamic solos.

When there is notation under the patterns, the key is as follows (same as key introduced on previous page): **If there is no notation, then the top line is the mouth and the bottom line is the neck, mirroring your holding of the bell as you play.**

1a=Open stroke on mouth of bell.
1b=Muffled stroke on mouth of bell.
2=Muffled stroke on neck of bell.
3=Semi-muffled stroke on edge of bell.

3–2 Clave Position

2-3 Clave Position

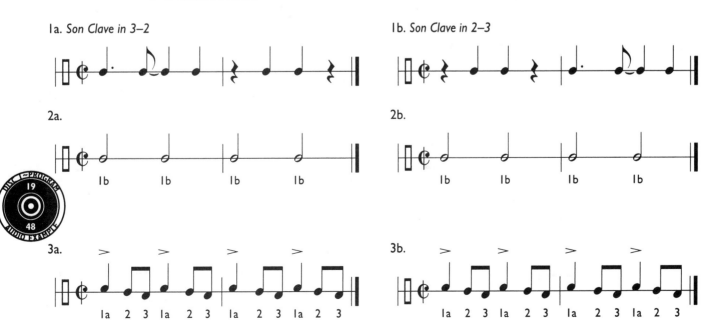

1a. *Son Clave in 3–2*

1b. *Son Clave in 2–3*

2a.

1b   1b   1b   1b

2b.

1b   1b   1b   1b

3a.

1a 2 3 1a 2 3 1a 2 3 1a 2 3

3b.

1a 2 3 1a 2 3 1a 2 3 1a 2 3

3–2 Clave Position

2-3 Clave Position

4a.
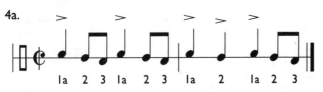

la 2 3 la 2 3 la 2 la 2 3

4b.

la 2 la 2 3 la 2 3 la 2 3

These next patterns—the same as the basic *Palito* or *Cascara* patterns—are commonly used during percussion solos. They are generally played on the mouth of the bell. First practice the pattern *without the accents.* When you can make that groove try playing the *accented notes on the mouth* and the *unaccented notes down towards the neck.*

How much distinction you can make partly depends on the tempo and your technique. At very fast tempos you basically play the whole thing on the mouth. At slower tempos you can bring the accents out more. Even when you play the whole thing on the mouth, the accents are an important inflection. They shouldn't disrupt the flow of the pattern.

3–2 Clave Position

2-3 Clave Position

These patterns are more syncopated variations that function the same as the last pattern. You can use these for percussion solos or during the *Mambo* or *Montuno* sections of arrangements. Since they are more syncopated, not all musi-

cal situations will accommodate them. When they're used also depends on what the timbalero's bell pattern is. ***Reminder: the top line is the lower pitch and is played on the mouth of the bell. The bottom line, the higher pitch, is played on the neck.***

3–2 Clave Position

2-3 Clave Position

la.

lb.

2a. **Note:** *Audio example 2a starts on the second bar.*

2b.
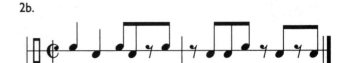

3a.

3b. **Note:** *Audio example 3b starts as written.*

3–2 Clave Position

2-3 Clave Position

The following patterns are various combinations for the Conga de Comparsa and the Mozambique. They are played on the *Cencerro* but in their traditional form are played on other types of bells (depending on the situation). For example, those for the *Conga/Comparsa* styles are played on an instrument called *Sartenes*—metal pans welded together—when played in the Cuban Carnaval parades. For all practical applications though, all of these patterns can be played on the *Cencerro*. These patterns are most commonly played with the *Rumba Clave*. In your phrasing of these rhythms you not only have to keep the clave in mind, but the *Bombo* note—the *and-of-two on the three-side of the clave* in order to project the right feel. ***Reminder: The top line is played on the mouth of the bell. The bottom line is played on the neck.***

3–2 Clave Position

2-3 Clave Position

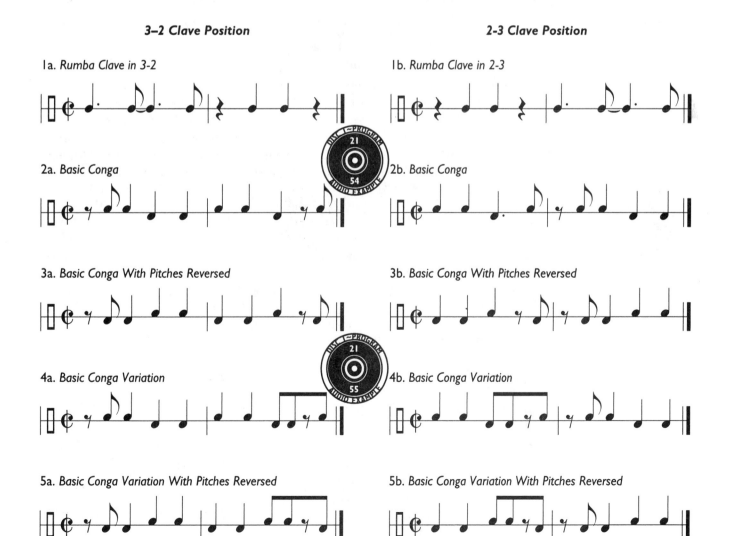

1a. *Rumba Clave in 3-2*

1b. *Rumba Clave in 2-3*

2a. *Basic Conga*

2b. *Basic Conga*

3a. *Basic Conga With Pitches Reversed*

3b. *Basic Conga With Pitches Reversed*

4a. *Basic Conga Variation*

4b. *Basic Conga Variation*

5a. *Basic Conga Variation With Pitches Reversed*

5b. *Basic Conga Variation With Pitches Reversed*

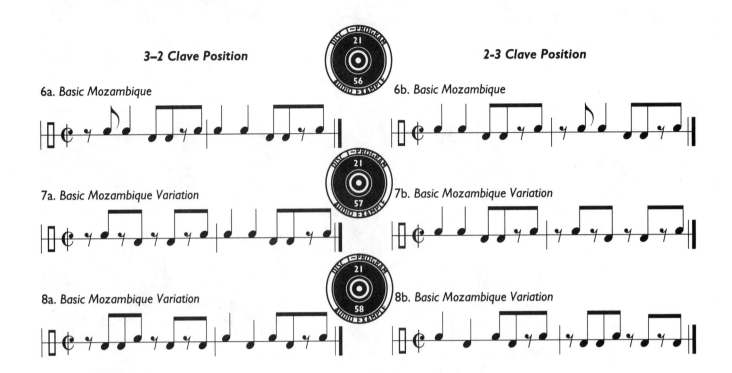

3–2 Clave Position

2-3 Clave Position

6a. Basic Mozambique

6b. Basic Mozambique

7a. Basic Mozambique Variation

7b. Basic Mozambique Variation

8a. Basic Mozambique Variation

8b. Basic Mozambique Variation

More bell variations for these two styles are in their respective drum set sections.

Now we move onto the *Mambo/ Timbale* bells. As previously stated, these bells are most often mounted and played by the *Timbalero* in his setup. There are *many* patterns and variations played on these bells, but we'll address the two most common here and present the rest later in the book. *Figure 1* on the following page shows a pretty common setup of the *Mambo, Cha-Cha* and *Charanga* bells on a set of timbales, along with a jam block functioning as the woodblock sound. *Figures 2* and *3* show the playing of the mambo bell. It is virtually impossible to notate or photograph all of the nuances of playing the patterns on this bell. I mentioned earlier that cowbells are like cymbals in that no two are alike in sound. Playing a ride pattern on this cowbell is like playing a jazz ride on a cymbal with all its many variations and nuances. You don't play all of the strokes with the tip of the stick; you play with varying depths of the shoulder and you certainly don't play all your strokes in one part of the cymbal. You play some in the center, some on the edge, some near the bell, on the bell, and so

on. These same factors are a part of playing the *timbale* bell. Generally the opening of the bell faces to the right so you have the entire top of the bell's surface to play on. Try using different parts of the stick (timbale sticks or dowels, not drum sticks with beaded tips)—the tip, a little down the shoulder, the whole shoulder—and different parts of the bell—the neck of the bell, near the clamp, all the way to the edge, and the mouth. Notice how the tone changes. Try playing some completely open tones where the bell rings, and try dead-sticking the bell so the tones are dampened. This multitude of sounds and articulations are essential to getting the right sound and feel.

We'll look at two very common patterns: first the *Palitos* pattern presented in the last chapter, also known as the *Cascara* or *Paila* pattern, because it is the pattern most commonly played on the sides of the timbales, (which are also known as *Cascara* and *Paila)*; And second, a common *Mambo* pattern played on this bell by the *Timbalero* during a *Mambo* songstyle or during the

figure 1

figure 2

Montuno section of an arrangement. *More specific details about the playing of these patterns as well as other variations are presented later in the Timbales Section as well as in the Songstyles Section.* Both rhythms are listed with the clave in both the 3–2 and 2–3 positions. Also notice that accents have been notated. In the first pattern try playing the accented notes as open tones (tones that ring more), and the unaccented tones as *dead-sticked* strokes. In general try to make a tonal/timbral difference as well as a volume difference between the accented and unaccented notes. In the second pattern the open and closed tones have been specifically notated

figure 3

along with the accents. Even though this is a very close notation of the rhythm, you must learn the true articulation by ear from the audio recording provided with this book and, most importantly, from listening to as many artists as possible.

3–2 Clave Position   **2-3 Clave Position**

MAMBO~TIMBALE BELL PATTERNS

Following are several of the most common patterns from Son-derived styles. Applications of these patterns within each specific style are presented and discussed in Part II. For now, try to memorize them all and get them to groove with all the correct inflections. Listen to some recordings and play the patterns along with them to help you get the right feel. As mentioned on the previous page, keep in mind the many variations in inflection that are played within each pattern and the many nuances that each particular player adds. Listen to the recording and to the masters for the true reference. All examples are presented in both clave positions.

3–2 Clave Position　　　　　　　　　　　　　　**2-3 Clave Position**

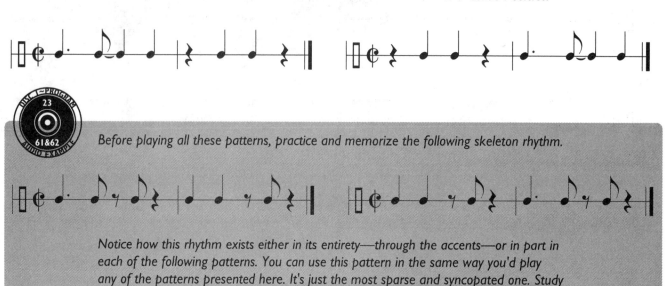

Before playing all these patterns, practice and memorize the following skeleton rhythm.

Notice how this rhythm exists either in its entirety—through the accents—or in part in each of the following patterns. You can use this pattern in the same way you'd play any of the patterns presented here. It's just the most sparse and syncopated one. Study it because it is the underlying fundamental rhythm and accent of all these patterns.

Examples 1a & 1b are here for review since they are the two most common patterns. They were presented on the last page. Use these to start practicing and to get the groove going. Three through fourteen are a few common variations.

3–2 Clave Position　　　　　　　　　　　　　　**2-3 Clave Position**

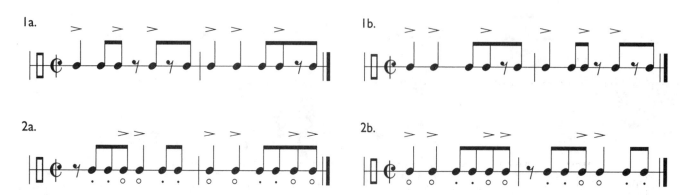

3–2 Clave Position

2-3 Clave Position

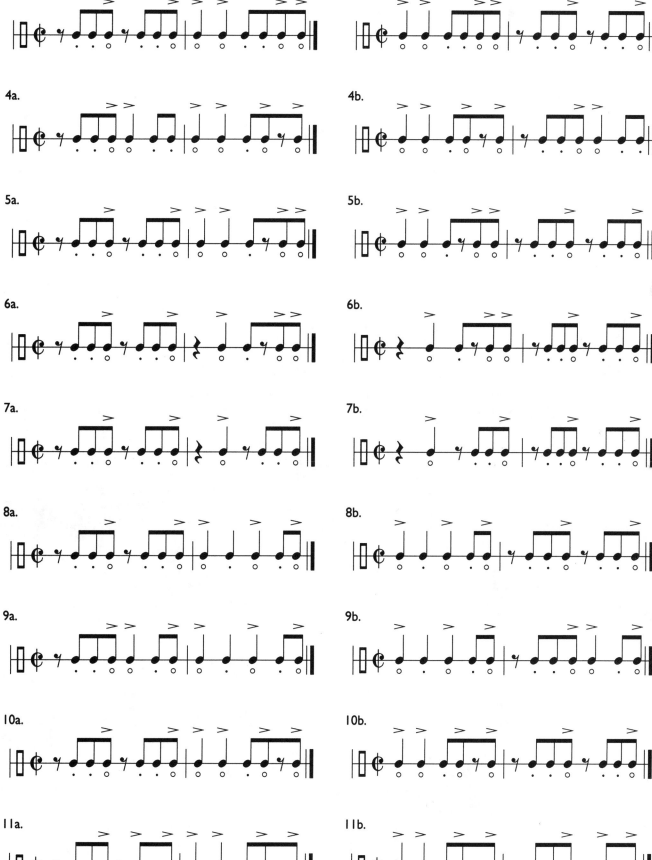

3–2 Clave Position   **2-3 Clave Position**

12a.   12b.

13a.   13b.

14a.   14b.

The *Cha-Cha* and *Charanga* bells are the smallest and highest pitched bells and are almost exclusively used for these two styles and also the *Guajira, Bolero* and other slower, quarter note pulsed $\frac{4}{4}$ styles. (Most *Charanga* interpretations are slightly faster and "in two.") These bells are mostly played with the shoulder of the stick on the mouth of the bell. Sometimes the stroke is dead-sticked, producing a muted tone and sometimes not, allowing the bell to ring. In rhythmic patterns that consist of more than just quarter notes, the tip of the stick is used to strike more towards the center top of the bell. Which strokes and patterns are played is dependent on the style and/or the section of a particular piece.

As shown in the timbale setup of the previous page, the *Cha-Cha* bell is usually faced directly away from the player (with the mouth facing forward and away from the player—towards the audience) or facing left (opposite the mambo bell) if the woodblock is not used. The *Charanga* bell is usually clipped to the rim of the timbales with the opening of the mouth facing the player.

Figure 1 shows the stroke toward the center of the bell with the tip of the stick (this stroke sweeps forward towards the mouth stroke), and *figure 2* shows the stroke towards the mouth of the bell with the shoulder of the stick.

figure 1

figure 2

The two most common patterns played on these bells are the following: the first is played on the mouth of the bell with the shoulder of the stick. The second is played with a combination of two sounds and strokes. Play the quarter notes on the mouth with the shoulder of the stick and the eighths on the body with the tip of the stick. *Since these are one-bar patterns repeated, the pattern itself does not spell out the clave so you have to be aware of which direction the clave is in.*

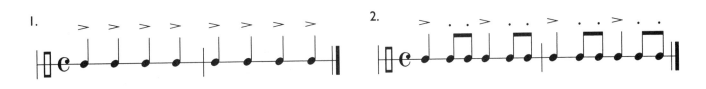

The final bells we'll mention are the *Comparsa/Conga* bells. During the *Carnaval* parades the actual bells used are called *Sartenes* (they are actually frying pans welded together), *Agogo*-type bells and *brake drums*. Basically you need two different pitches to play the patterns. There are many varieties of bells and many patterns that are layered over the basic one. A cencerro is also commonly used and the neck and mouth are played for the two different pitches. Here are two illustrations (*figures 3 & 4*) and a basic pattern is written below. (The Conga style is addressed in detail in its own section. Other similar bell patterns are also presented in the Mozambique section since this style emanated from the Conga tradition. Additional variations were also presented earlier in this section.)

figure 3

figure 4

Clave

Top line notes on the mouth of the bell— (figure 4).
Bottom line notes on the neck of the bell— (figure 3).

You could also mount the bell or mount two bells to emulate the sartenes or brake drums and play the following pattern:

CONGAS~TUMBADORAS

CONGA DRUMS—OR TUMBADORAS—AS THEY ARE TRADITIONALLY CALLED, ARE DIRECT DESCENDANTS OF THE CONICAL HAND DRUMS— MAKUTA DRUMS—OF THE CONGOLESE AFRICANS. They have undergone many incarnations since their inception, resulting in an extremely wide variety of shapes, sizes, makes, and models, each producing its own distinct sound. While many cultures throughout the world use what we loosely refer to as congas, none has taken conga drumming to the technical levels that have resulted from their use in Cuban folkloric styles, and all of the popular Afro-Latin musical styles. Their use in styles connected to Batá ritual music and the folkloric rumba and carnaval styles has taken the playing of conga drums to an unprecedented level, and their use in popular dance styles has yielded a high level of performance and craftsmanship. To a serious conguero or tumbador the playing of these drums is nothing to be taken lightly. The fact that the playing of the instrument is physical goes hand-in-hand with the fact that the precedent for performance includes a big, fat, and strong sound. While without a doubt a staple of Afro-Cuban folklore, the congas began their trek to worldwide popularity with their addition to the *Conjunto* format—an ensemble format derived from the *Septeto* in the 1940s. (Also added at this time were trumpets and more vocalists that usually also played maracas and clave. *More on these ensembles in the Songstyles Section of the book.*) Congas are present in not only most Afro-Latin ensembles and songstyles today but have become an accepted instrument in most popular music throughout the world.

Tumba, Quinto, Segundo

Though there are many sizes and types of these drums, we'll be dealing with three sizes and types (and every variety of size will fit into one of these three). The three most common and familiar names for the three types are— from largest to smallest—the *Tumba, Conga* (or *Segundo*), and *Quinto*. Each of the three drums is sometimes called by a different name depending on the style it is being played in, and these names sometimes also correspond to the rhythm played by that drum in that part. As explained earlier, if someone says "play palitos," you play not only the sticks and the gua-gua (or whatever instrument or sound is being substituted for it), but also the rhythm. Likewise, if someone in referring to the tumbadoras says, "play the *Tres Golpes*," you would play the middle drum and the middle part of the *Guaguancó* rhythm. If they said "play *Salidor*," you would be playing the low drum and the corresponding part but only if referring to *Guaguancó*. If you were playing for a *Comparsa*, the *Salidor* is the high drum and its part. This can get a little confusing, but you get used to hearing certain names used for certain drums and parts, and that is all part of the terminology of this style.

figure 1

figure 2

figure 3

The drums are most commonly played one, two, or three at a time and the three drums together cover the primary parts of all of the styles we discuss in this book. Pictured in *figures 1, 2, 3,* and *4* are the three most common ways the drums are set up with *figures 3* and *4* being the two most common three-drum setups. (Many artists of the congas also use many more drums for their performances.) Again, what each drum is called, and whether played individually or in a set of two or three, depends on the musical setting. We'll establish some common terminology to get things going. The Quinto is almost always referred to as such, except when it functions as the high drum in the *Conga/Comparsa,* where it is called the *Salidor* (unless there is an actual Quinto soloing, in which case the next highest of the drums is called the Salidor and the Quinto remains as the Quinto). It is also referred to as the *solo drum* or *primero,* due to its role in the *rumba* styles where it solos and is the primary "interactor" with the vocals and dancing. The middle drum is called the *Conga* or *Segundo*—the most common all-around names—*Tres Golpes in Guaguancó,* and *Rebajador* in the *Conga/Comparsa* styles. The lowest

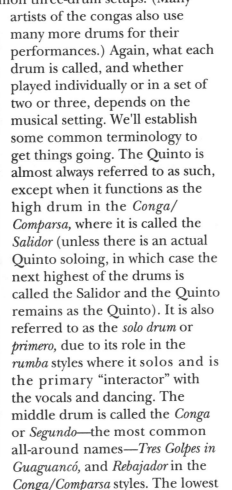

figure 4

figure 5

figure 6

and the largest drum in the set is called the *Tumba*—the most common all-around name—and the *Salidor* in the *Guaguancó.*

If you're playing only one drum, then you could be playing any of the three depending on the songstyle. If you're playing a set of two, then you're more than likely going to be playing the *Conga* and the *Tumba.* If you're playing three, then it would be the *Tumba, Conga & Quinto.* Setups are pretty much a personal thing but illustrated above are the four most common drum arrangements. A one drum setup is obvious but you also have to hold the drum correctly, so let's cover that now.

The *Tumbadora* is held in the instep or between the heels of your feet in such a way that you can lean the drum slightly away from you and play on it with both hands freely (*figure 1*). You also help hold the drum with your legs as it leans. This leaning away from you is to create space between the opening and the floor so the drum will resonate more. (If you are playing on a carpeted floor then you should place the drums on a wooden board large enough to accommodate all the drums you are playing. This especially helps the resonance of the drums you aren't holding—the ones sitting directly on the floor.) You must also hold them tightly enough—or be able to apply enough grip with you're feet—to lift the drum up several inches off the floor. This is commonly done when playing bass tones—to allow them to resonate more—or when playing open tones—to get a pitch bend effect (*figures 5 & 6*).

If you're playing one drum you obviously hold that one drum. If you're playing a set of two—*Conga* and *Tumba* or *Salidor* and *Tres Golpes*—whatever you call the two—then you generally hold the smaller of the two and place the larger one to your right assuming you're right-handed. If you're playing a set of three then you generally hold the *Quinto* and place the other two off to your right as shown in figure three with the *Tumba* directly right and the *Segundo* forward. The alternate setups for the three drums could be to hold the *Quinto* and place the *Conga* and *Tumba* on either side of you, figure four—both are common—or hold the *Conga* with the *Tumba* to your right like a set of two, and place the *Quinto* to your left.

There's one final topic to touch on before continuing with the exercises and that's the tuning of the drums. Again, this is a very personal and subjective thing from player to player but there are a few guidelines you can follow that stem from some common practices. First, each drum head should be in tune with itself, meaning that at each lug point the pitch of the drum is the same. If you have a preference for lower or higher pitches that's fine, but keep in mind that each drum size and head has as optimal resonance area where the drum will speak best. Don't choke the sound by tightening too much and don't lose tone and resonance by tuning too low. Since weather affects the natural hide of the heads the drums should be tuned for each playing and then the heads should be loosened to preserve it for a longer period. For two drums try some specific intervals—a fourth is very common and gives you a tonic-dominant relationship between the drums. You can even try to tune to general tonal areas of a piece—as long as the harmony of the piece isn't complicated. If you're playing a traditional I-IV-V type *Salsa* style vamp then this works great. You can also try thirds, tritones, etc. Start with C and the G below it and then work from there. As you move to three and four or more drums, thirds and seconds become more common. For three drums you can start with a fourth between the *Tumba* and *Conga* and put the *Quinto* a second or major or minor third above that. Another very common three drum tuning is a minor third between the *Tumba* and *Conga* with the *Quinto* a major second above the *Conga*. As you deal with different musical situations the tuning issue will become second nature. As always with any style or instrument, listen to the masters for the ultimate guidance.

The next essential component is the playing technique. There are an infinite number of sounds that can be played on a *Tumbadora* with some being essential to the performance of specific patterns and other being more decorative and more commonly used in solo improvisation or for effects. Let's look at the individual sounds and how to play them. (*Developing each of the various sounds is essential to getting the patterns to sound right. You can't play the patterns without having the technique down so don't jump ahead.*)

The basic sounds that you have to master to play the drums are the following: *Heel–Toe Rocking Motion (sometimes called the Marcha or Manoteo), Open Tones, Palm (Closed) Tones, Slaps—three types: Open Slaps, Closed Slaps and Muted Slaps, the Tapado Stroke, and Bass Tones.* Other sounds include playing with the fists, nails, chin, elbows, sliding groans, fingertips, playing harmonics, playing with sticks on both the head and the sides and anything your musical imagination can conjure. Following is an illustration and specific instructions for the development of each sound.

Open Tones

Played with the fingers and palm towards the edge of the drum. These tones should ring and produce a nice round open tone. Practice developing these by landing the palm of your hand on the edge of the drum and letting your fingers bounce off the head, letting the tone ring. When you can get the sound consistently improvise some rhythms.

Closed/Palm and some variations of the Tapado Tones

Played with the palm and/or fingers on various parts of the head—center, edge or any place in between—depending on the sound desired. These tones are muted and don't ring. Practice playing these tones in various parts of the head. Slightly change the shape of your hand from totally flat and open to slightly cupped and notice how the sound changes. Also see Tapado under the Slap Tones.

Bass Tones

Played with the heel of the hand on the center of the drum—the stroke is actually just slightly off center. Another variation of the tone can also be played with the entire hand flat on the head. If you're playing sitting down and holding the drum with your legs, you can pick it up off the floor to get more sound. If the drums are on stands then they're already up off the floor and this isn't an issue.

Heel–Toe Motion~The Marcha

*Played by rocking between the heel and toe (fingertips) of the hand (although the true sound is really the entire palm of the hand for the heel strokes, and the fingers and palm for the tip strokes). These tones are muffled and do not ring. They are the double strokes and groove timekeeper of the hand drums. As the groove timekeeper it is referred to as the **Marcha** or **Manoteo**. As the double strokes they are used in soloing and as variations in patterns. Practice rocking each hand individually until you get a strong sound and some endurance. Then start playing combinations between the two hands. The motion is actually as much back and forth as it is up and down. Keep your forearm kind of parallel to the head of the drum. This should almost happen naturally if you're holding the drum at the right height.*

Following are some exercise combinations to develop the Heel-Toe motion. Play slowly at first concentrating on getting a strong attack and a good sound from both the heel and tip of the hand, then work on the speed. Notice that number eight has a different alternating pattern—HHTT. This is a very common and very important combination—especially in the Rumba styles. Make up exercises of your own to build more chops.

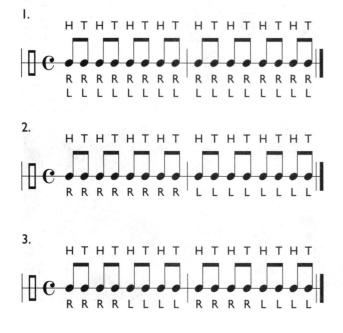

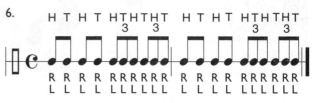

7.
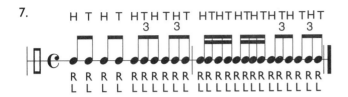

8.

Finally we'll address the sound that will probably take you the longest to build up—the slap. There are three general varieties of the slap—closed, open and muted—*tapado*. (The *tapado* stroke—the word itself means "capped" or "topped"—is a unique stroke in that it can be an accented sort of slap tone, but can also be a muted tone that still rings the fundamental of the drum but in a kind of "choked" or "covered" way.) While these sounds do require a lot of repetition to get right, they don't require you to beat your hands to death in order to get them. Force and loud volume do not get you the slap—or any other tone. The correct hand placement and stroke and attack does the trick. Endurance, power and a big sound come more from repetition than short stints of bashing. You're better off practicing each exercise slowly and more softly—*but for more extended periods*—than killing yourself for a couple of minutes and then not being able to play for a week. Some of the greatest conga players have relatively soft hands—not all of them—but those that have practiced good technique generally do. You will develop some callouses and you'll have to play on the pain a little to develop the endurance and technique, but remember, more repetitions for longer periods, with less force and correct hand placement and stroke types, will give far better and quicker results. Following are illustrations of the correct hand positions for each of the slaps and then some basic exercises. Later in the book are some advanced exercises for more technique, independence, multiple instrument playing and the like.

Closed Slap/Tapado

Open Slap

Muted Slap

The following exercises—as well as the *Heel/Toe* exercises from the previous page, others you acquire from other players, and those you make up on your own—should become part of a regular practice routine that you should run through before playing the specific songstyle patterns.

Conga Notation

In an effort to simplify the memorization of a notation scheme, multi-line examples are used only to signify different drums. All notation for a single drum is written on one line with one type of notehead. Which hand is playing and what stroke type it's playing is written above and below each note, respectively. All you have to memorize are the names of the tones and then the first letter of the name is written above the note.

*The rhythms are simple enough that you shouldn't have to read them so you can memorize the repetition pattern—i.e.: **O S P** above the note and **R R L** below it and the notes are **triplets** means play an **Open Tone** then a **Slap** with the **right hand** and then a **Palm Tone** with the **left hand** in **triplets**. Now you don't have to read the music. Look at your hands and make sure your hand placement is correct on the drum and listen to the sounds you're producing. Here's the notation key:*

R = Right Hand
L = Left Hand
O = Open Tone
C = Closed Tone—*meaning a muffled tone with part of your palm and/or fingers—one variety of the Tapado sound.*
P = Palm Tone—*Also a closed tone but more specifically a full palm tone towards the center of the head.*
S = Slap—*Play a Closed Slap to start. Later you can make distinctions between the Closed, Open and Muted types. This can also indicate a variation of the Tapado.*
H = Heel *of hand stroke—as in the Heel/Toe (tip) rocking motion*
T = Toe *or Tip of hand stroke—as in the Heel/Toe (tip) rocking motion*
B = Bass Tone

In exercises 1, 6, and 7 make one exercise out of each sticking line and then also practice alternating hands as you repeat—i.e.: in example 1 you would first practice all Rights then all Lefts and then repeat alternating between two bars of Rights then two bars of Lefts. The same applies to numbers 6 and 7. Also notice that exercise 8 is a different Heel-Toe combination. This is also a very common stroke combination so focus on it quite a bit.

Before continuing on review and practice the following exercises once again. They are the same exercises presented on pages 72 and 73. They should be memorized and become part of a regular practice and warm-up routine. These will strengthen your basic chops and endurance.

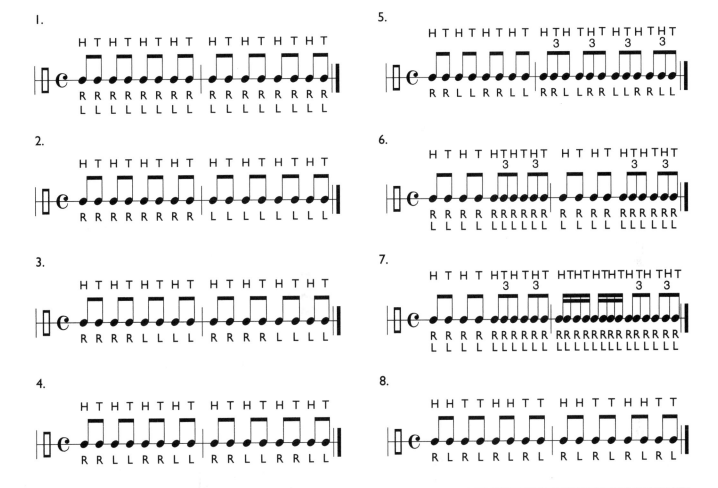

In these exercises each line is one separate exercise (to be repeated), so each example is five separate exercises. These exercises are great for developing the slap so don't bash. Focus on the correct hand position and placement and do many repetitions at a comfortable level. Your sound and endurance and strength will develop with time.

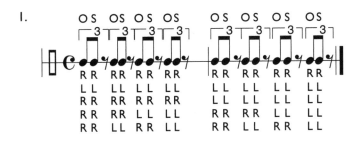

2.

3.

4.

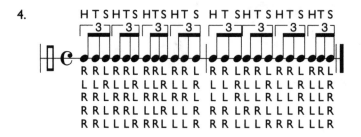

5.

Following are some more technical exercises that combine various stroke types—Open Tones, Slaps, Bass Tones and the Heel-Toe rocking motion.

1.

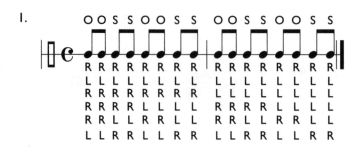

2.

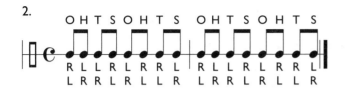

3.

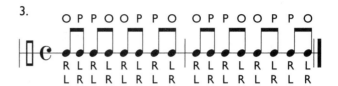

These next exercises are based on the rudimental rolls—five through fifteen stroke rolls. When played on congas, or any instrument played with the hands, the double strokes of the rolls are played with the Heel-Toe

rocking motion. You can work up enough speed and power practicing these that you're almost bouncing your hands—HTHT—as you do with sticks, and get very fast and fluid rolls on the congas.

1. *5 Stroke Roll*

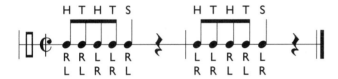

6. *10 Stroke Roll*

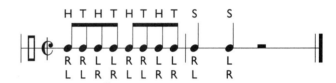

2. *6 Stroke Roll*

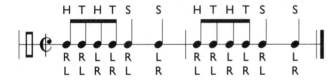

7. *11 Stroke Roll*

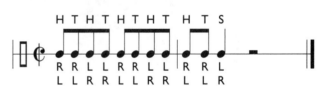

3. *7 Stroke Roll*

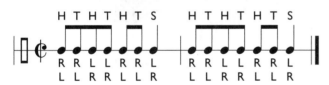

8. *12 Stroke Roll*

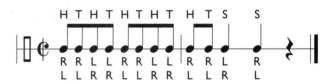

4. *8 Stroke Roll*

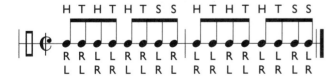

9. *13 Stroke Roll*

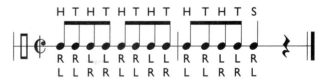

5. *9 Stroke Roll*

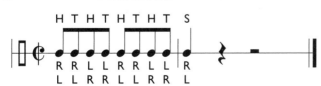

10. *15 Stroke Roll*

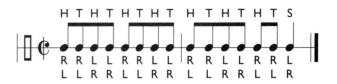

Finally here are some technical exercises which stress independence between the hands. These are good not only for conga playing but for general percussion playing as well. Illustrated in the photos are approaches for this. You can play the fixed rhythm with a stick on the side of the drum, or you can mount a bell or other instrument (as pictured below) and play it with your hand, while your other hand plays the rhythmic variations and improvisations. You'll also do exercises of this sort with one hand playing a fixed pattern directly on one drum, while the other plays rhythmic variations or improvisations on the other drums. This is actually a way of playing certain folkloric styles when one player is playing

several players' parts alone. Developing this will also give you a lot of facility in playing two or more different instruments simultaneously, as when you are playing percussion on a pop type of gig, where various colors may be necessary at the same time but there's only one percussionist. You can try this by playing guiro and congas, bells and congas, shakers and congas, or any combination you can dream up. Also remember you can rig things to play with your feet.

We'll begin by using some simple patterns working from the half note as an ostinato to more complex patterns. Take you're time with these. Getting these down the right way will really give you a lot of facility on the drums.

Practice the following with one hand playing the fixed rhythm line and the other playing the written variations. Then switch hands and do it the other way. You can start by playing these exercises as in the illustrations above. Also included in this section are exercises for two drums where you play two different tones—one as an ostinato on one drum and the written line on the other. The key here is not just the rhythms but the playing of the different tones.

The first four rhythms at the top of the next page are the fixed patterns—

the ostinatos—that you'll play with one hand while the other hand plays the exercises that follow.

The rhythms of the four ostinatos are the Son Clave, Rumba Clave, the Cencerro Bell pattern, and the Cascara pattern. The ostinatos for the $\frac{6}{8}$ section are the $\frac{6}{8}$ clave and the $\frac{6}{8}$ bell pattern.

If these ostinatos are too difficult for you at first, try starting with half notes and then quarter notes as your first two ostinatos. Once you get it with those you'll move to the others more easily.

Ostinatos 1

1. Son Clave

3. Cencerro Bell Pattern

2. Rumba Clave

4. Cascara Pattern

Exercises 1 This group of exercises focuses on the Heel-Toe motion and independence between the hands. Play each of the ostinatos above with the rhythms below.

1.

7.

2.
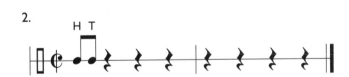

8.

3.
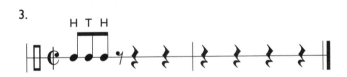

9.

4.

10.

5.

11.

6.
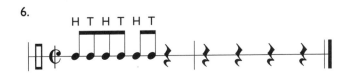

12.

13.

15.

14.

16.

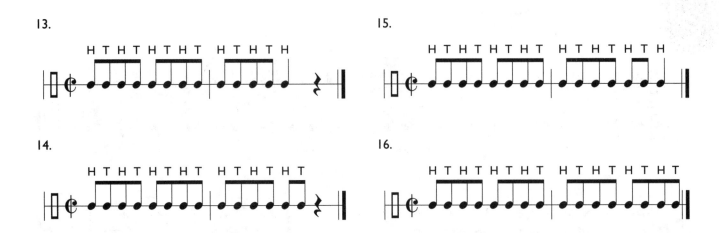

Exercises 2 *These exercises are written simply as a rhythmic table that you should memorize since this is a formula you can use to create a wealth of technical studies. Basically you should play the following rhythms with one hand against all four ostinatos in the other. Repeat every exercise many times until you are comfortable with it and then move onto the next one. In the end you should be able to play each one as well as move from one to the next and from any one to any other one without any disruption of the rhythmic flow. Use every stroke type with these variations. In other words, play through the entire exercise with slaps, then with bass tones, and gradually work with all of the sounds. When you can play it through comfortably with all the ostinatos in one hand and all of these rhythms with any sound in the other, practice improvising rhythms as well as stroke types.*

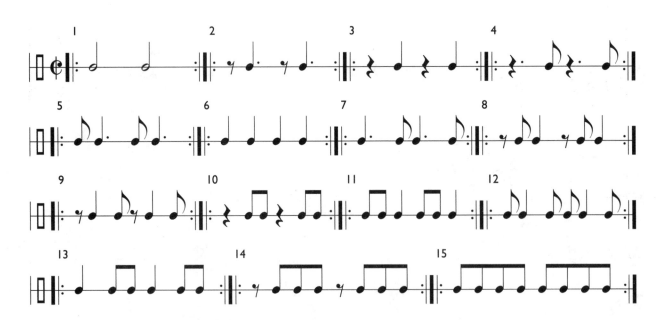

Improvisation 1 *Following is an example of an improvisation using the Rumba Clave as the ostinato in one hand and playing the rhythmic line on one conga drum with a variety of tones with the other. You can also play this on two drums and of course you can take it wherever you want. For musical examples of this listen to the Quinto improvisations in traditional rumba groups like Los Muñequitos de Matanzas, Los Papines, Totico y Sus Rumberos and the like. Many more are listed in the Suggested Listening section.*

Ostinatos 2

1. §Clave

2. §Bell Pattern

3. §Pattern

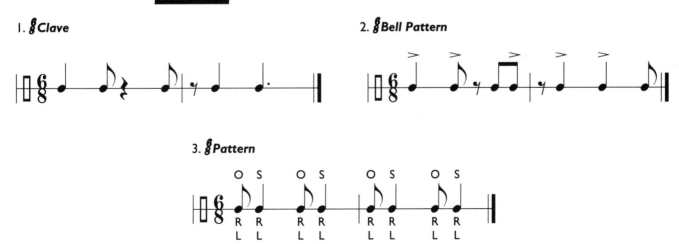

Exercises 3 *The following exercises represent the same approach as the last group but working in ⁶⁄₈. Use the same routine for these rhythms.*

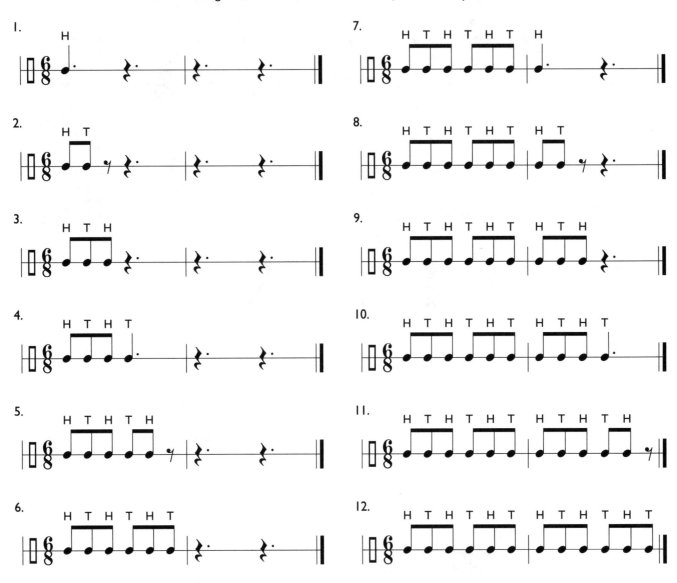

Exercises 4 *The following is a rhythmic table in ⁶⁄₈, (or triplets if in a duple meter). Use the same approach as with the last rhythmic table. Play with one ostinato in one hand and these rhythms in the other. Use all of the different stroke types, then improvise.*

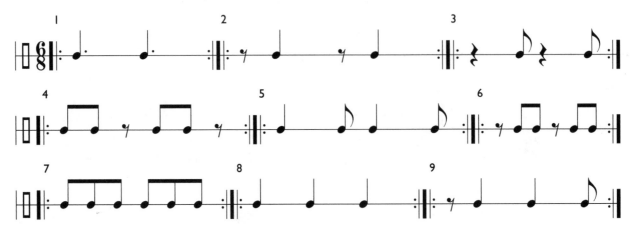

Improvisation 2 *Following is an improvisation using the previous ⁶⁄₈ rhythms. This could also be played on two drums with either the same or different stroke types. Again, refer to the listening list for examples of this type of playing. Keep working with all of these concepts until you can play freely incorporating all of this material.*

FUNDAMENTAL RHYTHM PATTERNS OF THE VARIOUS STYLES

THE TUMBAÓ

The most fundamental, common, and familiar pattern on the Conga drums is a rhythm called *Tumbaó*. It is the basic Conga drum rhythm for practically all of the *Son*-derived styles with the only basic difference in the pattern from style to style being the tempo. Played for the *Guajira, Cha-Cha, Son* (*Son Montuno*) and *Mambo*—from slowest to fastest— the pattern is essentially the same.

Patterns 1 and 2 are the basic one-bar patterns and patterns 3 and 4 have a slight variation. Since they are *one-bar* phrases, the patterns themselves are not spelling out the clave rhythm, even though *you are still in whatever clave position the piece is in.* Consequently any variation you play must still be *in clave.* Since the styles this rhythm is used for can vary drastically in tempo, the pattern takes place in both $\frac{4}{4}$ and $\frac{2}{2}$ time. Here it is notated in $\frac{2}{2}$, but practice it at all tempos. Again, since these are one-bar

patterns you are not denoting the clave with the pattern itself, but you must be aware of it nonetheless, since moving to a two-bar phrase requires syncing with the clave, and any variation of these patterns must be in clave. Practice the patterns starting in both the 3-2 and 2-3 clave positions.

These first four examples are the most common one-drum patterns. Only one thing differs from pattern to pattern, but that one small detail makes the rhythms feel very different. Pattern 1 is the basic Tumbaó with a slap on beat 2, open tones on 4 and 4+ and the Marcha (heel-toe rocking motion) in the left hand. Pattern 2 is the same as pattern 1 except that only beat 4 is an open tone. Patterns 3 and 4 mirror patterns 1 and 2 with the addition of the open tone on beat 2+. Practice each pattern until you have it down, then practice improvising phrases using all four of them.

Basic one-bar patterns for one drum

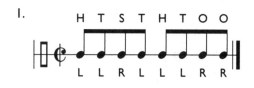

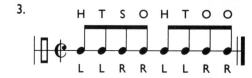

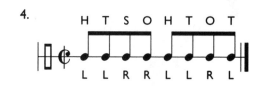

Next we move on to one bar patterns for two drums. Since they are still one bar patterns the same situation with the clave applies as in the previous examples but remember not to lose track of where you are in the two bar clave pattern. This is most important as you move onto combining the one bar patterns to make two bar (or longer) patterns and to improvising. Patterns 1 and 2 have the slap on beat 2 with the open tone on beat 2+ on the Tumba. The difference between the two is on beat four. Patterns 3 and 4 have the slap on beat 2, the open tone on beat 3 on the Tumba and the open tone variations on beat 4. Pattern 5 is the basic one bar pattern for the Son Montuno. Any of these patterns can be used as variations for any of the styles that use the Tumbaó.

Basic one bar patterns for two drums

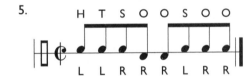

"A Caballo" pattern

Rhythms 6a and 6b are patterns used for a style called Caballo—horse—because the rhythm grooves like a horse trotting. This rhythm comes from a style called Pachanga which came from the Charanga style and ensembles. This pattern is often called for in orchestra arrangements. On the chart (perhaps at a bridge section) you might see a section marked "A Caballo"—like a horse—at which time you would play this pattern or the two bar variation on the next page.

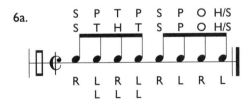

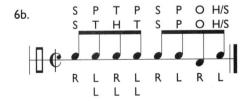

Bolero pattern

Rhythm pattern 7 is the basic pattern for the Bolero—a slow ballad form.

Practice all of the previous patterns at a variety of tempos—from *Cha-Cha* tempo to *Mambo* tempo. When you're comfortable with each, combine two of them to make a two bar phrase and use the others for variations in the time feel and to make longer phrases. Make sure you're able to go from any one to any other one without disrupting the flow and the groove.

Two bar variations for two drums

Now that we've examined the one bar skeleton patterns let's start working with some two bar phrases for these styles that use the *Tumbaó* rhythm. Here is where you really have to focus on the pattern you're playing and its relation to the clave. A two bar phrase only works one way with the clave. That is each bar of the pattern corresponds with each bar of the clave. You cannot reverse (invert) the bars or you've crossed clave. This not only applies to the pattern itself, but any variations to the pattern and any soloing also needs to be in clave (that is, cadence with the clave correctly). All of this will become more self-evident as you play more and listen more and gain more vocabulary in this style.

Here is the Son Clave in both 3-2 and 2-3 positions. Under it is the basic two bar Tumbaó rhythm. The pattern is for the Segundo and the Tumba. Note that when the pattern goes down to the Tumba it is with the three side and the *bombo* note of the clave. This is the way this pattern lines up in clave. (To say that it is never played any other way would be extreme, but you should learn it this way and get it down. Once you can play in clave then you can do whatever you want.) Practice and memorize this pattern in both clave positions. *Note: When the pattern is first started the first note is very often an **accented open tone**.*

3-2 Son Clave

2-3 Son Clave

A.

B.

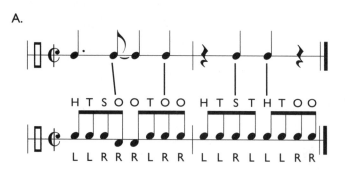

Following are some common variations of the Tumbaó rhythm. *They are written in 2-3 clave.* When you have them under control, practice them starting on the second bar so that you'll cover them in the 3-2 clave position as well.

1.

2.

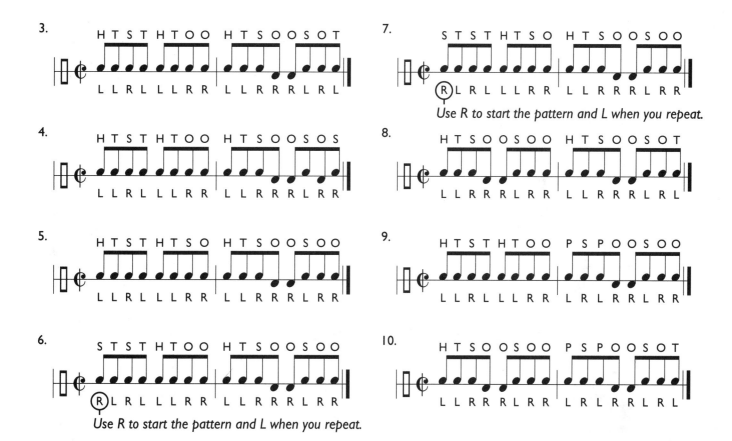

3.

H T S T H T O O   H T S O O S O T

L L R L L L R R   L L R R R L R L

4.

H T S T H T O O   H T S O O S O S

L L R L L L R R   L L R R R L R R

5.

H T S T H T S O   H T S O O S O O

L L R L L L R R   L L R R R L R R

6.

S T S T H T O O   H T S O O S O O

Ⓡ L R L L L R R   L L R R R L R R

Use R to start the pattern and L when you repeat.

7.

S T S T H T S O   H T S O O S O O

Ⓡ L R L L L R R   L L R R R L R R

Use R to start the pattern and L when you repeat.

8.

H T S O O S O O   H T S O O S O T

L L R R R L R R   L L R R R L R L

9.

H T S T H T O O   P S P O O S O O

L L R L L L R R   L R L R R L R R

10.

H T S O O S O O   P S P O O S O T

L L R R R L R R   L R L R R L R L

The possibilities for variations are endless. Once you get the one and two bar phrases presented here in your repertoire and you listen to some music in these styles you'll be able to improvise variations pretty easily and what to play in a particular musical situation will be pretty clear. You almost invariably use the basic Tumbaó rhythm to start and most of the time you just sit on that and make it groove. Everything else is just a slight variation. This is almost always the case in typical salsa and dance orchestras where the vocals are the feature. There are many groups that use more involved versions or mixtures of styles arranged into the pieces and if you're in an instrumental ensemble that features more improvisation then of course you're freer to experiment.

In the next section are listed specific patterns for each style. Again the variations to all of these styles are endless and new approaches to all of these are always being developed by players and ensembles. Here we'll examine the most common patterns and variations. Everything else will come from your own listening and experimentation.

Again keep a constant awareness of the clave as you play. A good thing to develop is the ability to sing the clave as you play the patterns. Learn the patterns and then play the pattern while singing the clave and keep singing the clave as you start to introduce variations and improvising. All of the patterns here are notated in 3-2 clave but practice and learn them so you can start the pattern on any side of the clave and even on any beat of the pattern. Remember these are the basic patterns only. Listen and study individual players and ensembles to develop your vocabulary. Also remember that all of the Son styles are based on the one bar Tumbaó. The rhythms presented here are two bar phrases in order to show them in a clave position.

SON

SON MONTUNO

CHA-CHA

BOLERO

GUAJIRA

PACHANGA~A CABALLO

DANZÓN

The traditional Charanga group's instrumentation had no Conga drums. It was added in the 1940s and the Tumbadoras would play only during the Montuno section (the D Section/Nuevo Ritmo) of the Danzón. This section and approach later developed into the Cha-Cha style. Shown here is the basic rhythm—tumbaó—for this section.

```
H T S O O P O O   H T S T H T O O
L L R R R L R R   L L R L L L R R
```

MAMBO

Shown here for the Mambo are three different patterns. The first is the basic two-bar Tumbaó. This is the primary pattern unless the basic one-bar Tumbaó is what the particular piece calls for. If this is the case then the two-bar pattern is what you would go to in the Montuno section of the arrangement. The second example is a slightly more intense version of the basic pattern but functions as a basic groove just the same. As long as the music calls for it, the first two are interchangeable. The third example shows a more modern version of what can be played. This can be used as the basic pattern, but it is most commonly used as the pattern for the Montuno section when coming from a basic Tumbaó, as shown in examples 1 and 2.

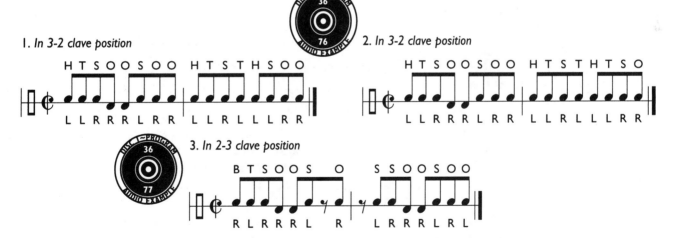

1. In 3-2 clave position

```
H T S O O S O O   H T S T H S O O
L L R R R L R R   L L R L L L R R
```

2. In 3-2 clave position

```
H T S O O S O O   H T S T H T S O
L L R R R L R R   L L R L L L R R
```

3. In 2-3 clave position

```
B T S O O S   O   S S O O S O O
R L R R R L   R   L R R R L R L
```

This concludes the family of song-styles that use the Tumbaó as the basic and primary rhythm for the conga drums. Keep in mind that what was presented here are some common varieties of the *fundamental* patterns. There are many variations that can be applied to any of these patterns and to any songstyle—some slight and some great. These can be the result of an individual player's style or approach to a style, or could be an arranging or compositional concept. Also, many variations are quite often brought about through the development of a new style or the evolution of an ensemble—as was the case with the Charanga groups developing the Danzón, and from there the Cha-Cha, and adding the congas to its instrumentation in the 1940s. This was a significant development for the congas in these styles. As always, analytical listening will be your best source for augmenting knowledge of these styles.

Next we move to the folkloric rhythms, beginning with the Rumba styles. These rhythms are traditionally played on two, three or four drums along with other instruments. (Refer to the Songstyles section for complete scores of all of the instruments.) The conga parts to these rhythms are first presented as individual parts on their corresponding drum; then a combined version is presented showing all the rhythms (or a condensed version) for one player playing all the parts.

RUMBA STYLES

There are three Rumba rhythm styles: **Guaguancó**, **Yambú** and **Columbia**. Originally the Rumba was played on the Cajones—wooden boxes in three different sizes—that functioned as the three congas do now. The Rumba Yambú continues to be played that way in folkloric settings. Presented here are the rhythms for the Tumbadoras. First each individual conga part for one player playing each drum, and then combinations for one player playing all the parts. Note and memorize the names of the drums in each of these styles because the rhythms themselves are also called or referred to by the name of the drum. The name *Salidor* in the Guaguancó is a different drum than in the Conga/Comparsa Carnaval rhythm. Also keep in mind that these rhythms are not possible to notate with total metric precision. The simultaneous duple and triple meter inflection and the improvisational language is best learned by analytical listening and aurally transcribing the performance with the drums in front of you and reproducing what you hear until you have the vocabulary under control. Don't hurry through this. It is very much a lifelong study.

GUAGUANCÓ

The Guaguancó has a wide variety of interpretations both in its conga drumming as well as its other percussion and vocal parts. Presented here are the two most common and basic approaches to the Habana and the Matanzas styles (one approach being from Habana, the capital city and the other from Matanzas, a province to the east of Habana). The rhythms notated for the Salidor and the Tres Golpes are the basic patterns. These two drums get into very intricate call-and-response patterns (conversations) between them along with the continuous improvisation and interaction the Quinto drummer has with the singers and the dancers. This leads to numerous very intricate patterns as the Guaguancó develops. Due to the improvisational nature of the performance it isn't possible to notate all of the specific playing. You learn the basic patterns from notation and you learn to play the rest from listening to other players and learning the style thoroughly.

The first two rhythms presented in this section are patterns the two drummers play to start the Guaguancó—as an ad lib introduction. With this feel started, the Salidor "calls" the Tres Golpes by playing its Guaguancó pattern and the full rhythm begins. This call-and-response used to start the piece can be a very intricate and arranged section or it can be very loose, with the Guaguancó patterns beginning right with the basic calls. (The Tres-Golpes is also called the Tres-Dos.) The Salidor is the largest and lowest-pitched drum. The Tres-Golpes the middle size and mid-pitched, and the Quinto the smallest and highest-pitched drum. The Salidor and Tres Golpes are usually tuned a fourth apart and the Quinto is

a third up from that, but this can vary between players and ensembles.

Here is the intro pattern for the Tres Golpes. It is basically a series of alternating heel and tip strokes. You just sit on this pattern and make it groove until the Salidor calls you by playing its basic pattern. Then you move on to the Tres Golpes rhythm.

Here is the intro pattern for the Salidor. There are two variations presented. The first has a straight, duple-meter inflection, and the second a triplet inflection. Either can be used in an arrangement but many times the real folkloric inflection is a combination of the two, or falls "in the cracks"

between the two. The triplet infection of this drum against the straight inflection of the Tres Golpes creates a beautiful rhythmic tension. Notice that both patterns outline the clave with a strong bass tone on the Bombo note of the three side of the clave.

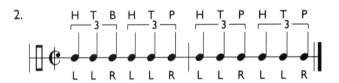

Next are examples of the three drums scored out for one player on each drum. This is the traditional way

this is played in the folkloric Rumba ensembles. You must have a thorough familiarity with all of the players' parts.

Example one is the Habana style and example two the Matanzas style.

In these styles the notes marked as Slaps (S) are played as what are called *Tapado* strokes. Basically they are slaps or higher pitched muted tones, but in general they are not as accented as a Slap would be. Again, the inflections vary during the playing. Some slaps would be more muted and some more accented depending on the effect sought by the player.

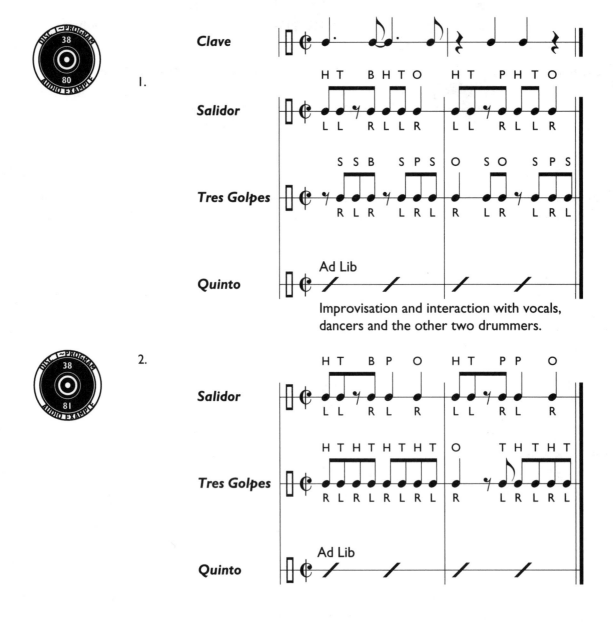

Improvisation and interaction with vocals, dancers and the other two drummers.

Following are examples of Rumba Guaguancó combinations for one player on two drums. Some examples are based on the Habana style and some on the Matanzas style. Unless you're playing in a folkloric ensemble all of the patterns are interchangeable.

Notice that although the variations between some patterns are slight, just one change of sticking or stroke type can really change the whole feel. Get each pattern down first and then work on mixing them up.

The complete picture for one player would involve a three drum setup also incorporating the Quinto drum and playing all the parts by improvising figures on the quinto while keeping the Guaguancó going on the Salidor and the Tres Golpes. Obviously this takes more technique and you have to leave some things out to put others in. You can begin working with putting the left hand figures from the patterns above on the Quinto and adding improvised variations as you can fit them in. Gradually you'll be able to play more solo figures. You can improvise on all three drums and you don't have to keep every note of the pattern going as you try to improvise. When played in ensemble the Guaguancó is a dialogue between the three drums, the voice, and the dancers. When doing this by yourself you are creating that dialogue between all the drums alone. A more advanced version of this would be to learn the words to a Rumba song and sing the parts while you accompany yourself playing the Guaguancó, and improvise variations on the quinto between your vocal phrases. Also do this with the Columbia rhythm that follows.

COLUMBIA

The Columbia is the fastest of the three Rumba styles and is played in $\frac{6}{8}$. Presented here are the rhythms for the three conga drums and combinations for one player.

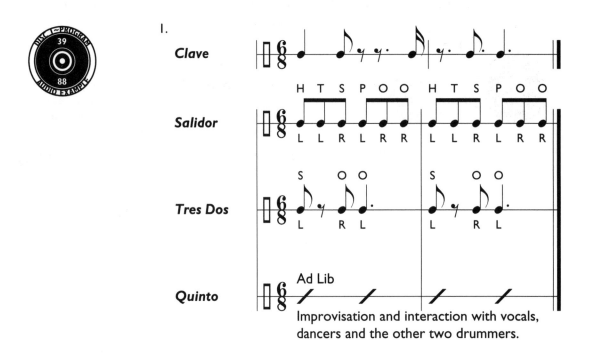

Improvisation and interaction with vocals, dancers and the other two drummers.

Following are some examples of the Columbia rhythm for one player. Since this results in a repeated one bar pattern, the pattern itself does not denote the clave. You must be especially aware of what's going on with the other instruments. Also work with incorporating a third drum into the patterns.

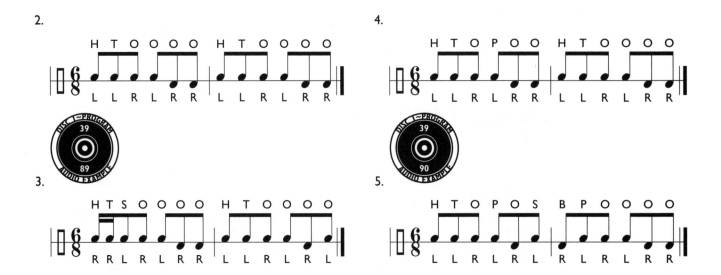

YAMBÚ

The Yambú is the oldest and slowest of the three Rumba styles and is traditionally played on the cajones—especially when played by folkloric ensembles—but can also be performed on congas. The timbres of the congas are much different than that of the cajones, so the groove isn't quite the same but the rhythm can still be performed this way. Here are the parts for the three drums as well as combinations for one player.

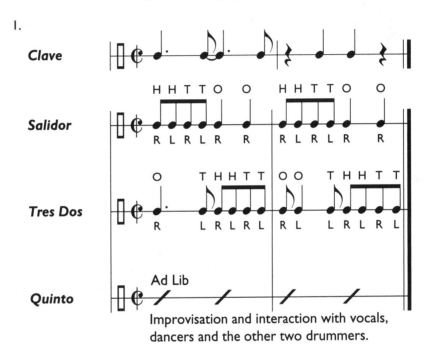

Improvisation and interaction with vocals, dancers and the other two drummers.

Here is an example of the Yambú rhythm for one player. You can also work with adding a third drum.

CONGA DE COMPARSA

These two terms are sometimes used to refer to the same thing but they are not. The Conga is a rhythm and dance associated primarily with the Cuban Carnaval celebration. The Comparsa or Comparsas refer to the ensembles that perform the Conga during Carnaval, and sometimes refers to the Carnaval parade itself. The Tumbadoras used in this style are as follows: The high drum is called the *Salidor*, (unlike in the Rumba Guaguancó where the low drum is the Salidor), the middle drum the *Conga* and the low drum the *Rebajador*. Sometimes in instrumental situations where improvisation and soloing play a key role, a quinto is also used and it plays the role of the soloist over the percussion ensemble. The first example represents the basic skeletal rhythms of the three drums. Keep in mind that many inflections and variations are improvised by each player.

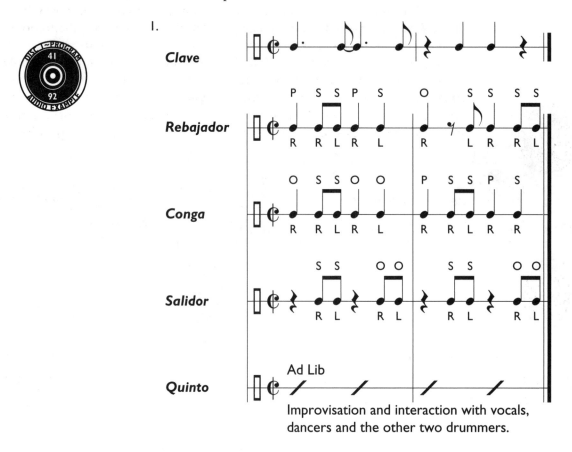

Improvisation and interaction with vocals, dancers and the other two drummers.

Following are examples of the Conga/Comparsa rhythm for one player. Once you have these under control try combining two patterns or repeating a pattern with a slight variation the second time to create a four bar phrase. This is also a very common approach. Also add a third drum and play the pattern over all three. You can start this by playing all of the non-open tones on the Quinto and all of the open melody tones on the Tumba and Segundo. Gradually work in more variations.

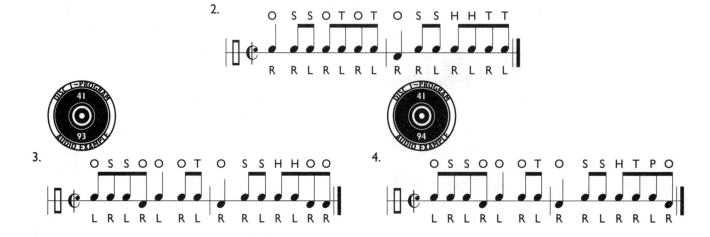

MOZAMBIQUE

The Mozambique is another Carnaval rhythm that evolved from the Conga and Comparsas. It was created and developed by Pedro Izquierdo (Pello El Afrokan) in the early 1960s. Over the years many adaptations of this rhythm have developed both on the hand drums and on the drum set, as well as within the percussion ensemble and full band settings. Some adaptations are more folkloric and others contain elements or influence from integration with other Cuban as well as non-Afro-Latin styles. The patterns below are all for one player on two drums and they are written in 2-3 clave position.

Many Mozambique patterns were actually either developed on three or four drums, or over time came to be played that way. Many are also four-bar phrases instead of the original two bars. Following are two examples: The first two orchestrated for three drums and the last two for four drums. The positioning of the drums also becomes an issue with patterns like this. In some instances the pattern develops around the player's personal choice in positioning the drums. Other times—like when playing an already established pattern or someone else's pattern, as in the following, you position the drums in the way they need to be to make the pattern work. Generally you'll have a couple of personal setups and you'll make small adjustments to accommodate other situations. Following are a couple of suggestions for how to set up the drums to play these next patterns as well as some of the multi-drum patterns that follow. Both of these three- and four-drum setups are very common with most players. Patterns one and two work best with this setup.

The notation for patterns 1 & 2 is as follows: **The top line is the Quinto—Drum #1. The middle line is the Segundo—Drum #2. The Bottom line is the Tumba—Drum #3. All of the stroke types and the hand combinations are above and below the notes.**

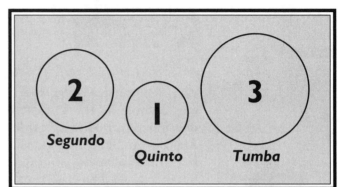

6.

7.

Patterns three and four are best played with this setup. The notation is as follows: **The top line is the Quinto—Drum #1. The next line down is the Segundo—Drum #2. The next line down is Tumba 1—Drum #3. The bottom line is Tumba 2—Drum #4. Stroke types and stickings are above and below the notes.**

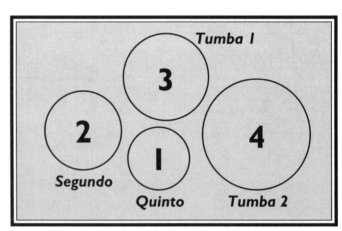

8.

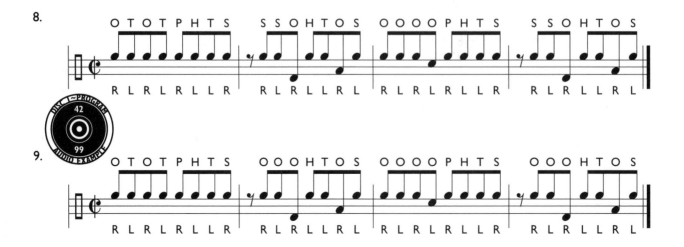

9.

PILÓN

The Pilón is another folkloric rhythm. It is commonly orchestrated on three drums set up like the three drum Mozambique patterns on the previous page. This rhythm is said to be a predecessor of the Songo. (In 2-3 clave.)

1.

2.

CHA CHA LOKUA FUN

This rhythm has variations in both duple meter (¢) and triple meter (⁶⁄₈). These patterns work best on three drums with the following setup. The notation is as follows: **The top line is the Quinto—Drum #1. The middle line is the Segundo—Drum #2. The Bottom line is the Tumba—Drum #3. All of the stroke types and hand combinations are above and below the notes.** (In 2-3 clave.)

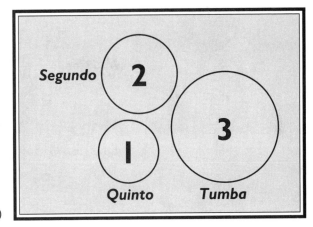

1.

2.

3.

105

ABAKUÁ

The Abakuá (a descendant of the African Calabar culture) was originally a sacred fraternal all male society that, among other things, performed the Abacuá rhythms in the course of their worship or ritualistic ceremonies. The fact that rhythms they play, or that emanate from them would also be called Abakuá seems obvious, but the number of rhythms that fall under this category is quite large, and even more so if you account for all the different societies, and all the varieties possible in these rhythms. Sometimes the many varieties will be in the form of different rhythmic variations in the drums them-selves, but often the drum patterns will be the same from one variation to the next and it will be other elements—the other percussion instruments, the vocal arrangements, lyric content, and geo-graphic regions of origin—that define the particular rhythmic variation, or a particular group's or society's adapta-tion of the style.

These song forms and rhythms greatly influenced many Cuban secular forms, particularly the Rumba styles. The first example is a score showing how three or four separate drummers would play a typical Abakuá rhythm.

1.

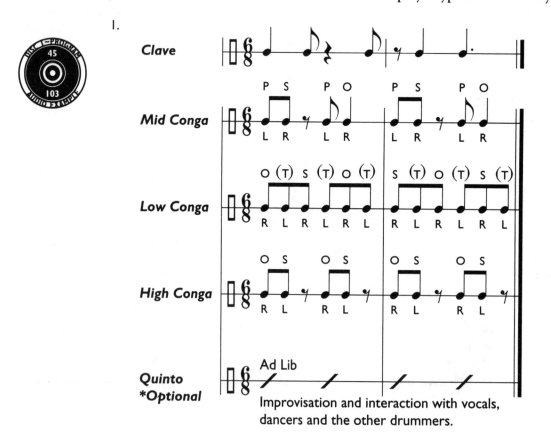

Improvisation and interaction with vocals, dancers and the other drummers.

Following are patterns for one player on three drums. These work best with the drums set up the same as for the Cha Cha Lokua Fun. The top line is the Quinto, the middle the Segundo, and the bottom the Tumba.

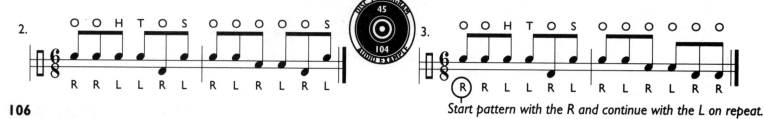

Start pattern with the R and continue with the L on repeat.

BEMBÉ

The Bembé is a folkloric festival with singing, dancing and drumming. In a traditional setting there is only a solo drummer on a low tumbadora playing improvised material that interacts with the vocals and dance along with the other percussion (similar to the way a Quinto player functions in a Rumba ensemble). Other instruments include the Hoeblade—the Guataca—and Shekerés. In more informal or colloquial terms the word Bembé is also used to describe a gathering or festivity that may be just an informal gathering, much like the term Rumba—while traditionally describing specific song forms and settings—is also loosely used to describe a percussion jam session or

a party or gathering. Consequently there are also rhythms commonly referred to as Bembé rhythms that are more generic ⅜ rhythms that maintain the flavor of the traditional Bembé performance but are set for two, three and four congas along with other percussion. Following is an example of a section of hand drums playing a Bembé or folkloric ⅜ style rhythm. Many of these generic patterns might draw from other ⅜ folkloric styles as well and in the course of playing one of these patterns there would be elements of Abacuá or Guiro or other ⅜ styles. Following is an example of this type of rhythm. ***Note: the audio example is of only a single drum improvising over a bell and shekeré pattern.***

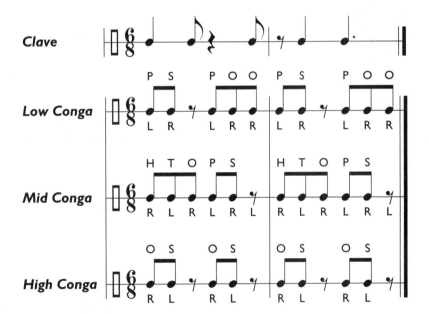

GUIRO

The Guiro rhythm got its name because it was originally performed on beaded gourds called Guiros—later called shekerés. A bell and a single

conga drummer were first added and later interpretations came to include all three tumbadoras. Other percussion is also sometimes added.

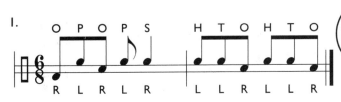

SONGO

The Songo is probably Cuba's most well known and interesting mix of the folkloric and contemporary styles. It is a blend of the Son and the Rumba styles, as well as the Cuban Carnaval rhythms (the Conga de Comparsa and the Mozambique), the Pilón, the Cha Cha Lokua Fun, and many other influences including funk and jazz styles. Next to the Son styles, there is probably no Cuban rhythm which has gotten as much attention and been imitated as much by drummers throughout the world. A percussionist by the name of Jose Luis Quintana—Changuito—of the Group Los Van Van is credited with being the father of the Songo, although like most rhythms and styles it evolved through the input of a variety of sources and players. Since Songo has so many influences it also has an equally vast number of approaches. Being a contemporary rhythm it also has the influence of the drum set and instrumental music. While there are certain patterns that are considered standard, the approach to the style is generally very free. Following are a variety of patterns. The first eight are written for two drums and the last three for three drums. Any of the patterns could be made to work for more or less drums by simply reorchestrating the melody tones around your particular conga setup. *All of these examples are written in the 3-2 clave position. In the audio examples they are started on the two side of the clave. Practice them starting on either bar.*

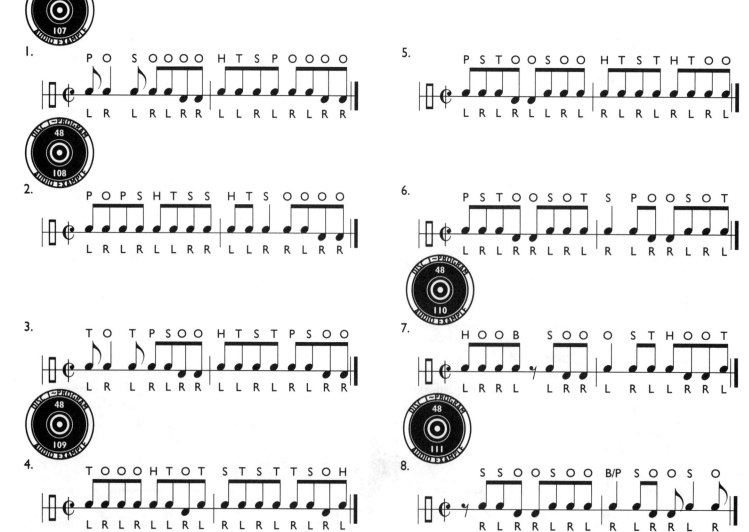

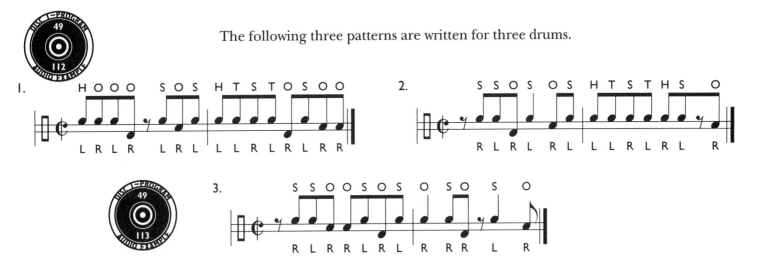

The following three patterns are written for three drums.

1.
```
H O O O   S O S   H T S T O S O O
L R L R   L R L   L L R L R L R R
```

2.
```
S S O S   O S   H T S T H S   O
R L R L   R L   L L R L R L   R
```

3.
```
S S O O S O S   O   S O   S   O
R L R R L R L   R   R L   R
```

The following are non-Cuban styles but still fall under the general category of Afro-Latin or Afro-Caribbean music and most are quite well known and influential throughout the world.

MERENGUE

The Merengue hails from the Dominican Republic and is basically it's national dance and musical form. The primary percussion instruments of the Merengue are the Tambora and the Guira, though in large orchestras two congas are also common. In an ensemble that is not exclusively a Merengue ensemble but plays some Merengue selections, the Conga drummer would play the Tambora parts on one Conga. Following are the actual Conga drummer's parts. Refer to the Tambora section for those patterns. You should learn the Tambora patterns and be able to play them on a Conga drum should the need arise. Examples one and two are one-drum patterns, three and four are two-drum patterns. Both are to accompany the basic Merengue groove. The fifth pattern is the conga accompaniment to the Pambiche or Apanpichao section of an arrangement. This is like the Montuno section or the breakdown of the piece. (The Pambiche is also a type of approach to the Merengue.)

1.

```
P S P O P S P O
L R L R L R L R
```

2.
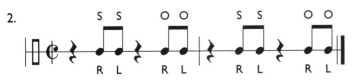
```
S S   O O   S S   O O
R L   R L   R L   R L
```

3.

```
O O   S   S O O P S P O O
R L   R   L R R L R L R R
```
Start pattern with the R and continue with the L on repeat.

4.
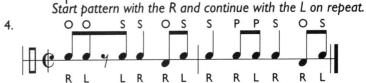
```
O O   S S   O S   S P P S O S
R L   L R   R L   R R L R R L
```

5.
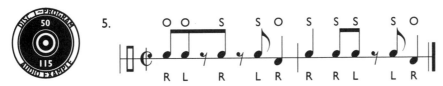
```
O O   S   S O S   S S   S O
R L   R   L R R   R L   L R
```

BOMBA

The Bomba is a folkloric style from Puerto Rico and is played on Conga-like drums called Bombos. They are generally shorter than Congas. The rhythms are generally one-bar phrases so they don't denote the clave, though a band arrangement of a Bombo would have it's melodic structures in clave. The names of the two drums are the Buleador, which plays the roll of the Tumba, and the Requinto, which plays the improvisational role of the Quinto. Following is a basic pattern for both drums.

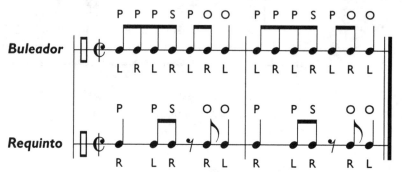

The Requinto improvises freely or plays this pattern with variations.

PLENA

The Plena is another folkloric style from Puerto Rico. It is normally played on tambourines called Panderetas, but is also interpreted on the Congas. The following two-drum pattern is a combination of the two Pandereta parts.

CALYPSO

The Calypso originated in Trinidad and is another rhythm which has undergone many transformations and has been integrated with and changed into many different styles and offshoots. Following are some basic patterns.

1.

2.

3.

BONGOS

THE BONGOS ARE A PAIR OF SMALL HIGH-PITCHED DRUMS ATTACHED SIDE BY SIDE AND HELD BETWEEN THE LEGS OF THE SEATED PLAYER. THEY ARE ALSO MOUNTED ON STANDS IN CONTEMPORARY multi-percussion setups. The smaller and higher pitched of the two drums is sometimes called the *Macho,* and the larger and lower pitched drum is called the *Hembra*—male and female, respectively. They originated in Cuba, in the Province of Oriente, with the *Changui* and *Son* groups and their musical traditions. They were the original—and only—drum of these popular music groups until the *Tumbadora* was added to the *Conjunto* in the 1940s. Pictured in *figure 1* are the *Bongos* and the *Campana*—the large hand-held bell played by the *Bongocero* (the bongo player) in an orchestra. (More on this later).

The basic rhythmic pattern of the *Bongo* is called *Martillo.* The word literally means hammer in Spanish, and in its most skeletal form the pattern's quarter note or half note pulse marks the groove with that type of strength—hammering. The Martillo consists of a string of eighth notes. There are three quarters on the high drum and the fourth quarter—beat four—on the low drum (these four notes are the pulse—the hammer). The fourth note is the same note that the congas accent in the *Tumbaó*—though the congas generally accent both beats *four* and *four-and*—but because the bongos are tuned much higher than the congas, it does not sound like patterns are being duplicated. The left hand "fills in" time with a *heel–toe* (actually thumb-finger) rocking motion to create the eighth-note pattern. Because they are tuned very high and their timbre is not as heavy as that of the congas and timbales,

figure 1

the bongos also have a very improvisational role in its timekeeping, playing many variations to the *Martillo* and creating a syncopated rhythmic texture. Though this can be very rhythmically active, it never disrupts the stability of the groove or the roles of the other instruments or vocalists. These variations and improvisations are called *repiques* and the action is called *repiquiar.*

The *bongocero* (bongo player) in an orchestra has two roles—one playing bongos and one playing the campana (the large hand-held bell). The bongos are generally played during the introductions and verses, as well as in lower dynamic accompaniments like for piano or bass solos. During the *Montuno* section of an arrangement, as well as during higher dynamic solos or percussion solos, the player switches to the campana. A player may switch between the bongo and campana several times within a piece of music.

Figures 2, 3, and *4* at the top of the next page show the holding position, the playing position, and the switch to the bell. It is also very common to stand while playing the bell especially if the player sings or dances with the *Coro*—the background vocal sections.

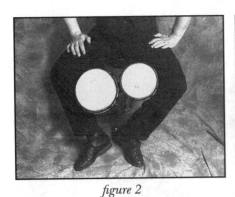

figure 2   figure 3   figure 4

Note: A right-handed player will place the small drum on the left and a left-handed player will place it to the right.

Following is the stroke sequence for the *Martillo* rhythm. The eight basic strokes are illustrated in rhythmic sequence, but keep in mind that there are a wide variety of stroke types and tones played in a real performance situation. These include a variety of open and closed tones, ghosted notes, slaps using one, two, or three fingers, or the whole hand, as well as many other variations.

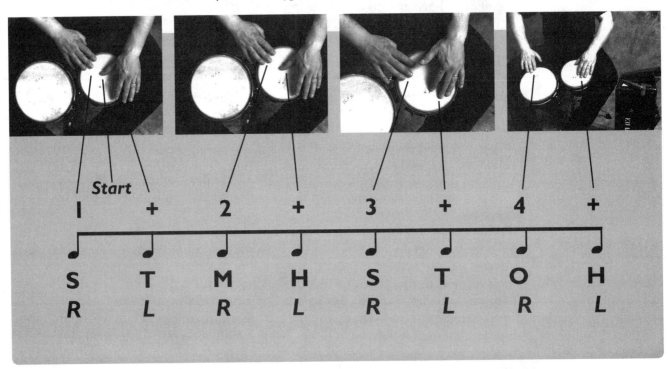

Stroke 1 is an accented high-pitched stroke with one, two, or three fingers (depending on the volume you want) of the right hand with the thumb of the left hand down on the head. This is how the pattern starts. *Stroke 1+* is a left-hand toe stroke—the tips of the fingers come down and strike the head. (The position looks like the stroke for beat 3+.) *Stroke 2* is also a finger stroke with the right hand, but is less high pitched, less accented, and more muted than the right-hand stroke on beat one. *Stroke 2+* is a heel stroke with the thumb/heel of the left hand. *Stroke 3* is the same as stroke 1. *Stroke 3+* is the same as stroke 1+. *Stroke 4* is an open tone on the low drum with the right hand. *Stroke 4+* is the same as stroke 2+, or is also very often an accented high-pitched stroke with the left hand on the small drum as pictured here.

Practice all of the stroke types and technical exercises from the section on congas. (Adjust your hand placement for the smaller bongo drums. It's not the same instrument as congas but the technical studies apply to both.) For variations and improvisations, play along with recordings and transcribe the licks you hear. This is the best way to get the vocabulary on this instrument. Here is the notated version of the *martillo* rhythm along with some variations. The variations and additional rhythms listed are not patterns *per se*. The *martillo* and the rhythm for "a caballo" are the basic patterns. Every-thing else is a variation of the *martillo*. It is impossible to write out every nuance of the playing of this instrument because of the improvisational nature of its role in an orchestra. Your best bet is to play along with records and pick out the licks and get them in your own playing.

Listed below are the basic rhythms and some common variations. It is not inconceivable that in the course of a given piece of music all of the following material would be played throughout the piece, starting with the basic *martillo* pattern and using the other material as variations as you move through the piece.

Basic Martillo Pattern *Beats 1 and 3 are marked S for slap but in the course of the timekeeping pattern are not really slaps but stronger accents than beat 2. This creates a feeling of a strong two pulse.*

Following are some one-bar variations of the basic rhythm. Work until you can play phrases combining all of the examples as well as improvising variations.

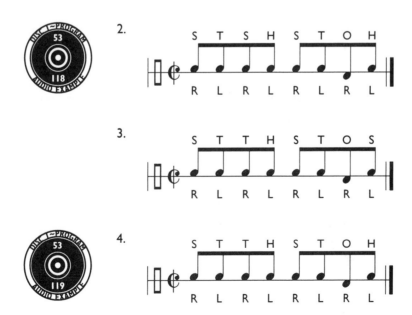

5.

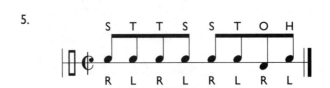

6.

This pattern also works for the "a caballo" style.

Following are four two bar combinations.

7.

9.

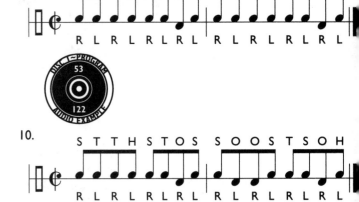

8.

10.

Following are two four bar examples.

11.

12.

TIMBALES AND TIMBALITOS

THE TIMBALES AND THE TIMBALITOS ARE PAIRS OF TUNABLE DRUMS MOUNTED ON A STAND AND PLAYED WITH STICKS AS WELL AS A SPECIFIC STROKE played with the bare hand. The basic setup consists of a pair of two drums ranging in size from 10″ to 15″. A pair of 14″ and 15″ or 13″ and 14″ are the most common for an orchestra. Also included in the setup is a cymbal used for both riding and punctuating, as well as a woodblock and at least two cowbells—the Mambo and Cha-Cha bells. In a Charanga group the Charanga bell would also be used, and in contemporary setups a wide variety of other percussion instruments can be combined.

The timbales, as we know them today, are considered an instrument of Cuban descent, but they evolved directly from an offshoot of the European orchestral timpani called the *Timbales Criollos (Creole Timpani),* which originally looked exactly like the European timpani. The Timbales Criollos were used to accompany the *French Contredanse* (then popular in Haiti). In 1791 the slave rebellion in Haiti resulted in a large number of Afro-Haitian immigrants settling in the eastern Cuban province of Oriente. Their *Contradanza* evolved into the Cuban *Danza*—also the *Danza Habanera* or simply *Habanera*—which then developed into the modern-day Danzón. It was in this evolution from the Contradanza to Danzón that this instrument went from Timbales Criollos to the present-day timbales. The timbales basically evolved parallel to these musical developments.

These early musical styles were first interpreted by ensembles called

Orquestas Típicas (traditional orchestras), whose instrumentation consisted of woodwind and brass instruments (clarinets, bassoon, cornet, trombone, and tuba), a string section with violins, violas, cellos, and the contrabass, and a percussion section which consisted of the Timbales Criollos and the guiro. Originally all of the performance took place directly on the heads, just as the traditional timpani are played.

The appearance of the Danzón in the early 1900s, along with the concurrently evolving Son traditions, marked the beginning of the development of Afro-Cuban commercial dance music. This period introduced a variety of different ensembles, each with their own unique approach and instrumenta-

tion, and each introducing new sounds and musical styles as well as new percussion instruments or new approaches to existing ones. In terms of the timbales, the most significant of these new ensembles was the *Charanga Francesa*, which appeared in the 1900s as the primary interpreter of the Danzón style. This group's instrumentation consisted of flute, piano, bass, violins, guiro, and timbales—called pailas, pailitas or Timbales Criollos—smaller versions of the European timpani. As the Danzón gained popularity with the general public, and especially in the dance halls of white society, the Charanga groups grew to be much in demand. The continued evolution of their sound and their instruments led to the birth of the modern-day timbal. They came to exist partly from a musical evolution and partly out of necessity, as it was limiting to carry the European kettle drum to a gig. Calfskin heads were mounted with tension keys onto metal canisters and the canisters mounted on a stand at about knee height. These original timbales were played sitting down. At this point the timbales did not have cowbells, woodblocks, or cymbals and were played just as the timpani were. All of the rhythms were played directly on the heads of the drums with a combination of open and dampened strokes and the later introduction of the rim click sound. This was (and is) known as the baqueteo. This is still the way the Danzón is played today.

The Danzón and other dance hall styles continued to develop and gain popularity, and in the late 1930s and early 1940s bassist/composer Israel "Cacháo" Lopez created a new section—the *Nuevo Ritmo* —which was a vamp section added to the end of the arrangement. This section became the montuno section. This musical development marked the introduction of a cowbell onto the timbales. The bell was played only during this section and the rest of the piece was played with the baqueteo. At first this was a single small

bell, but as this section developed and spawned styles of its own (most notably the Cha-Cha and later the Mambo), larger bells and a woodblock were added to the setup. As larger dance orchestras developed and began gaining popularity, the function of the Latin rhythm section further evolved and with it the setup and function of the timbales.

In the 1940s in New York, Latin dance orchestras were also being influenced by the developments of the jazz big bands. Because these *Orquestas* often also played non-Latin songstyles for dancing (foxtrots, waltzes, and the like), the timbales sometimes functioned like a drum set would in a big band. Sometimes both were played for different pieces throughout an orchestra's performance. It was during this period that the final refinements and developments in the instrument took place. Through the orchestras of Machito and other significant figures of that period, a woodblock and another larger bell was added as well as a cymbal on a stand. It was also during this period that a new figure emerged on the scene, Ernesto (Tito) Puente, and brought the timbales into the limelight within the musical community as well as with the general public.

The approach to playing the timbales continues to develop and has grown to see many new developments and many great artists and soloists. It has also made its way into other cultures and styles of music and has become a member of the pop percussion instrument repertoire as well. All the while, the traditional Charanga ensembles maintain their original conventions in performance with the baqueteo of the Danzón.

As just mentioned, the original approach to playing the timbales was the baqueteo of the Danzón, played with both sticks directly on the drums. This accompaniment was played mostly on the large drum (the hembra—female; to the left for a right-handed player), while the small drum (the macho—male; to the right), was used for accentuations. The left hand would muffle the head while the right hand played a combination of muffled and open tones and rim clicks. Following are two examples of the basic baqueteo. Notice all the tones are muffled except for beat four. In the first example all the main strokes are played by the right hand while the left hand muffles the head and releases on beat four for the open tone.

1.

In the next example the left hand both muffles the head and fills in the rhythm with either rim clicks or muffled tones directly on the head. These were the original approaches to the timbales.

2.

As time went on and the *montuno* section was added, the playing on the bell and the sides came into place along

figure 1

with one other very important sound, the *abanico* (*figure 1*). This is the accent and roll which is used to lead the ensemble into an upcoming section—and especially into the montuno section of an arrangement. The abanico would be used to lead the ensemble into this new section, and the timbalero would then switch from the sides and play on the large bell. The abanico is an extremely important aspect of playing the timbales and should be gotten under control early on. The word abanico means *fan* in Spanish and the sound or feel of the roll is similar to that of a fan opening or unfolding. It is hard to describe in words how this effect sounds since the abanico is played with a personal approach by each player and one can't notate the sound of how the time seems to stretch or pull back during the short roll and how the downbeat brings the ensemble in like nails. Listen to recordings. It's the best way to get this happening. A particular player's approach to the Abanico has the same individuality as a jazz drummer's approach to a ride cymbal. (The same holds true for a timbalero's approach to riding on the cowbell.)

Following are two basic examples. Notice that the accent of the *Abanico* syncs with that of the clave. The first example is in the 3-2 position and the second in the 2-3 direction.

3.

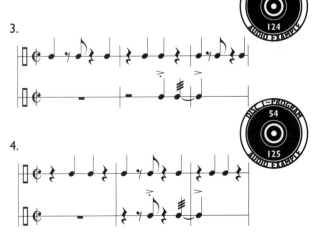

4.

There are several ways to approach playing the abanico roll and they are as follows:

1. *The left stick can be dropped on the high timbal letting the stick bounce and buzz. You end the roll by playing a rim shot with the right hand on the downbeat.*
2. *Both sticks can be dropped and allowed to buzz or roll and this roll is capped with a rim shot with the right hand on the downbeat.*
3. *Using the standard rudimental approach, a press roll can be played terminating with the rim shot on the downbeat. The tempo of the piece and how much you want to stretch the time determines wether you play a five, seven, or nine stroke roll.*
4. *Again using the standard rudimental approach, an open roll can be employed with the same considerations as in number three above.*

More information on the abanico can be found later in this chapter with the rhythm style examples.

The next topic to be addressed is the standard comping or timekeeping approach. As mentioned earlier, with the introduction of the *Nuevo Ritmo* section to the Danzón, a cowbell was added to the setup. With this, a new approach began to develop which has taken many directions over the years, but one basic element remains and that is the function of the left hand.

When comping (accompanying or keeping time for the ensemble) in any of the Son styles, the left hand plays the following figure (notated below): a muted tone on beat two and an open tone on beat four. This mimics the tumbaó of the conga drums.

5.

after the stroke so that the tone will ring.

This left hand pattern can also be played with a stick in the left hand playing both muted and open tones directly on the head (pictured below), or by playing a rim click (cross-sticked) on beat two and the open tone on beat four.

Here the sequence is shown with the right hand playing time on the side of the high timbal—called *playing paila* or cascara. In the first picture the left hand plays the muted stroke in the center of the head and in the second it plays the open tone towards the edge so the head can ring freely.

Following is an illustration showing the ride on the cowbell with the left hand playing the muted stroke that takes place on beat two of the comping pattern. Beat four would be closer to the edge with the hand coming off the head

There are many figures the left hand can play both with or without the stick, and those are presented later in the chapter with the actual rhythm styles.

I'll also mention here that though this material may appear simple it isn't to be taken as trivial, and by no means is it optional. It is an integral part of playing the timbales in an ensemble. As you can see from the examples, this left hand comping element is used whether the right hand is riding on the sides or on the bell, meaning it is used throughout virtually the entire arrangement.

Next we'll examine the actual ride, or comping patterns on the timbales. We've already established the baqueteo of the Danzón as the original or initial approach to the timbales. Next down the road is the playing on the sides of the timbales. The sides—called Cáscara or Paila—are the primary place where time is played for introductions, vocal verses or instrumental "A sections," piano solos or any other low dynamic part of a piece. This sound (which was basically a wood sound on the original timbales and is now a metal sound on today's brass or other metal shell timbales) was derived in part from the playing of the sticks on wood in the folkloric styles—such as the palitos on the Gua-Gua in the rumba styles.

There are two basic approaches to playing the sides. The first involves the right hand (or left for a left-handed

player playing a reversed setup—the small drum on the left), playing the basic cáscara pattern along with the basic left hand comping pattern just described (notated and picture below). Also notice in the picture the index finger on the stick. This is a way of dead-sticking. A common sound for this is achieved by pushing the stick into the sides and not letting them ring. Also notice in the two pictures the two different places where the stick is hitting. Both of these will give very different sounds and are both used in actual playing.

6.

The second approach to the cáscara involves a two-handed combination. Many variations are played but the basic pattern is the following at the top of the next page. Keep in mind the dead-sticking, placement of the sticks and the accents. This is integral to the pattern having the right sound and grooving correctly. Here is the basic pattern and an illustration of the playing position. The top line of the pattern is the right hand and the bottom the left. (Reverse for a left handed player.)

8.

7.

During the montuno section of an arrangement, the timbalero moves up to the bell. In the case of a Mambo or Son Montuno, it would be the large bell (Mambo bell). In the case of a Cha-Cha or Guajira it would be the small Cha-Cha bell. In the case of the Charanga it would be the even smaller Charanga bell. Regardless of the style, a bell is played during this section and the left hand would still play the same basic comping pattern.

Following is the basic pattern for the montuno section of a Mambo, Son-Montuno or Guaracha style arrangement and an illustration of the playing position. (The part above the line is the right hand and the part below the line is the left.) There are many variations to this pattern. These are presented in the next part of this chapter.

Here is a basic example for the Cha-Cha and Charanga. These would be played on their respective bells with a position like the one in the illustration above. (The part above the line is the right hand and the part below the line is the left.)

9.

10.

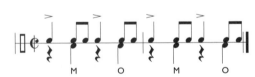

This concludes the introduction, history and fundamentals of the timbales. Now let's move on to specific patterns for each of the specific styles.

DANZÓN

As mentioned earlier, the Danzón style was one of the first to be played on the timbales. The Charangas that played the Danzón developed the baqueteo, which is the primary timbale part for this style. These groups also eventually added the cowbell and were responsible for the early developments of the Cha-Cha and the montuno section in arrangements, and thus the modern day approach to the timbales.

Following are two basic approaches to this style. The first pattern is the basic rhythm played on the low timbal. The right hand plays all of the rhythm and the left muffles and unmuffles the tones as marked. In the second the right plays the rhythm and the left both muffles and plays rhythms on the rim (cross-sticked). These are the foundation rhythms and all variations stem from here.

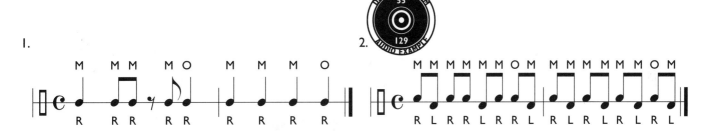

SON & SON-MONTUNO

The Son was originally played without timbales, and when played by the *Tipico* style Son groups it is still played with the original instrumentation of bongos, clave, maracas and guiro. It is sometimes now played with the timbales and the *Son Montuno* does include them as well as the Congas. Following are the basic patterns. The first is the basic two-handed paila (cascara rhythm) played on the sides. The second is the cascara with the basic left hand comping pattern.

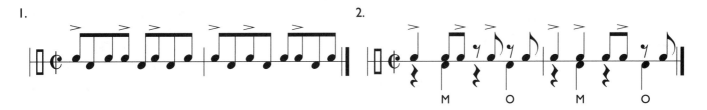

Before moving further with other styles we'll examine the playing of the cascara, also called paila. The word cascara in Spanish means shell. Playing the sides was called playing the shell. "Playing paila" is the most basic timekeeping pattern in the Son styles. It is used in practically every introduction, verse, piano solo or any other low dynamic section. Other than the

patterns played during the montuno section it is what you will play on the timbales most of the time. Following are several very common approaches to playing the cascara. Since you'll use these in one format or another in practically every Latin music application it's best if you get these in your repertoire now.

CASCARA/PAILA

Cascara is not a style but a method needed to play in a variety of styles. Following are several common ways to play the cascara with the two-handed approach. They are presented here in the 3-2 clave position. Practice them starting

on the second bar also. In real applications you need to be able to start playing from any note anywhere in the pattern—3-2 or 2-3 position. In all of these patterns the part above the line is the right hand and the part below the line is the left.

1.

5.

2.

6.

3.

7.

4.

8.

9.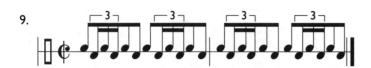

CHA-CHA

The Cha-Cha developed from the montuno, the improvisational *Nuevo*

Ritmo section that was added to the Danzón. Following are two basic patterns.

1.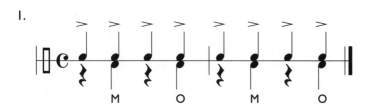

2.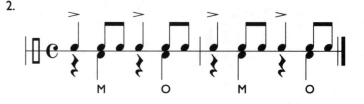

MAMBO

The first example is the basic pattern for Mambo. All of the rest of these bell patterns are variations that can be played instead—as long as the music accommodates it. ***Practice all of the variations with the basic left hand comping patterns as well as with the Son Clave in the left hand.*** Make a workout out of this. Practice all of this in both the 3-2 and 2-3 positions. These examples are presented in 3-2.

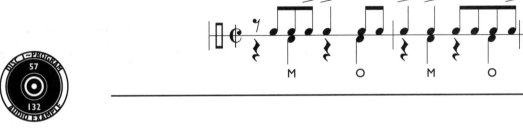

DISC 1 PROGRAM 57 / **AUDIO EXAMPLE 132**

1.

2.

3.

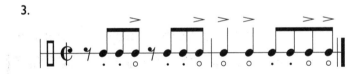

4.

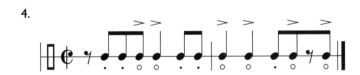

5.

6.

7.

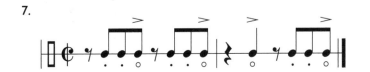

8.

9.

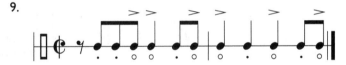

10.

11.

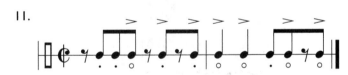

12.

13.

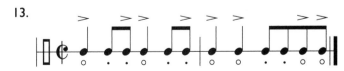

14.

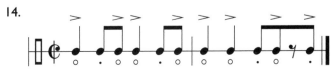

GUARACHA

The Guaracha is a rhythm resembling the Son Montuno and Mambo and is often the rhythm associated with the generic blend of styles used in the Salsa style. Like the Son and Mambo it is pulsed in two and the timbalero would play *paila* during the verses and go to the bell during the montuno. The first two patterns are the cascara for the lower dynamic sections and the third is for the montuno. Virtually all of the variations from the previous two pages could be applied in this type of playing as long as the particular arrangement accommodates it.

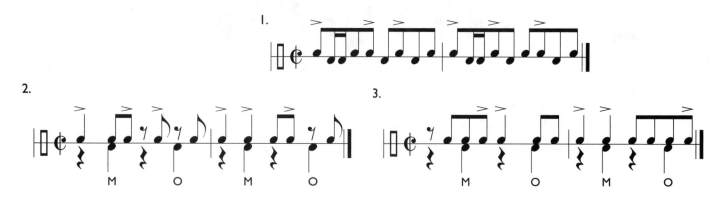

PACHANGA~A CABALLO

The Pachanga style (in which you play the Caballo rhythm) and the Caballo rhythm itself (also used in other arranging styles) is a *two beat half note pulsed rhythm* that got its name from the feel that it emulates—the trot of a horse. Caballo is the Spanish word for horse and the rhythm creates that feeling.

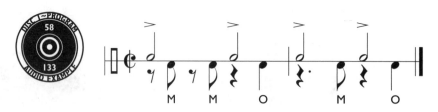

BOLERO

The Bolero is a ballad form that is usually the torch song of the Latin show. The themes of these songs are often about love, loss of love or the like.

GUAJIRA

The Guajira can be compared in essence to the blues style of North America. It is a style that was born in the fields and developed by the struggling peasant class while in their states of oppression. The themes generally portray the difficulties of that life, or can deal with political commentary, melancholy romantic issues, and other similar motifs. It is generally slow to medium slow and usually a major or minor key I-IV-V progression.

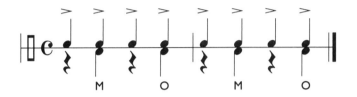

CONGA & THE COMPARSA

As mentioned in the section on the conga drums, the terms Conga and Comparsa are sometimes used to refer to the same thing, but though closely related, they are not. To review, the Conga is a rhythm and dance associated primarily with the Cuban Carnaval celebration. The Comparsa or Comparsas refer to the ensembles that perform the Conga during Carnaval, and sometimes refers to the Carnaval parade itself. In the traditional Carnaval groups (Comparsas) there are no timbales, but contemporary ensembles and orchestras that play music based on these Carnaval styles do incorporate them.

There are a variety of ways that you could play the Conga rhythm on the timbales. How you approach it depends on what other percussion is present and what those parts are. If you are playing with just a conga drummer and the timbales, you would probably play the main cowbell part and the bombo (bass drum) pattern on the low timbal. If another percussionist is playing the main bell, then you could play a secondary bell part and the bombo, or the clave rhythm and the bombo. If another percussionist is playing the bombo, then you can play the primary bell part and the clave.

In the following patterns the cowbell parts can be played two ways. One would be to play the entire pattern on one bell, using the neck and mouth of the bell for the high and low (long and short, open and closed) sounds to give the pattern the right color. The second way would be to break up the pattern between two bells, playing the high and low parts on the respective bells. In these examples the pattern is written for two bells. The lower line is the low bell and the upper the high. The low notes are long notes and the high notes are short. If you play these patterns on only one large bell, then play the low notes near the mouth and the high notes near the neck. You need to produce two distinct sounds.

The first group of examples shows the basic bell patterns over the basic bombo pattern. The bombo should be played on the low timbal. The notes marked "o" are open and the notes marked "m" are played as muted or dampened strokes. These are played by *dead-sticking* the stroke into the head. This first set of examples is written in 3-2 clave. Be sure to practice starting them on either bar and, ideally, from any point of either bar.

You could use these patterns if you are playing timbales along with a conga drummer and no other percussion, or another percussionist playing clave and/or another secondary bell part. You are covering the primary bell and the bombo.

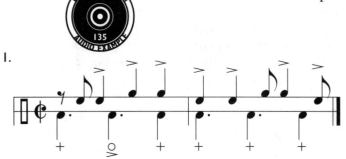

1.

2.

This is an alternate bombo pattern you can play with the two examples above.

3.

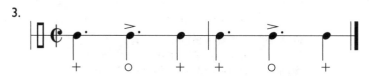

The following are alternate bell patterns that can be played if someone is already covering the primary cowbell parts above. These are the patterns played on the *sartenes* (frying pans) or on *brake drums*. These are two-handed patterns and are ideally split up on two bells but can be played on one bell using the neck and mouth for the high and low sounds.

4.

5.

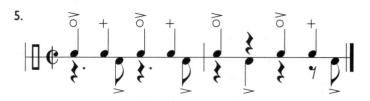

Here are four more alternate bell patterns that can be added to an ensemble. These are also better split up on two bells but can be played on one.

6.

7.

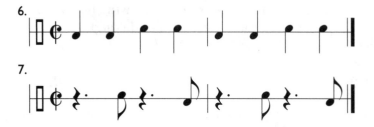

8.

9.

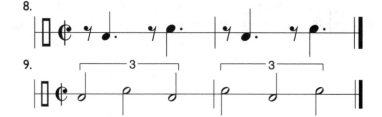

If the bombo is already played by another percussionist then you can play the following combination of clave and bell. Which hand plays which part is up to you. Ideally you should be able to do it both ways.

10.

11.

MOZAMBIQUE

The most significant offshoot of the Conga style is the Mozambique rhythm, developed in the early 1960s by Pedro Izquierdo (Pello El Afrokan) and a group called Los Afrokanes. This group used the Conga rhythms of the Comparsas as the basis for its band arrangements creating the Mozambique style. This rhythm has influenced many later Afro-Latin styles and found its way into many jazz, funk, and fusion settings as well. It has been used in the arrangements of many contemporary Cuban groups as well as those of New York-based Latin Jazz groups like those of Manny Oquendo and Eddie Palmieri and many others since the mid-1960s. It was also developed into a drum set style by both Latin and non-Latin drum set players.

This rhythm has a number of inter-

pretations that have resulted in a variety of patterns and approaches to the style. We'll look at a few of the basic patterns and then put them together into parts for the timbales.

The first group of examples shows four basic cowbell parts along with the clave. They are written with a high and low line, indicating either high and low bells or neck and mouth strokes on one bell. It is very important to articulate this correctly. Either hand can play either part. These would be used with a conga drummer and if the bombo part is being played by another percussionist. You then cover the cowbell and clave. Which bell pattern you play depends on the specific musical situation—which type of Mozambique, what type of ensemble and the instrumentation of the ensemble.

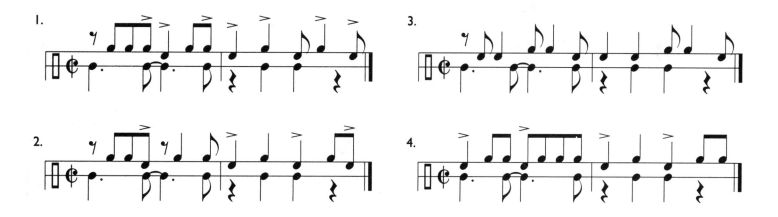

The following is another pattern for the cowbell. This is actually two bell parts for one player and comes from one of the Mozambique approaches of

Pello El Afrokan. For this pattern to really work you need to have the corresponding bombo parts.

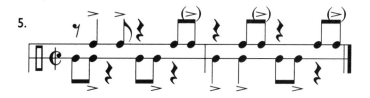

Next are the bombo patterns along with the clave. There are two main bombo patterns and they take place simultaneously (in some settings) and require one player for each. You can use these patterns if there is a conga drummer, and another percussionist is playing the cowbell part. Observe the open "o" and closed "+" tones.

6.

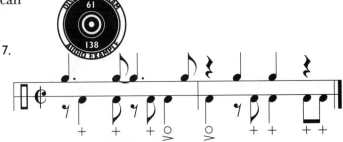

7.

This a variation of the first bass drum pattern above.

8.

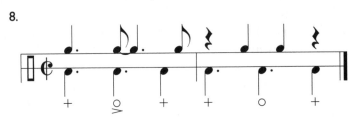

The bell patterns can also be combined with the bombo played on the low timbal. Use this if there is a conga drummer and another percussionist playing the clave. If there is only one bombo it is usually the first pattern but you can use either if it works musically.

Below are examples of the cowbell parts combined with bombo. Depending on the musical setting you can combine any bell part with any bombo part. The following show bell pattern #3 with bombo variation #1 and #2.

9.

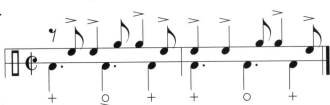

10.

The bombo pattern can also be split up between the high and low timbal. The first example shows bell pattern #3 and bombo #1 split up between the high and low timbal. The second example shows bell pattern #4 with bombo pattern #2 played between the high and low drums.

11.

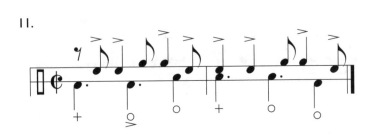

12.

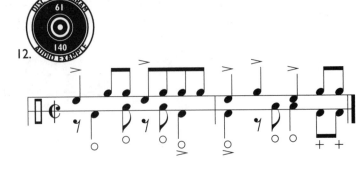

There are a number of bombo variations that you can play. Some come from patterns and some are simply improvised in the course of playing. Following are a few bombo variations shown with bell pattern #2.

The ideal scenario is that you can combine any bell pattern or clave with any bombo variation. *After playing the following as written do it again with the other two cowbell variations and then with clave.*

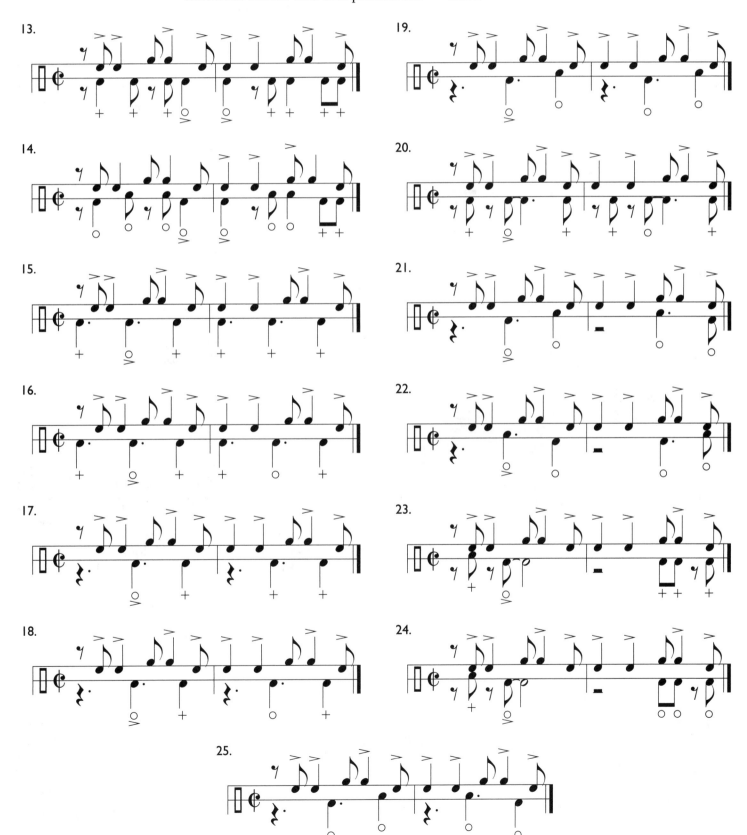

Make sure to go back and play every bell pattern and the clave with every bombo variation. This will not only be a great technical workout but will give you a lot of rhythmic vocabulary to use in this style.

You can also create different variations of the four basic bell patterns by combining one bar from one pattern with one bar from another. Following are two variations created from the previous patterns and shown here with one of the bombo variations. In traditional settings you pretty much have to stick to the basic patterns but in nontraditional or non-Latin settings you can basically create any combinations that work with the music you're playing.

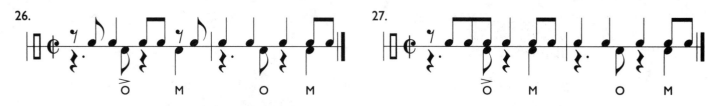

RUMBA STYLES

As discussed in the previous chapter, there are three Rumba styles: **Guaguancó**, **Yambú** and **Columbia**. Originally Rumba was played on the cajones—wooden boxes of three different sizes—that functioned as the three congas do now. The primary instrumentation of the Rumba does not include timbales so if you're playing timbales and performing one of the rumba styles you would play one of the palito or bell rhythms and perhaps the clave and the bombo note on the low timbal. Listed below are some possibilities for each.

GUAGUANCÓ

The first combination is the basic palito rhythm. You can play this on the timbale sides, the woodblock, the cowbell or combinations of the three throughout the particular piece you're playing. The second example is the same as the first but with the left hand also playing the bombo's open accented note on the low timbal. The third example is the basic one-handed cascara rhythm in one hand and the rumba clave in the other. You can play the cascara on the sides or bell with the clave on the woodblock. The fourth is the same as the third but with the left hand also playing the bombo note on the low timbal.

YAMBU

For the Yambu we have the basic palito rhythm in one hand and the rumba clave in the other.

COLUMBIA

For the Columbia we have the basic bell pattern in one hand and the $\frac{6}{8}$ clave in the other. Then we have the same pattern but with the left hand playing the bombo note of the clave on the low timbal.

CHA CHA LOKUA FUN

For this rhythm one possibility would be the basic $\frac{6}{8}$ bell pattern with the clave in the left hand, or an alternate variation (example 2) where the left hand plays the upbeats of the triplet. This can be played in the rim (cross-sticked), on the sides, woodblock or subtly on a small cowbell, or as a muted note on the low timbal. The last three examples are the same as the first but with various bass drum notes played on the low timbal. Keep in mind that these folkloric rhythms do not have timbales in their instrumentation so you're essentially taking a variety of stick parts or fragments from other instruments and developing a supporting part that compliments the ensemble and the piece you're playing.

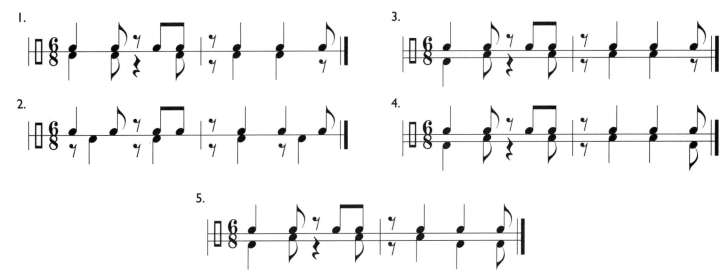

ABAKUÁ

The Abakuá (also spelled Abakwa and Abacuá) is a sacred ritual rhythm from the Abakuá society—a secret fraternal (traditionally male) society that descended and evolved from the African Calabar tribes—the Carabalí. Again, there are no timbales in the traditional instrumentation so you're performing combinations of bell parts. The lower line of the first example is the basic traditional bell part shown here combined with the basic $^6_8$ bell pattern. The second, third and fourth examples are not specifically Abakuá patterns (they are more generic $^6_8$ rhythms) and should only be played if the musical situation allows. They should be played with the top line on the large bell and the bottom on the small bell. The fifth pattern is the pattern of the guagua but sometimes played on a small bell.

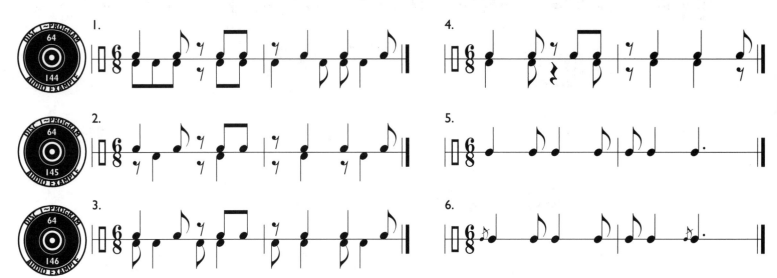

GUIRO

Practically all of the previously introduced $^6_8$ patterns can accompany this style. In all of these folkloric styles it is generally the Tumbadoras and the lyric style that define the style and many of the bell patterns are the same from one style to another with only a slight detail differing in one of the parts.

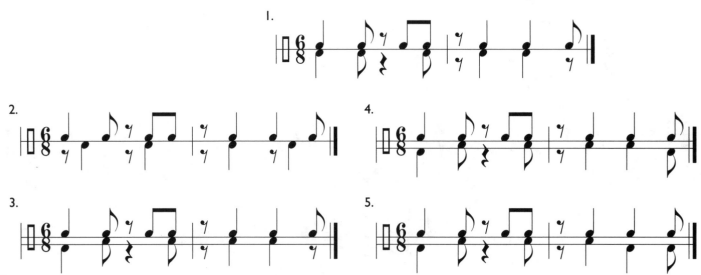

BEMBÉ

For the Bembé all of the previously introduced ⁶₈ parts can be used depending on the musical setting. Shown here is the basic pattern and one bell pattern that is often played on a small cowbell.

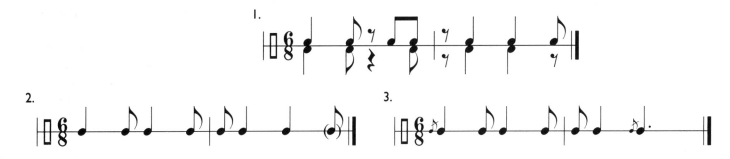

PILÓN

The Pilón is a predecessor of the Songo. Notice the similarities in the patterns. You basically need to project a similar feel for both. The notation for these is as follows. The top line is the cowbell with the right hand. Observe the accents. The accented notes should be toward the mouth of the bell and ring (long notes). The unaccented notes should be toward the neck of the bell and be more closed (short notes). Of the two bottom lines, the middle is the high timbal and the lowest one the low drum. The note marked WB means woodblock. The accented note in the middle line means a rim shot on the high timbal. These examples are in the 3-2 clave position. The notes enclosed in parenthesis are optional.

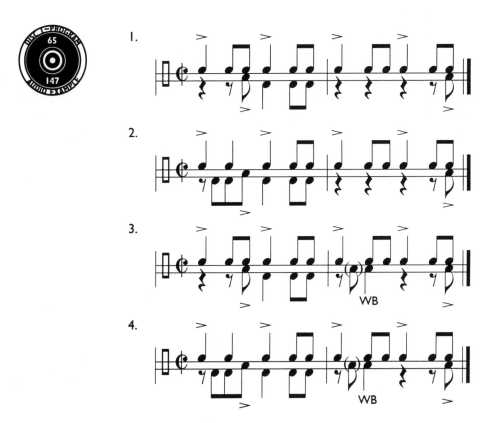

SONGO

The Songo is probably Cuba's most well known and interesting mix of the folkloric and contemporary styles. It is a blend of the Son and the Rumba styles, as well as the Cuban Carnaval rhythms—the Conga de Comparsa and the Mozambique—the Pilón, the Cha Cha Lokua Fun, and many other influences including funk and jazz styles. Next to the Son styles there is probably no Cuban rhythm which has gotten as much attention and been imitated as much by drummers throughout the world. A percussionist by the name of Jose Luis Quintana—Changuito—of the Group Los Van Van is credited with being the father of the Songo but like most styles it also evolved from the input

and influence of many styles and players. Since the Songo has so many influences it also has an equally vast number of approaches to playing it. Being a contemporary rhythm it also has the influence of the drum set and improvisational music, and while there are certain patterns that are considered standard Songo patterns, the approach to the style is generally very free. Following are various possibilities for the timbales.

The first two patterns are pretty standard orchestrations for the timbales. The third and fourth are really combinations of two different cowbell patterns played simultaneously.

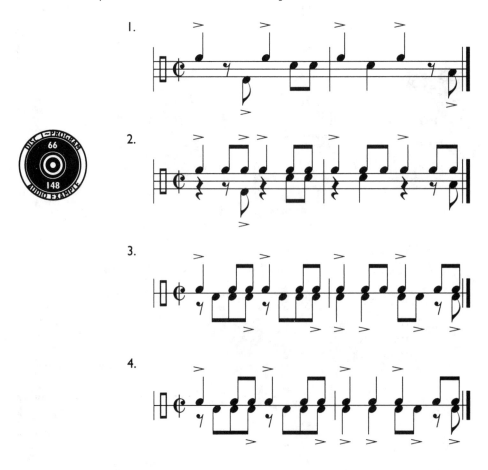

The following rhythms are non-Cuban styles but still fall under the general category of Afro-Latin or Afro-Caribbean music and most are quite well known and influential throughout the world.

MERENGUE

As mentioned earlier, the Merengue hails from the Dominican Republic and is basically it's national dance and musical form. The primary percussion instruments of the Merengue are the Tambora and the guira. The timbales are not part of the traditional ensemble. In large dance orchestras that are not exclusively Merengue groups, but do play this style in their repertoire, congas, bongos, timbales, and even a drum set are sometimes used. Basically anything you would play on the timbales would be extractions from the standard percussion parts, so in learning those you are giving yourself more vocabulary for any other instrument you might play in this style. Following are three patterns, one for each of the basic styles or sections of the Merengue. The first example is the basic Merengue pattern, the second is for the Jaleo, and the third for the Pambiche.

Additional notation is shown for these examples and is as follows: The top line is the left hand, either Muted (marked M), or Slap (marked S). The next line down is the right hand, playing either Rim (or woodblock or small cowbell) (marked R). The next line down is either a right or left stroke as marked, played as an open tone on the low timbal. The suggested sticking for the pattern is written below each example.

PLENA

The Plena is a folkloric style from Puerto Rico. It is normally played on tambourines called *panderetas*, the *guicharo*, and cowbells. It is also interpreted on the congas. Following is a basic pattern for the timbales, a combination of two cowbell parts.

BOMBA

The Bomba is another folkloric rhythm from Puerto Rico played with the hand drums—the *buleador* and *requinto*, and the small guiro called the guicharo, and the *cúa* (a wood sound). The cúa part has come to be played on bells also. The bell part would be played by the timbalero if the timbales were included in the ensemble, but they are sometimes not and the bell is simply hand held. Following are some basic patterns. The first is a basic bell pattern with a left hand part played on the low timbal. The second is the same but using the high timbal as well. The third is a combination of two cúa patterns. You can play these on a bell and wood sound or two bells.

CALYPSO

The Calypso originated in Trinidad and is another rhythm which has undergone many transformations and been integrated with, and changed into, many different styles and offshoots. Following are some basic patterns. The first is for two cowbells, a high and a low, duplicating the brake drums used in the traditional pan ensembles. The second and third are common orchestrations for the timbales with the top line being the bell and the bottom the high and low timbales.

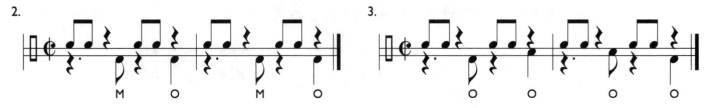

GUIRO

THE GUIRO IS A GOURD WITH RIDGES CARVED INTO THE FRONT AND PLAYED BY SCRAPING THE RIDGES WITH A THIN WOODEN STICK. SOMETIMES OTHER SCRAPERS — BAMBOO OR METAL — ARE USED with a variety of different guiros (like the smaller guiros of the Bomba and Plena traditions). Being made of a natural material, the original, traditional guiros come in many different shapes and sizes. Specific sizes and types are used in specific musical styles. Today many of the traditional gourds are manufactured of synthetic materials—plastics and metals—since the gourd is somewhat fragile and easy to break. The ones made of gourd have a warmer more natural tone while the plastic ones are more road-worthy.

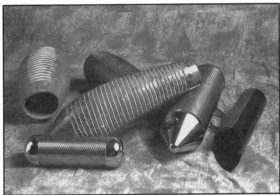

The guiro emanates from the Changui and Son groups as well as the Charanga traditions and is now used in virtually all types of Latin popular music ensembles as well as in folkloric settings. The sound, rhythm and texture it provides is an indispensable part of the groove and in the Son styles the ensemble would sound thin or empty without it.

The notation of patterns played on the guiro cannot accurately capture the nuance of the articulations required to make these patterns groove right. You must listen but you must also *see* someone do it in order to understand the technique involved. Yes, you scrape downstrokes and upstrokes in quarter and eighth note combinations, but there is a sweeping motion made on certain downstrokes that actually results in a upstroke sound that is very long and sort of pulled back from the pulse (but certainly does not slow down the tempo). In addition to providing this texture it also accents the pulse of the rhythm. It's also hard to describe this in words and musical notation, so again, have someone who knows play this for you so you can *see* what's going on.

The following illustration shows the playing position followed by examples of the basic patterns. The first figure shows the stroke on beat one—the downstroke—the *long* downstroke.

The second figure shows the end of that stroke. Notice the "down-up" arrows on beats one and three in the following examples. The attack on these beats is a downstroke that sweeps upward, to create the longest scrape possible within the tempo of the piece. The first example is the basic patterns for all of the Son styles. Examples two through four are three variations for the Danzón style. The last two examples are patterns for the Rumba.

The Dominican *guira* is a metal canister with ridges scraped with a metal multi-pronged scraper. It is used in the Merengue styles and its playing can be very complex because of the improvised variations of the basic pattern and the sometimes very fast tempos of some Merengues.

Again, the basic pattern strongly emphasizes the pulse but like in the previous examples, the actual nuance and all the variations played are impossible to notate. You have to actually see someone play it and have them show you the actual motions so you can practice correctly. Following are two basic patterns.

MARACAS

THE MARACAS ARE CANISTERS FILLED WITH BEADS MOUNTED ON A HANDLE . THE ORIGINAL CANISTERS WERE MADE OF A HARDENED HIDE OR THIN WOOD. MANY TODAY ARE made of plastics. Emanating from the Son tradition, this instrument provides a subtle but vital element of the groove of these styles.

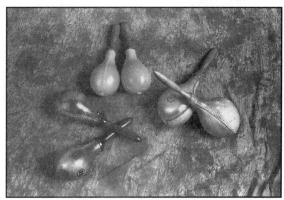

The basic pattern consists of eighth notes but the articulation of these eighths cannot be notated. You have to listen to capture the feel. Another very common pattern is the addition of a triplet, but this is not a strict triplet. The notes are slurred in a very unique way that you can only capture aurally. In an orchestra this instrument is usually played by one of the vocalists. Following are three common patterns.

1.
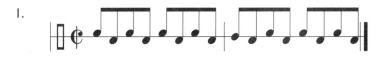

2.

3.
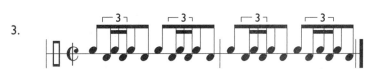

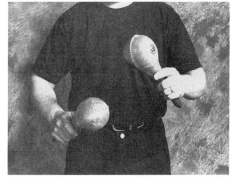

QUIJADA & VIBRA-SLAP

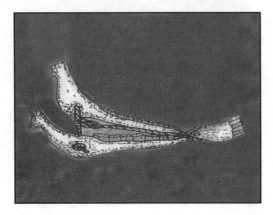

THE QUIJADA IS AN INSTRUMENT ORIGINALLY MADE FROM THE JAWBONE OF A DONKEY, MULE OR HORSE. IT'S SOUND GENERATES FROM THE CLATTERING OF THE TEETH FROM THE bottom of the jaw being struck against the top. It is the original predecessor of today's *Vibra-Slap*. Musically it is used mostly to punctuate rhythms on the downbeats of bars or phrases. Sometimes it is also played in an improvised fashion as a percussive or textural sound effect.

SHEKERÉ~AGBE

THE SHEKERÉ (ALSO SPELLED CHEKERÉ), OR CALLED AGBÉ (THE TRADITIONAL YORUBAN NAME FOR THIS INSTRUMENT), IS A GOURD (CALABASH) WRAPPED with beads. They range in size from very small to very large ones, with the larger ones producing beautiful bass tones when the base of the gourd is struck.

The playing is done by a combination of shaking and bouncing between the hands in both an up and down and circular motion. This allows the beads to strike the head and rattle and rotate around the head. Other tones (slaps, bass tones) are produced by striking the gourd itself on the bottom with the palm or heel of the hand or on the top (neck) with the heel of the hand.

The Shekeré is used in folkloric groups as well as in contemporary instrumental groups. Following are illustrations of playing positions and some basic patterns for both $\frac{6}{8}$ styles and the Rumba. The notation RH stands for Right Heel and OB signifies Open Bass tone played with a heel stroke on the bottom of the gourd. (Shown in figure 1.).

figure 1

figure 2

figure 3

1.

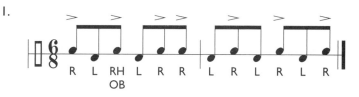

2.

3.

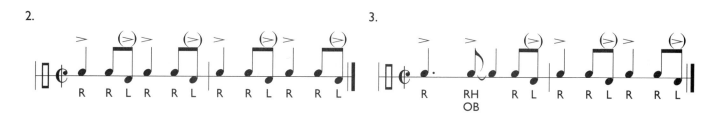

TAMBORA

THE TAMBORA IS A TWO-HEADED DRUM FROM THE DOMINICAN REPUBLIC USED IN THE MERENGUE STYLES. THE TAMBORA IS HUNG AROUND THE NECK WITH A STRAP AND SITS on your lap. It is played with a thick stick in one hand, which strikes both the head of one side of the drum and the wooden shell or rim of the drum. The other side is played with the hand. Shown below are illustrations of all of the stroke types and playing positions.

Figures 1 and 2 below show the two main right hand strokes. Figure 1 shows the playing on the side of the drum. (This drum has a block attached to the shell to play the shell stroke on), and figure 2 shows the right hand stroke directly on the head.

Figures 3 through 5 show the left hand strokes. Figure 3 shows the slap, figure 4 the open tone, and figure 5 the palm or bass tone. This position can also be played as a slap in the center of the head. Following the illustrations are several common patterns for this instrument. Also keep in mind that there are improvised variations to these patterns.

figure 1

figure 2

figure 3

figure 4

figure 5

The first of the following is the basic pattern for the Merengue. This pattern could be played in the *Paseo* (traditional introduction if there is one), and any verse sections. The second is the basic pattern for the Jaleo, the second section of the arrangement and the third and fourth are variations of this pattern. The fifth and sixth patterns are for the *Pambiche* or *Apanpichao* sections.

1.

2.

3.

4.

5.

6.

SUMMARY~PART I

HAVING COMPLETED THIS SECTION YOU SHOULD NOW HAVE A PRETTY THOROUGH KNOWLEDGE OF THE CLAVE RHYTHM AND HOW IT FUNCTIONS, AS WELL AS HOW every instrument, rhythm and part of the ensemble functions with it. You should also have a strong grasp of the rhythmic components of the styles presented, and at least a basic technique on each of the percussion instruments presented.

You need to have a thorough understanding of the Clave section in order to really benefit from the study of the rhythm section and the songstyles in the next section, and you must have a thorough understanding of the percussion instrument parts in order to really excel with the drum set stuff in Part III. The same holds true as you move into improvisation and development of your own approaches to this material.

All of this is no light task. There is a lot of information presented here and the Afro-Latin percussion instruments and musical repertoire provides a wealth of material to study and explore, and it should be approached and enjoyed as a lifetime endeavor. Don't feel compelled to try to digest all of this in a small amount of time. Keep in mind that this music has developed over centuries, existed for all this time, and continues to develop today. As you read this right now there are players playing and developing new innovative approaches to this material that will undoubtedly affect many musical styles and approaches to instruments in the future.

Be diligent and patient with your study. It takes time to learn but it especially takes time to assimilate. Don't be disappointed if you don't get it all right away. No one does. Now we move on to the rhythm section and the songstyles.

PART II

THE RHYTHM SECTION AND THE SONGSTYLES

INTRODUCTION~PART II

AS A PERCUSSIONIST OR DRUMMER, ONE OF YOUR MAIN CONCERNS IS TO FOCUS ON AND ANCHOR THE RHYTHM SECTION, AND THUS THE ENTIRE ENSEMBLE. THE MORE FAMILIAR you are with each instrument's part and role in the ensemble, the better you will be able to do this. Also, it is very common in these styles for percussionists to play all of the percussion instruments, and many times switch from, say, congas to bongos in a given situation, or play different gigs on different instruments. You'll always excel at one or some instruments more than others, but you should be able to cover on all of them.

This section of the book is divided into three parts: **Section I**: *The Rhythm Section*; **Section II**: *Arrangements, Charts, Terminology and Notation*; and **Section III**: *The Songstyles and Scores*.

Section I contains the introduction of the rhythm section instruments—bass, piano, tres, and guitar—as well as the horns and strings. There is some historical information on each and some of the most common approaches and patterns played on them. This is presented for specific styles on each of the instruments.

Section II consists of an arrangement of a piece and presents some arranging conventions through showing an actual score, and defining what each player and instrument's function is at each point in an arrangement (within a given songstyle). This section introduces terminology that you need to be very familiar with. Terms such as *Tumbaó, Paila, Montuno, Mambo,* and *Moña* are used in chart writing to describe specific sections or instrument parts of arrangements. This section explains these and other relevant terms and what to do at each section of a piece on whatever instrument you happen to be playing.

Section III contains reduced scores for many Afro-Cuban songstyles as well as styles from other Latin American countries that directly developed from the Afro-Cuban traditions. These show a complete ensemble's instrumentation for each of the songstyles presented.

PART II SECTION I~THE RHYTHM SECTION

The Bass and the Tumbaó

The Piano and the Montuno

The Tres and Guitar and the Guajéo

The String Section and the Guajéo

The Horn Section the Guajéo & the Moña

THE BASS AND THE TUMBAÓ

THE USE OF THE STRING BASS IN AFRO-CUBAN ENSEMBLES EVOLVED FROM TWO INSTRUMENTS, THE *Marimbula* AND THE *Botija*. THE MARIMBULA IS A LARGE THUMB PIANO (LIKE A KALIMBA), FROM THE *Congolese Bantú* tradition. It is built onto a large wooden box over a hole cut into the box for very big and low resonance. The player sits on the box and plucks the metal prongs to get the bass notes. The *Botija* was a large clay jug originally used to import olive oil to these regions. The jug had a large opening at the top and smaller holes on its sides. The holes could be cupped and struck with the hands and the player could also blow into the holes; all combined to produce bass tones. These were the first bass instruments of these musical traditions.

The string bass entered the picture through its use in the string section of the early Orquestas Tipicas and the Danza traditions (these groups initially were comprised of primarily European instruments—winds, brass and full string section), as well as eventually replacing the marimbula in the Son groups. The Changui groups (the original Son groups) did not adapt the string bass and to this day maintain the marimbula and the original traditions. Today both the traditional acoustic string bass, an electric version called the baby bass, and the standard electric bass are all used in Afro-Cuban popular music groups with the baby bass and the electric bass being the most common.

The fundamental pattern of the bass is also called a *tumbaó*—the *bass tumbaó*. It is a repeating pattern based on notes extracted from the *clave* rhythm. Like the percussion instruments previously presented, the bass can also play either a one bar or a two bar (or

longer) pattern as its fundamental accompaniment in a piece. Like all of the rhythms and instruments presented in *Part I*, it too must adhere to the foundation established by the *clave*. Consequently the patterns and any variations that are improvised, must also be in sync with the clave, as well as address all of the harmonic and melodic considerations of the piece.

The most common and well known *rhythm* of the bass tumbaó is the following:

Sometimes the first note is played only when beginning the pattern and then is tied when repeating. Sometimes the pattern also begins with an anticipation on beat four or four-and of the previous measure, so beat one is sometimes never stated. The notes of the line tend to center around the roots and fifths of the harmonies with other notes added as passing tones or improvised variations. This of course depends on the style. In a very traditional salsa-oriented setting you might play mostly roots and fifths, but in a Latin-jazz setting the harmonic and melodic vocabulary would be much more sophisticated. Regardless of the style, the bass is still depended upon for the bottom of the harmonies—the roots—as well as the bottom of the groove.

In looking at specific examples we'll start first with the simplest tumbaós and move to more syncopated variations. Notice that the more complex patterns are developments of the fundamental patterns and not necessarily new inventions. Also keep in mind that the older style patterns presented are still in use today not only when played in their native styles, but are used in modern styles as a basis for a new rhythm created by virtue of adding other variations or more complex harmonies to the basic parts.

The following two examples represent the early tumbaó of the traditional Son style. Though almost a century old it is still played today both in its traditional version as well as modernized versions that include other improvised variations. The first pattern attacks the one of each bar and the second ties beat one to beat four of the previous measure.

The next example is the standard basic tumbaó rhythm used most commonly in Afro-Cuban styles.

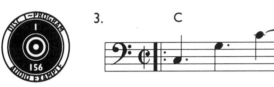

The next two examples are common for the Cha-Cha and for some older styles of Mambo.

These next three examples are combinations based on the patterns above. (In 3-2.)

The next example is a common riff for the Guajira style. (In 2-3.)

The next two examples show the standard bass tumbaó applied to two very common chord progressions. The first is a II-V-I-VI vamp with one chord per bar. The second is another very common progression with two chords per bar. (Written in 3-2.)

10.

11.

These two examples show the same chord progressions used in the two examples above, but with a freer rhythmic approach to the lines. Though the choice of notes still centers around the roots and fifths of the harmonies, note what a difference a simple variation of the rhythm makes. Lines like this are usually improvised by the player as variations to the basic pattern. More variation and interest is created by the players choice of plucking or slapping or damping certain notes. These examples can be used for standard Son styles but start to move towards more modern approaches, and can be used for some more contemporary Mambo and Songo styles. (In 3-2.)

12.

13.

The next two examples show an eight bar tumbaó played over one chord. This is a more freestyle tumbaó and would generally either function as an improvised variation to a more basic timekeeping pattern or as part of an arrangement that calls for this type of line. It might also be used as a vamp for one section of an arrangement. These approaches can be used for more modern Mambo, Songo, Mozambique, or arrangements that incorporate these styles. They can also be "funked up" with slaps and the like. You can also use just two or four bars of the line as a pattern. For practicing percussion or drums, you should sequence or record these patterns and practice playing along to them and improvising over them. (In 3-2.)

These two examples show a similar approach as the previous two but over different sets of chord changes. (In 3-2).

The following are examples of a vamp called a Descarga. The word Descarga means "to unload" and this is generally what a soloist does over a Descarga. It is not necessarily a full solo, although it can be. It can be an arranged vamp section of a piece but is also often improvised. Bassist and composer Israel "Cacháo" Lopez was a master of improvising bass lines in this style. Both of these examples are lines commonly associated with Cacháo. (In 3-2.)

The following examples, though not Descargas, can be used in a similar way—as vamps to improvise over. You can begin by improvising in the holes left in bars three and four, and then gradually stretch out and blow over the whole thing. Any instrument can be featured. These lines are in the style of the very influential Cuban group Los Van Van. (In 3-2.)

The following are examples of bass tumbáos in ⁶⁄₈. The same clave considerations apply in these as well. (In 3-2.)

Next is an example of a bass tumbaó over the chord changes to an F blues. Since the only rhythm used in the line is the basic tumbaó, this example would work in either 3-2 or 2-3 clave.

27.

Here is an example of a bass tumbaó over the chord changes to "On Green Dolphin Street." (In 2-3 clave.)

28.

THE PIANO AND THE MONTUNO

THE PIANO'S CURRENT ROLE IN AFRO-LATIN POPULAR MUSIC BEGAN EVOLVING IN THE EARLY PART OF THIS CENTURY WITH THE DEVELOPMENTS OF THE DANZÓN—although it wasn't officially added to these ensembles until the late 1930s and early '40s. Originally the piano's role in the Danza tradition was that of long-note accompaniment with little rhythmic activity, but as the Son traditions also developed, the piano began to develop an identity as a rhythm section instrument—especially in the *Conjunto* settings. It began adapting the rhythmic structures of these styles—especially the *Guajéos* of the Tres—and through this developed what became the *piano montuno*.

The montuno is perhaps the ultimate combination of the percussive and harmonic/melodic elements of this music. It can be rhythmically very complex or very simple, but must always strike a perfect balance of rhythmic interest and foundational strength for the rhythm section. Like all the other instruments' patterns, the montuno must also adhere to the clave—whether playing one-, two-, four-bar, or longer phrases. In this section we'll examine the fundamentals of the montuno. You should sequence or record these patterns to practice playing with them.

Keep in mind that although there are several montuno patterns written here, montunos are almost never written out in a score or a piano part—any more than conga parts or bongo parts. A player with knowledge of these styles simply knows what to play and when. Most players would frown upon being given a written montuno. If you are arranging music and you know the player that is going to play it, you would never write out the montuno for them. Although there are numerous "standard" montuno combinations that you hear over and over, there is still an improvisational element that must be left up to the player.

Montuno playing has been developed to a very advanced degree by artists of this style. This section shows basic approaches, but the variety of ways that montunos can be approached are as varied as the artists who play them. Nonetheless, there are several "rules" you should be familiar with that will strengthen your familiarity with these styles, and with elements of the clave, and will help you play better as a percussionist in the rhythm section.

A montuno is a repetitive riff or vamp that provides a rhythmic element to the rhythm section, as well as the harmonic elements to the song. In its most basic form, it is an arpeggiation of the harmonies of a piece, or a section of a piece, played mostly in two-bar phrases. This basic approach evolved directly from the Son Guajéos of the Cuban Tres, which will be covered in the next section.

Let's look at this basic example and point out some key elements that you must be thoroughly familiar with. All of the examples presented in this section are consistent with the examples in the bass section. That is, there are examples of similar styles over similar chord progressions. You can put these piano montunos together with the bass tumbáos from the last section and create vamps for practicing drums and percussion.

The following example represents the most basic montuno over a single harmony. It is written in the 2-3 clave position. It is a two-bar phrase that is repeated. Notice that it begins on the beat—the first bar of the phrase, the 2 side of the clave—and that the second bar is all upbeats. There is no downbeat in the second bar of the phrase—the 3 side of the clave. It is essential that you grasp this because this is one indicator of what is going on in a piece of music in terms of clave direction. This is not to say that you will never hear anything different, but this is a basic rule. If you play it the other way around you are crossing the clave. This basic pattern is essentially arpeggiating a first inversion major 6th chord.

1.

Now the next essential point: Following is the same montuno as above but written the way it really should sound—legato. The notation used above is going to be used throughout this section for the sake of rhythmic clarity, but you must remember to execute these as if they were all notated like this. A montuno is not staccato but legato, fluid and smooth.

2.

Now let's look at this same montuno but in 3-2 clave. Since this is only a vamp on one chord, we don't have a harmonic issue to address so we simply reverse the pattern as follows. The catch is that you are beginning with an upbeat and you must be in the pocket with it.

3.

There are two other basic ways to handle this montuno in 3-2 clave. Which of these three you'd use depends on the musical situation. The previous pattern is the bottom line. Of the two that follow, the first gives you a downbeat to start with. You just simply play the one when you start the pattern and as you repeat it you are no longer stating the one and you are in 3-2 clave. This pattern would work fine at the beginning of a piece or section. The second begins the phrase with a pickup. Basically this is the last note of the pattern so you're just starting a beat early. This pattern works fine if the rhythms section is also "pushing" this kick, but even if they're not, you can anticipate these rhythms and use this pattern as a transition between two sections or some similar situation, but not to start a piece. There you must use one of the other two patterns.

4.

5.

Next we introduce what is probably the most common harmonic progression in Latin music, the I-IV-V. (Both major and minor keys are equally popular.) We are using the same approach as in the previous montuno but now adding notes to outline the harmonies. Notice that the rhythm is exactly the same. This first example is written in 2-3 so it begins and continues with the downbeat at the beginning of each two bar phrase.

6.

Now the first clincher. The following example is the same montuno as above but in 3-2. Notice that *the rhythm is reversed to work with the clave but the harmony is not.* The progression remains the same so you must play the right notes of the chord but reverse the rhythm of the montuno. Notice the downbeat of the first bar in parenthesis. We are using this to start the phrase but it is not played again when the two-bar phrase repeats. Also notice that the downbeat is played in the second bar because that's where it goes, with the 2 side of the clave.

7.

The next two examples are identical to the last two, but with the addition of an octave doubling in part of the line. This is also a basic approach to the montuno. The first example is in 2-3 and the second in 3-2.

8.

9.

C   F   G   F   C   F   G   F

Most montuno playing is played with both hands. In its basic form, both hands double the same pattern with perhaps the addition of an octave doubling of certain notes. In its real performance, the player will double and harmonize as well. This creates a richer harmonic texture and a fatter groove. Following are the same examples shown for two hands and written in the 2-3 position.

10.

C   F   G   F   C   F   G   F

As a reminder, look at this pattern notated the way it should sound when you play it—legato.

11.

Now that we've established some fundamentals, let's look at some other ways to play montunos. Following is another very common approach to the I-IV-V vamp. It is shown here in 2-3 clave in both C major and C minor.

12.

CMaj

13.

Cmin

Another very common vamp is that of playing over a single Dominant 7 chord. Following are three variations. The first shows both hands doubling the same pattern—basically a second inversion G7 chord. The second is the identical rhythmic pattern and both hands are doubling the rhythm but the notes are now harmonized. The third shows another harmonized variation. All three are written in 2-3 clave. Practice staring on the 3 side also.

14.

15.

16.

Next we move to montunos over a variety of common chord progressions. The following example is over a II-V-I-VI vamp. (The VI is really functioning as a dominant V of II).

17.

Following are montunos to two other very common chord progressions in these styles.

18.

19.

Last we'll check out two staples of the Son tradition, the Cha-Cha and the Guajira. Following are two examples for each of the styles. The first two are for the Cha-Cha and the third and fourth for the Guajira.

20.

21.

Note: In the Guajira it is very common to begin these lines with pickups. The audio examples contain the pickup notes G A B (*Sol La Ti*) leading to the C (*Do*), the tonic note that starts the riff.

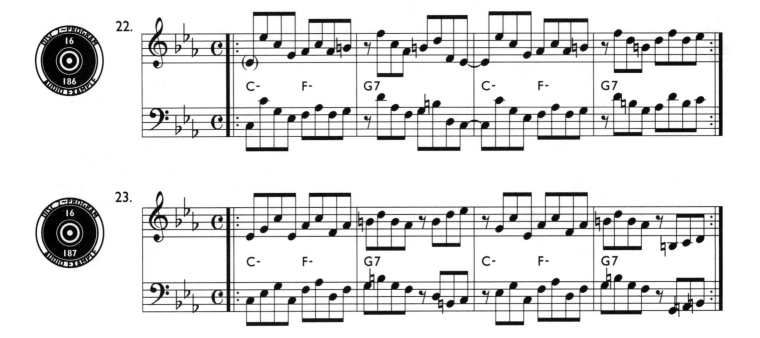

THE TRES AND GUITAR AND THE GUAJÉO

THE TRES IS A THREE NOTE SIX-STRINGED INSTRUMENT. IT IS BASICALLY A SMALL GUITAR WITH THREE SETS OF TWO STRINGS BOTH SOUNDING THE SAME NOTE. (THE ORIGINAL TRES had three sets of three strings, and was a nine-string guitar.) Another instrument along these same lines is the Puerto Rican *Cuatro*, which has four sets of two (or three) strings.

The *Tres* was the original harmonic instrument of the Son tradition and always served the dual harmonic and melodic role, playing the Guajéo, which was the harmonic (and rhythmic) accompaniment, as well as playing melodies and/or improvising within an arrangement. Because the Guajéo is a rhythmic part, the Tres, like the piano, is not only a part of the rhythm section, but can also be seen as a percussion instrument within the ensemble.

The Guajéos of the Tres are the predecessors of the montunos of the piano, and are essentially responsible for the development of that approach on the piano, as the piano's original montunos were adaptations of the Tres' patterns. In some ensembles—specifically the *Conjunto* instrumentation of the 1940s—both the piano and the Tres performed similar roles within the ensemble—in the playing of the guajéos or montunos during the mambo section of arrangements. The Tres' open strings sound a third-inversion C-Major triad without a third—G below middle C, middle C, G above middle C.

The role of the Tres, Cuatro, and later the guitar, remain pretty traditional in the Salsa setting, but the guitar has taken a much broader position in the Latin-jazz instrumental settings where it not only plays variations of the traditional guajéos, but plays a large role in improvisation.

Following are some basic Guajéo patterns for the Tres. They can also be played on the Cuatro or the guitar. (In 2-3 clave.)

THE STRING SECTION AND THE GUAJÉO

The use of strings in Afro-Cuban popular music emanated from the early Danzas and Orquestas Tipicas and evolved with the Danzón and Charanga tradition, where their role was (and remains) threefold. Not in any order of priority, first the melodic role includes playing the melodies of the arrangement. Though these are often lead melodies or features, in the Charanga instrumentation it is also very common for the strings to play contrapuntal and background lines for the flute. Second, they perform a harmonic and textural "comping" to provide a chordal foundation for the flutes and vocals, and third, a rhythmic role in which they play *Guajéos* in the montuno or mambo section. In this last sense the strings also become part of the rhythm section. Most common in these ensembles are two or three violins, but cello is also used as well as full string section arrangements. The examples below work well with three violins or two violins and a viola.

The examples below are in the style of the string parts of *Orquesta Aragón*, one of my favorite Afro-Cuban ensembles performing the Charanga traditions, Danzón, and other Son styles. I highly recommend listening to this ensemble not only for its use of strings but for its capturing and rendering of the beauty and elegance of these styles.

THE HORN SECTION THE GUAJÉO & THE MOÑA

THE HORN SECTION IN AFRO-CUBAN POPULAR MUSIC ENSEMBLES FLOURISHED FULLY IN THE CONJUNTO SETTING AND FROM THE INTEGRATION OF ELEMENTS FROM THE JAZZ BIG BAND traditions that were in full swing at the time. Like the strings and guitar, the horn section also has a multifunction role providing melodic lead lines, background lines and improvisation, as well as functioning with the rhythm section in its performance of what can also be thought of as guajéos for the horn section. These can be written and/or improvised and there is almost always an arranged section—usually during the mambo section of an arrangement—which features the horn section playing a *moña*. These are layered horn parts with staggered entrances with a variety of harmonic, melodic, and rhythmically syncopated elements that intertwine as parts are repeated and more parts enter, building the intensity of the interlude.

The instrumentation can range from three trumpets and a trombone (a very common salsa dance band horn section) to combinations of woodwinds and brass, to a full big band.

Following are examples of moñas. In these examples the bottom line, here played by trombones, would repeat their line four times, and then the trumpets (and possibly saxes) would enter with the top line and repeat that another four times, and then a cue or a written indication to go to another section or back to the montuno would be given. The next time around there might be a cue to another moña and then another cue to the top or another repeat back to the montuno for another solo or coro (chorus).

Section II~Arrangements-Charts, Notation, and Terminology

THIS SECTION DEFINES THE TERMINOLOGY USED IN AN ARRANGEMENT OF AFRO-LATIN POPULAR MUSIC STYLES; OFTEN REFERRED TO AS SALSA STYLE CHARTS. IT PRESENTS a short arrangement of a simple piece with all of the sections and individual instrument parts defined. A percussion part is then extracted from the same arrangement. This is what you would be handed as a drummer or percussionist in an ensemble or on a recording date. Study the score to get a better understanding of what the things on the percussion part mean. I'd also strongly suggest you study piano, bass, lead trumpet and entire horn section parts. Sometimes these give you a better picture of what's going on than a drum part. Also remember that a good player knows all the parts even if he or she doesn't necessarily play all the instruments.

We'll begin by defining each section, and the essential terminology that runs through the arrangement. A typical Salsa arrangement's progression is as follows. Keep in mind that the rhythm styles used in the arrangement—unless of a specific tradition like a Danzón—can include Cha-Cha, Son Montuno, Mambo and/or include anyone of a number of rhythms or styles. This medium to medium up tempo salsa groove based on the Son, Son Montuno and Mambo is also sometimes called a *Guaracha*. These rhythms may be written into the arrangement or possibly improvised by the player. Regardless, the general format is as follows.

Arrangements begin with an *Intro Section*. This sets up the *A Section*—the verse, which generally features the vocal or instrumental rendering of the main melody of the piece. Next there is a bridge section, the *B Section*. These sections might or might not be labeled specifically as A and B, but the important thing to remember is that they form the verse (A) and bridge (B) of the song. The bridge section generally leads to the *Montuno Section*. This is the vamp section used for lead vocal improvisation and vocal choruses, as well as instrumental solos. In standard vocal arrangements that do not feature the instrumentalists as much as the vocals and the song itself, the montuno is usually played a fixed amount of times—for example an eight bar section repeated four times. In situations where improvisation and instrumentalists are featured the section is often open and then "cued out" to the next section. This leads to the Mambo Section which features new arranged material and generally serves as an interlude between repeated Montuno sections, as well as a bridge back to the top and on to the ending section. These Mambo sections generally feature horn section parts entering in staggered and layered fashion. These horn section parts are called Moñas. The section is repeated a number of times until the entire section is in and the intensity is quite high. It then usually cues back to the Montuno section for another vocal chorus or instrumental solo. From the repeated Montuno you would then go back to another Mambo section but have another set of Moñas that would be played, or you might see another Mambo section arranged in its entirety. From this last Mambo the cue can be back to the Montuno or back to the top for a DC al Coda or other arranged material leading to the **Ending Section**, which in popular dance music arranging is usually a return to the intro material with an ending written in. It can also be an arranged ending that is completely different from the intro material. In our arrangement, the second Mambo returns to the Montuno a third time and the last Montuno cues to the top for a DC al Coda consisting of the Intro material arranged with an ending Coda. Each instrumentalist has a specific part and/or instrument to play at *each* of these sections, and each has specific responsibilities for the transitions between sections and the setups or entrances at each point.

There will also almost always be what I'll call *virtual changes* in the direction of the clave from section to section, caused by virtue of sections arranged with odd numbers of bars. I call it *virtual* because the direction doesn't really change. Remember the information from the *Clave* section. The direction of the clave never *really* changes. If there was an odd number of bars, you were simply starting a section on the second bar of the clave (or the first bar if you had been playing with the second bar first up until that point). This is all definitional and semantic, and all of this should become transparent once you understand and can hear all of this. Then you'll just simply play it right without giving it much thought.

Before looking at the chart, let's define what each percussion instrument does at each of these sections. Keep in mind that at times this will vary but this is the most common scenario.

Intro Section:
Bongos: *Martillo with variations.*
Congas: *Tumbaó, basic on one drum.*
Timbales: *Cascara or bell with LH tumbaó or clave on the woodblock or two-handed cascara pattern.*

A Section
Bongos: *Martillo with some variations.*
Congas: *Tumbaó, basic on one drum.*
Timbales: *Cascara or bell with LH tumbaó or clave on the woodblock, or two-handed cascara pattern.*

B Section
Bongos: *Martillo with variations.*
Congas: *Tumbaó, basic on one drum.*
Timbales: *Cascara with LH tumbaó or clave on the woodblock, or two-handed cascara pattern. Sometimes but rarely the bell.*

Montuno Section
Bongos: *Starts with Martillo with improvisation and moves to the Hand Bell.*
Congas: *Tumbaó on two drums.*
Timbales: *Mambo Bell with either tumbaó on low timbale with left hand or clave on the woodblock with stick.*

Mambo Section
Bongos: *Stays on the Hand Bell. Possibly changes bell to more or less active pattern depending on the arrangement.*
Congas: *Tumbaó on two drums.*
Timbales: *Mambo Bell with either tumbaó on low timbale with hand or clave on the woodblock with stick or move to the ride cymbal.*

Ending Section
Bongos: *Martillo with variations.*
Congas: *Tumbaó, basic on one drum.*
Timbales: *Cascara or bell with LH tumbaó or clave on the woodblock or twohanded cascara pattern.*

This is the general approach. If it's a vocal-oriented Salsa arrangement this is almost always what you'll hear. You'll hear a particular player's approach to the tumbaó on the congas, variations of the martillo, and a variety of bell patterns on the timbales and the hand bell, but essentially all the players will follow these guidelines.

None of these patterns are actually written into the percussion charts with the exception of perhaps an occasional bell pattern to indicate clave direction at a particular section or because an arranger might want a specific pattern or feel like "a-caballo." It is up to the player to know what to do and this is where knowing the style integrally really comes into play. It's the same as playing a jazz gig and seeing a chart that says "two feel." The two feel is never written out. The player is expected to know how to play it and lead into the next section, etc.

Now let's look at the actual chart and then its respective percussion part. We'll assume this arrangement is for a recording session for a Salsa record. We'll also say it's a vocal feature so all of the instrumental parts play a more subdued role than they might on a Latin-Jazz date. There are also few instrumental features on our hypothetical recording session.

As you look at the music itself, here are some things to keep in mind: The clave is written on the bottom line of the score *for reference only.* Although it can be played throughout a piece (usually by one of the vocalists if it is played), it seldom is in this type of arrangement. (That usually takes place in the folkloric styles.) It is written throughout this score to make clear what happens when a section is in 3-2 or 2-3. As you can see from the score, the timbalero does a pickup—an abanico—on the three side of the clave and brings in the intro on the two side. With this now established, the direction in clave never changes, even though some sections begin in 3-2 and others in 2-3. (This will be noted specifically at each section.) There is no *arbitrary* change in clave direction. Any *virtual* change happens solely for musical reasons. In our case it is the arranging of material with odd-numbered phrases and breaks—that lead into and out of sections—which give us a certain clave position in that section because the musical material in that section works in that particular clave direction. What works best is determined by the composition and is also a matter of arranging technique and artistic preference of the

composer and/or arranger—in this case yours truly. One example in this arrangement is that the intro is in 2-3 but the A Section—the verse is in 3-2. This is because the intro material is in 2-3 as defined by the musical material—the melodies—and thus the rhythm section is arranged and plays it that way. The melody and musical material of the A Section is in 3-2 as defined by the music itself. Notice that though the Intro began in 2-3, the last bar of the intro is the 17th bar of the phrase—an odd number of bars—and on the two side of the clave. This sets up the A Section to begin in 3-2. These types of transitions happen often throughout the score and were purposely arranged this way to illustrate this concept. You should practice playing all of the percussion instruments along with the audio recording so you'll be comfortable with these types of transitions.

It is critical that you understand this material for this music to make sense to you in performance. If this isn't clear, go back to the clave section and review. Also listen to commercial recordings of arrangements while playing/following the clave all the way through the piece. Without a solid grasp of this material you'll be in the dark and guessing at every section change every time you play this music, and *every time* you play this music you will encounter these types of transitions and these perceived changes in the clave's direction.

Some technical notes about the score:
—It is assumed that you are familiar with all of the standard notation and terminology used in chart writing and arranging—endings, repeats, codas, signs, and the like.
—Not every voice of every horn part was written out, so as you listen to the score you'll sometimes hear more voices than you see written. What is written is essentially a complete representation of what you'll hear. The piece is scored out for two trumpets, two trombones and rhythm section.

INTRO SECTION

The intro section begins with an abanico from the timbalero on the 3 side of the clave and sets up the Intro to begin on the 2 side at the first double bar—bar 1. The intro is essentially 16 bars of music with a break on the 17th bar which sets up the melody pickup to the A section. This odd number of bars sets up the A section to begin in 3-2.

All of the instruments are playing the basic parts described earlier. The piano plays a basic montuno over the chord changes, the bass player plays a basic tumbaó over the chord changes, the bongocero plays the martillo with some improvised riffs, the conguero the basic tumbaó on one conga and the timbalero plays two-handed cascara along with fills and setups. (You also will hear accessory percussion—maracas, guiro and clave throughout the piece but this is not notated and basically never is.)

A SECTION/VERSE

The A section is in 3-2 and is 16 bars long. The rhythm section plays basic time on their respective instruments—cascara, tumbaó and martillo—with slight improvised variations in the martillo and with the timbales sometimes lightly emphasizing background orchestrations. The bass plays a basic tumbaó and the piano a basic montuno comp. The horn section plays written backgrounds in the holes between the vocal phrases. The rhythm of the melody line is not played exactly as written. This is up to the creative interpretations of the vocalist or player of the melody instrument. Since this section is 16 bars long it leads into the B section with no transitional clave changes. There is simply arranged material leading into the bridge.

B Section/Bridge

The bridge continues along in the same fashion as the A section but is only 15 bars long. Notice the break on beats 2+ and 4 of the 15th bar. In the clave section we established that this was a very common rhythmic point for breaks, accents and the like. Since there is no 16th bar in this section—which would be the 2 side of the clave—it now becomes the first bar of the next section—a piano break to set up the montuno—and the next section—the montuno is played in 2-3.

© 1996 Ed Uribe

BREAK TO MONTUNO SECTION

The break for the montuno section is in 2-3 and is 8 bars long. The piano plays a solo guajeo over the chord changes and the percussion improvises some fills under the piano. There is a horn section and rhythm section accent on beats 2+ and 4 of the 8th bar leading into the Montuno.

Break to Montuno

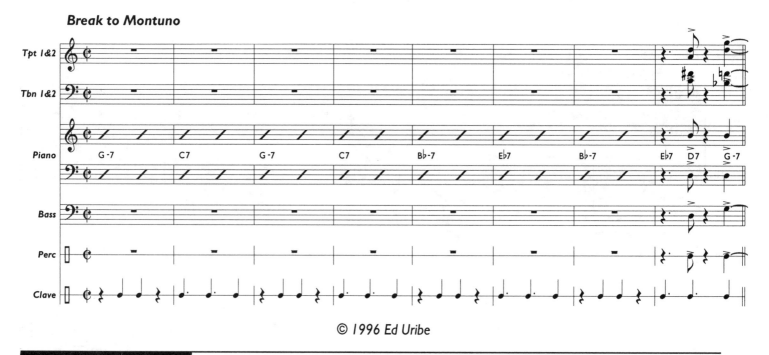

© 1996 Ed Uribe

MONTUNO SECTION

The Montuno section is in 2-3 and is played 3 times in this arrangement so it is written here with 3 endings. The 1st time it is played—now, following the B section—it goes to the 1st ending. Notice it is a 17 bar phrase and notice the material in the 15th through 17th bars. The rhythms are right with the clave and set up the entrance of the following Mambo 1 section in 3-2. When the montuno starts the bongocero plays some riffs on the bongos and then moves to the Campana (the bongo bell or hand bell). The conguero plays a tumbaó on 2 congas and the timbalero moves to the large bell.

The second time the Montuno is played it is returned to from the Mambo 1 section. The Mambo 1 is 19 bars long making the 19th bar the 3 side of the clave and setting up the 2nd Montuno in 2-3 once again. This time the Mon-

tuno is played to the 2nd ending—a 16 bar phrase—making the entrance of the Mambo 2 continue along in 2-3 clave. Notice the rhythmic break in the last 2 bars of the 2nd ending. The rhythm is right with the clave and the last bar has the accent on beats 2+ and 4 once again, leading into the Mambo 2 section.

The 3rd and final time through the Montuno section is a return from the Mambo 2 section. This time it is played to the 3rd ending. The Mambo 2 section is in 2-3 so we're back into the Montuno with no clave transitions. Once again the Montuno is played in 2-3 but this time to the 3rd ending. From here we DC al Coda. There is a rhythmic break in the last bar of the 3rd ending on the 2 side of the clave and that sets up the DC to the Intro which is also in 2-3. From there you go to the Coda for the ending. Every one of the 3 times through the Montuno section the rhythm section basically plays the same patterns on their respective instruments. The patterns might vary slightly at each repeat and if there were to be more repeats or open sections for more solos there would be more variations and interaction in the rhythm section parts.

As you listen to the recording you'll have to flip back to this page from the Mambo 1 section, then flip to the Mambo 2 section, then back here to the Montuno then to the DC al Coda section at the end.

© 1996 Ed Uribe

MAMBO 1 SECTION

The Mambo 1 section functions as an arranged interlude between the repeated Montuno sections with new material introduced in the arrangement. This musical material is in 3-2 clave and the break on the 17th bar of the 1st ending of the Montuno section set up the beginning of this section. Here the piano and bass have a written line they are doubling so there is no montuno from the piano or tumbaó from the bass. The timbalero is playing the cymbal as indicated and setting up the ensemble kicks. And though not indicated in the chart, the bongocero switches to a different pattern on the hand bell. In this section the bongocero sometimes doesn't play bell at all and either lays out or moves back to the bongos and picks up the bell again on the return to the Montuno section. The conga continues a 2 drum tumbaó with some variations. This is a 19 bar section and the arrangement of the last 4 bars sets up the return to the Montuno section in 2-3. Again notice the accent on beats 2+ and 4 of the last bar to set up the entrance of the 2 side of the clave on the return to the Montuno.

MAMBO 2 SECTION

The Mambo 2 section also functions as an arranged interlude between the repeated Montuno sections but adds a *Moña* in the horn section. This consists of some written lines that you see in the score and some improvised by the players. This musical material is in 2-3 clave and the break on the 16th bar of the 2nd ending of the Montuno section set up the beginning of this section.

The Montuno repeat to the 2nd ending was only 16 bars long so there was no clave transition into this section. The rhythm section functions exactly as it did in the Mambo 1 section

The Mambo 2 section is 16 bars long so it moves back to the Montuno for its 3rd and final repeat without any clave transitions.

© 1996 Ed Uribe

DC AL CODA

The DC al Coda from the 3rd ending of the Montuno section puts you here—the Intro section with a transition to the Coda. The 3rd ending of the Montuno set up the entrance to this section in 2-3, thus no clave transition. At this point all of the players return to the instruments and patterns that were played at the beginning of the arrangement. From here you just read to the Coda and end.

Intro as Ending (DC al Coda)

© 1996 Ed Uribe

PERCUSSION PART

This is the percussion part to the arrangement. Listen to the recording and follow the part. You can reference back to the score to see why things are or aren't in the part. Notice that the part is basically a rhythmic outline of the score and does not notate any of the specific percussion parts. Each player knows what to play and what to do at each section. The only rhythmic patterns are the cues for the timbale player's cascara, bell and cymbal and those aren't really essential to notate, they're just cues. You'll also hear things that aren't notated and that's also part of a player's just knowing how to play the style.

SECTION III~THE SONGSTYLES AND SCORES

TRADITIONAL ANALYSIS AND HISTORICAL STUDY OF MUSIC GENERALLY PLACES ALL STYLES WITHIN THE REALMS OF TWO CATEGORIES—SECULAR AND SACRED. Every aspect of a particular music is then defined as emanating from and belonging to one of these two areas. While it is true that any music from a given background can be generally assigned to one of these two groups, these categories and terms really evolved from the traditional western methodology for analysis and study, and don't necessarily account for the cultural aspects and societal functions of musical styles in their categorization. This type of analysis, which developed primarily in the European culture and conservatories, worked well in defining the European styles because the lines were clearly drawn in those cultures in terms of what was secular and what was sacred. From the thirteenth through nineteenth centuries, Christian religion—either Catholic or Protestant—prevailed, as did the Vatican and later the Lutheran church. Religion and the Vatican had the power of government in this time. It was during this period that the European styles that we today generally categorize as European classical music developed. The church, having the position that it did in society at large, very clearly defined what was secular and what was sacred. While folk or peasant music of these times was defined as secular music, it was not sanctioned by the church, often not acknowledged and sometimes even forbidden. The terms secular and sacred basically defined the sacred music of the church and the secular music commissioned for the entertainment of the courts.

If we use these two categories to define the styles we are looking at in

this book, then practically all of the music presented is secular music—with perhaps the exception of the Abakuá styles, and music played in some Bembé celebrations—and some of these are secular and some are sacred, in that they are sometimes used in religious worship or festivities and sometimes just in general festivities. This brings us to one glitch in using these terms to define Afro-Cuban music (or any associated African or Afro-Latin style).

The Christian doctrine teaches worship of one god (monotheism) with an ultimate goal of salvation through life after death. With the exception of praying and honoring specific saints and holy figures, one did not deviate from or improvise an interpretation of this doctrine. In the early period of Western musical development (the twelfth through nineteenth centuries, and certainly over an even earlier period of history in general), you were either a Christian or you were a heretic. The lines were clearly drawn throughout society. In music, there was the music of the church and there was the music of the courts and the music of the peasants, and all of it was heavily regulated and censored by the church.

Many African cultures (as well as many other cultures throughout the world) have religious doctrines that are much more tied in with folkloric aspects and daily life activities. Thus, their folkloric aspects and daily life activities are much more tied in with their religious doctrines. Many of these types of religious doctrines have not one but a variety of gods (pantheism). These gods are prayed to, honored, or worshipped at different times and for different reasons, often primarily dictated by the folkloric practices and daily activities and needs of the particular society. Some of these may include the worship of an almighty and supreme god for purely spiritual reasons, the worship of a god of healing, god of love, god of the harvest, of war, the mountains, rivers, and so on.

While the music performed in these cultures to honor and worship these deities can certainly be defined as religious or sacred music, it is also secular in that it is used by and serves the purpose of the society at large, and is thus closely integrated with the folklore of a particular society. Music is a much more integral and indispensable part of the daily functioning of these cultures and is consequently a more integral part of the religious practices as well. While there certainly is music in these cultures that is used for entertainment and celebration, it too is not extraneous or optional as it is in European and American culture. Thus in examining these types of musical styles, I believe the line between the secular and the sacred is more transparent than in the analysis of music based on the traditional European classical styles. In the European approach folkloric music is always secular, but in these styles the folkloric music is often both sacred and secular. While some Afro-Cuban styles are strictly sacred, many are really sacred/secular or more accurately religious/folkloric in origin, and these styles spawned another category of nonreligious/folkloric styles.

In the settlement and development of Cuba and all of Latin America, the European, African and native Indian people formed the culture of today. A general look at this evolution in Cuba shows the Europeans—particularly the Spanish and French—contributing the elements of the Christian musical definition, along with the music of their courts, or the bourgeoisie. This was European sacred and secular music. The other European (secular) style was the peasant music brought by the

peasant workers who accompanied the early explorers. The African slaves provided the multi-deity (pantheistic) religious practices that were coupled with the folklore of their African regions of origin. This was the sacred/secular or religious/folkloric element just described. The native Indians provided much the same in this area as the African slaves did, but were less influential because of their early exposure to the European settlers and the religious conversion imposed upon them by their clergy.

In Cuba this religious/folkloric element was contributed most predominantly by the Yoruba people of West Africa. In the first half of the nineteenth century history shows some 600,000 African slaves entered Cuba. The Yoruba people represented a major percentage of this group. Others were the Dahomeans (who were initially brought to Haiti by the French but entered Cuba in large numbers after the Haitian slave rebellion in 1791), Congolese and Abacuá (Carabalí) people.

Due to the ethnic diversity of the various African tribes many customs were transformed and integrated. The Catholic Church also laid claim to the practices of these slaves and though some permissiveness was granted for the religious/folkloric practices of the slaves to continue, the goal of the Church was their eventual conversion to Christianity. Thus regardless of the attempts of a particular people to maintain their traditions intact, this cross-cultural integration resulted in the development of new indigenous religious/folkloric (secular/sacred) customs.

The various deities of the Africans are called *Orichas*. Depending on the permissiveness of the church towards a particular group, these Orichas were either worshipped openly or often camouflaged to appear as a Catholic saint. Other religious or sacred practices were camouflaged as folkloric or secular festivities. This allowed many traditional practices to continue in their original forms. (This camouflaging also took place with musical instruments. Partly due to these societal constraints, and to the need to develop instruments from whatever materials were available, instruments like the cajones, cucharas, palitos and guagua used in the Rumba styles came to exist.) Various African cultures and customs were integrated with each other and then further reintegrated with the Europeans (the Spanish in particular). All Afro-Cuban music evolved from these cultural and religious combinations, and these form the basis for the stylistic categories presented in this book.

While the primary traditional Western religion of Cuba (and all of Latin America) is Catholicism, the religion of *Santeria* is probably the largest, most popular and most influential African-based religion. Santeria now exists in various iterations due to even further integration and spread throughout the world. There is the primary or original West African or Yorubaland tradition, then there is that of Cuba, that of other Caribbean and Latin American regions, and that of New York. In Cuba it is from these religious traditions that many of the present-day folkloric styles developed.

We'll now apply these concepts to arrive at three general classes in which to place the musical styles: the sacred, but really sacred/secular or *religious/ folkloric*; the secular/folkloric or *nonreligious/folkloric*; and the *popular*, which includes all of the folkloric styles that were eventually commercialized and used purely for entertainment outside of the originating cultures. Following is a list of styles and their categorization based on these concepts.

The songstyles and instruments of the *Santeros* are without a doubt sacred when practiced in the context of their religious ceremonies as are other rhythms that are direct descendants of these traditional religious practices. Since this book does not deal specifically with the religious practices of Santeria, we'll only put the rhythms of the Abakuá and music played in Bembé celebrations in this category as they are the only religious styles presented. These would be the *religious/folkloric* styles. At this point the line gets a little obscured because many groups play sacred rhythms or derivations of them purely for musical entertainment. (The sacred drums would not be used in these scenarios but the rhythms and chants are.) Even traditional ensembles do performance presentations of sacred or religious music and of folkloric styles.

Under the *nonreligious/folkloric* category we'll put the Rumba styles— Guaguancó, Yambú, and Columbia— the Conga de Comparsa and related Carnaval styles, the Mozambique, Guiro, and Pilón. The Bembé and Abakuá and related styles could also live here when not used in a strictly religious sense.

Under the category of popular music we put the Danzón, the Son, and all of its offshoots—the Cha-Cha, Guajira, Bolero, Son Montuno, and Mambo. While these styles also initially began as folkloric traditions, (the Guajira and the basic lyric songstyle *Cancion* from the Spanish peasant class, Son style from the Changui and Son groups, and the Danzón from the Orquestas Tipicas), they underwent major integration and transformation into a wealth of other styles and ensemble instrumentations, and all ended up under the larger umbrella of Salsa in New York and other Caribbean and Latin American regions.

Yet another category called folkloric/ popular could be introduced to describe styles such as the Songo and Mozambique since they are results of influences of folkloric as well as popular Cuban styles, plus they've both undergone many transformations in their integration with jazz, funk, fusion and other styles.

The non-Cuban styles presented here are the Bomba and Plena, nonreligious/folkloric styles from Puerto Rico, and the Merengue from the Dominican Republic. Like all the other Afro-Latin styles, these too had folkloric beginnings, but are now highly commercialized.

One final aspect to bear in mind: until the 1960s, and especially during the '40s and '50s, there was constant exchange between Cuba and the U.S. After the embargo was set upon Cuba in the early '60s by the U.S., this interaction stopped. The result was that these styles now developed separately from each other.

This music and new developments in it continued to flourish in Cuba as it always had, but now it was not in constant touch with the major developments of the music scene of New York. Here a large Latin American population (not just Cubans) were actively continuing to develop these styles, contributing their indigenous elements, and combining them with the influences of the jazz, funk, and rock styles, but now without the constant Cuban presence and influence. Essentially this formed two separate musical cultures each developing these styles apart from each other.

This eventually developed into the general category of Salsa and was heavily commercialized in the 1970s and continues as such. The Latin American communities of New York and much of the Caribbean claimed this music as their own indigenous style and to some degree the integration of all of these traditions was in fact new. But the Cuban perspective—having been shut off from all of this—was that this was all merely a copy and commercialization of the Son traditions which they developed and had existed intact

in Cuba for generations. Now in the 1990s it seems it has come full swing and a new awareness, recognition, and acknowledgment is being given to the Cuban musical traditions.

A very similar situation exists with the Santeria traditions. Much of what developed in New York and in other areas of the Caribbean was a derivative of the Cuban traditions. The New York traditions have developed a strong identity as have some throughout other Latin American regions. Regardless though, the Cuban Santeros developed before the Americans. But the traditions go back before Cuba and there are native Africans living in America who look past Cuba to Africa for the original ideals of these practices.

In conclusion, in examining all of this information the goal is not to categorize purely for its own sake, but to understand where styles developed from and what they are connected to, so that a deeper understanding of their musical and cultural vocabulary can be achieved. On a more practical level, as players of this music in what many times are nontraditional, integrated scenarios, this information will give you a clearer understanding of these styles.

The scores shown here are skeletal representations of each instrument in each of these styles. They show the basic patterns of each of the instruments and the essential elements that would serve to identify the style. The metronome markings show the general tempo range in which these styles are played, as well as the range in which these written examples will sound best. Listening-analysis and the learning of many interpretations of one particular piece are essential to truly learning these songstyles.

THE SON

THIS SCORE SHOWS THE BASIC INSTRUMENTATION OF THE SON. THE SON IS THE ROOT OF MANY AFRO-CUBAN POPULAR STYLES. EMANATING from the Cuban peasant class and the Changui style, it is the foundation for the majority of Afro-Latin dance music.

In an original and initial group the piano would not have been present—only the Tres or guitars. The bass was originally played on the Marimbula or Botija, a tradition still maintained by the Changui. The string bass replaced these in the early 1900s.

SON-MONTUNO

THE SON MONTUNO IS THE NAME USED TO DESCRIBE THE STYLE OF SON PLAYED BY THE CONJUNTO ENSEMBLES OF THE 1940S AND '50S. IT IS BASICALLY A SON WITH MORE intricate arranging and larger instrumentation, open sections (Montuno sections) for *Soneos* (vocal improvisations), and perhaps instrumental improvisations.

Two scores are presented. The first score shows the rhythm section function during the lower dynamic sections—verse and chorus, as well as during a piano solo or other low dynamic section. The second score shows the rhythm section during the Montuno and Mambo sections, as well as any other high-dynamic and high-intensity section. The same piano montuno is shown for both sections. Though it could be played this way, it is more probable that this too would change from section to section. Since our focus is on the percussion, only those parts have changed. The bongo player switches from the bongos to the campana, the conga player switches from a one-drum tumbaó to a two-bar pattern and the timbalero moves from the sides—the cascara or paila—to the large cowbell and plays the written pattern or one of its variations.

SHOWN HERE ARE TWO SCORES
ALSO—ONE FOR COMPING FOR THE
VOCALS AND LOW DYNAMIC SECTIONS,
AND ONE FOR THE HIGHER DYNAMIC
MONTUNO SECTION. The rhythm section
changes between one section and the
other are very similar to those of the Son
Montuno style on the previous page, but
some slight variations in patterns are
presented here. Also the tempo of the
Mambo is faster. Very often what distin-
guishes one of these styles from another is only
the tempo. The Mambo is generally the
fastest of these types of interpretations.

The Mambo evolved partly from
the Son traditions and from a vamp
section added to the end of the Danzón called *Nuevo Ritmo*. This extended
vamp section, over which instruments
were solid or improvised, became the
Montuno section and later became a
style of its own—the Mambo. The
Mambo gained tremendous popularity
in the 1930s, '40s and '50s both in
Cuba, the Caribbean, and New York as
it developed as a musical genre as well
as a dance.

 Danzón

Unlike the peasant class roots of the Son traditions, the Danzón developed in the ballrooms and courts of the aristocracy. It evolved from a combination of European court dances and instrumentation and African rhythmic elements. The European instruments—woodwinds, strings sometimes brass, and tympani—(the tympani were replaced by the timbales as the rhythm section developed) were coupled with a rhythm section where the African elements were most prevalent.

It is an intricate compositional and arranging format and is the only Afro-Cuban setting that features this instrumentation of flutes and violins.

Originating from the Contradanza, the Danza and the Habanera, it was originally a three part ABAC form. The A is called the *Paseo*, the B is the main *Melody*, the Paseo then repeats, followed by the C section, called the *Trio*, which is played by and features the violins. A fourth (D) open vamp section (originally called the *Nuevo Ritmo*) was added which featured additional instrumental writing and/or improvisation in the strings, flute and piano in particular. This section spawned the Mambo as well as the Cha-Cha styles.

The first of these scores shows what would commonly be an A (or possibly a B) section. Notice in the first score the timbales are playing the *baqueteo* and there are no congas playing. This represents the traditional and initial instrumentation.

The second score has the timbalero switching to the bell—in this case the small bell (which is smaller than the Cha-Cha bell and is called the Charanga bell) and the addition of the conga drums. This represents what might be played during the D section (Nuevo Ritmo or Mambo section).

This presents only the skeletal parts. The string and flute writing and arranging is quite intricate in this style. These are short excerpts showing typical passages.

CHA-CHA

THE CHA-CHA EVOLVED FROM THE MAMBO SECTION OF THE DANZÓN AND REACHED ITS PINNACLE OF POPULARITY IN THE 1950S AS BOTH A MUSICAL STYLE AND a Latin dance craze.

Shown below are two scores. The first shows the comping for the vocal and lower dynamic section and the second has the bongocero moving to

the campana for what might be an open vamp or higher dynamic section.

Both piano parts presented are very common for this style and have existed for some time, but the first is almost a cliche at this point, having almost instant recognition due to its popularity gained as the intro to Santana's rendition of Tito Puente's "Oye Como Va."

RUMBA GUAGUANCÓ

RUMBA IS A FOLKLORIC MUSIC AND DANCE STYLE TRADITIONALLY PERFORMED WITH PERCUSSION, VOCALS AND DANCERS. THERE ARE ALSO REGIONAL INTERPRETATIONS of the Rumba within Cuba; the two prevalent ones being the Habana and Matanzas styles.

The Guaguancó is in duple meter (¢ time) and is performed at medium to very fast tempos. The Clave, Palitos and the Bombo lay the foundation and the Salidor and Tres Golpes provide the melody of the Guaguancó. The Quinto does not play any specific patterns but improvises with the vocal passages and the dancers providing punctuation and accentuation to the musical phrases and the movements of the dancers. All three of the drummers also improvise in call-and-response fashion with each other.

The dance to the Guaguancó is usually danced by couples but is sometimes danced by a single male dancer. The theme of the dance can depict a number of scenarios from the (symbolic) sexual conquest of the female by the male dancer to dramatic or comical themes portrayed by a solo dancer.

There is much complexity in the juxtaposition of the rhythms created by the interaction and improvisation of the percussionists and the vocals but the style is always very fluid and flowing.

RUMBA COLUMBIA

THE COLUMBIA IS THE FASTEST OF THE THREE RUMBA STYLES AND IS PERFORMED IN ⁶⁄₈ TIME. THE ROLES OF THE PLAYERS ARE THE SAME AS for the Rumba Guaguancó but the dance is usually danced by a single male or two males in a sort of challenge.

CONGA DE COMPARSA

THE CONGA IS A CARNAVAL RHYTHM OF CUBA. COMPARSA REFERS TO THE GATHERING OR GROUP OF PEOPLE WHO DANCE AND SING AND MARCH IN THE PARADE, OR SOMETIMES to the march or parade itself. Sometimes the term Comparsa is used incorrectly to describe the rhythm that actually accompanies it, called Conga. As with Rumba, there are also regional interpretations of this style—such as the Conga Habanera, Conga Santiaguera, and Conga Matanzera—representing the Carnaval rhythm interpretation of three different regions of Cuba. This style is played in ¢ time at medium to very fast tempos and features call-and-response passages between the lead vocalist and the chorus. It also features melody lines and improvisations played by trumpets.

*Improvises and solos but not always included in the ensemble.

MOZAMBIQUE

THE MOZAMBIQUE IS A DIRECT OFFSHOOT OF THE CONGA DE COMPARSA RHYTHM STYLES. IN THE EARLY 1960S PEDRO IZQUIERDO—PELLO EL AFRO-KAN—PUT TOGETHER an ensemble called Los Afrokanes which took Conga rhythms and other Comparsa accompaniments and interpreted them with the addition of the rhythm section—piano and bass. This style came to be known as Mozambique. It was further developed and interpreted by Latin Jazz artists in New York in the 1960s. Some notable renditions of the New York style are those of Eddie Palmieri's groups of the 1960s with Manny Oquendo on timbales, as well as those of many other groups adapting this sound at the time. This style was one of the most commonly combined with funk, fusion, and rock styles and was adapted by many drum set players. The Mozambique and many of its derivations continue to be used quite frequently in arrangements of contemporary Cuban groups.

The first score shows one variation of the Mozambique with a traditional percussion setting: the clave, cowbell, both bombo patterns, and the congas scored out for five players. The second score shows the same parts but the bombo rhythms are combined with the clave and cowbell parts so that three players could play this on perhaps the drum set, timbales and congas. In the first two examples, although the bell and bombo parts are only two bars long, the conga drum part is four bars long, so the phrase is a four bar rhythm.

2.

This is another variation of the Mozambique. The conga drum and bell parts change rhythms and the entire phrase is only two bars long.

3.

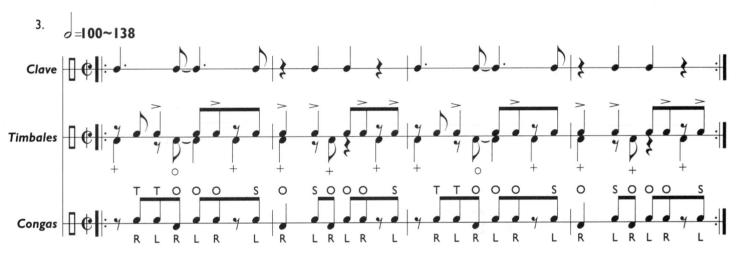

SONGO

THE SONGO IS A COMBINATION OF THE SON AND RUMBA STYLES. IT IS PLAYED IN ¢ TIME AT MEDIUM TO VERY FAST TEMPOS. A PERCUSSIONIST BY THE NAME OF JOSE LUIS QUINTANA—ChanAfro-Cuban Rumba and Son percussion instruments as well as with the drum set. It also carries the influences of funk and fusion drum set and bass styles. It is probably the most imitated and inteP
guito—is credited with the invention of this style but it is important to remember that it is usually a number of people and influences that contribute to the development of a style over a period of time so there are many sources and players to look to for study.

This style is played with the standard
grated Afro-Cuban rhythm to date.

It is a very free style in the sense that the basic patterns only provide basic skeletons of the rhythm and the players are free to improvise and interact with a wealth of variations—whatever the music calls for, or that they are at liberty to create.

These voicings vary on the first repeat in the audio recording.

GUIRO IS A FOLKLORIC $\frac{6}{8}$ RHYTHM ORIGINALLY PLAYED USING ONLY THE SHEKERÉS AND THE COWBELLS. A TUMBADORA IS ALSO ADDED and this is a common type of rhythm in a Bembé celebration.

Two scores are presented here. The first shows the traditional instrumentation of the shekerés, bells and the cajon which preceded the use of the tumbadora in these styles.

The second shows an adaptation for the standard section of timbales, congas and bongos along with the shekeré. Practically speaking, this second score shows a generic version of what could be used to play a variety of $\frac{6}{8}$ rhythms.

THE ABAKUÁ IS A SECRET MALE SOCIETY IN CUBA WHOSE RELIGIOUS MUSIC GREATLY INFLUENCED THE DEVELOPMENT OF THE RUMBA and other Cuban folkloric styles. Shown below is an example of one approach to the Abakuá style. Notice the juxtaposed duple and triple meter rhythms in the bell and tumbadora parts. This is typical of these rhythms as they are adaptations that evolved from the ritual drumming played on the batá drums.

BOMBA

THE BOMBA IS A FOLKLORIC STYLE FROM PUERTO RICO. IN ITS PURELY PERCUSSIVE FORM THE RHYTHMS ARE ONE BAR PHRASES AND ARE NOT IN CLAVE BUT WHEN A PIECE of music is arranged in a Bomba style then the arrangement functions in clave.

In traditional percussion interpretation the cúa functions as the clave and the Requinto functions as the quinto

does in a Rumba style with the buleador playing the foundation rhythm. The traditional bomba drums are large barrel shaped drums and are larger than regular congas, but today regular conga drums are more commonly used in ensemble settings.

The score below shows the rhythm section parts to what might be a section of a full ensemble arrangement.

THE PLENA IS ANOTHER FOLKLORIC RHYTHM FROM PUERTO RICO THAT IS TRADITIONALLY PLAYED ON TWO *Panderetas*—TWO TAMBOURINE SHAPED FRAME DRUMS without jingles.

The score below shows a full rhythm section, but the piano and bass parts are not specific to the Plena. The percussion parts are imitating the role of the traditional percussion, with the congas and timbales imitating the parts of the Panderetas.

The themes of this style are often of social commentary or political satire.

THE MERENGUE HAILS FROM THE DOMINICAN REPUBLIC AND IS PROBABLY THE MOST POPULAR FORM OF LATIN AMERICAN DANCE MUSIC TODAY IN ALL OF LATIN AMERICA, as well as the United States and the Caribbean. Along with Salsa it is the most commercialized Afro-Latin songstyle. This score shows the basic function of the rhythm section during the verse sections. You should also refer to the Tambora Section for other variations to the basic Tambora pattern, and for combinations for the Pambiche, Apanpichao, and other sections of the standard Merengue arrangement.

PART III

AFRO-CUBAN DRUM SET

INTRODUCTION~PART III

WE NOW MOVE TO THE DRUM SET— THE NEWEST INSTRUMENT IN THE CUBAN PERCUSSION FAMILY. THE DRUM SET WAS NOT ORIGINALLY PART OF THE CUBAN OR AFRO-LATIN instrument repertoire, but has now become an integral part of many Afro-Latin ensemble settings and specific rhythms— most notably the Songo. Other Rumba and ⁶⁄₈ oriented hybrids have also been partly developed on it as well as for it. It is very common in contemporary Cuban groups to have both a drum set player with a set of timbales to one side of the set, as well as a timbalero/percussionist and a conguero/percussionist, and perhaps even another percussionist that may play bongos and shekeré and other percussion. Of course in Cuban jazz groups there is pretty much always a drum set player as well as a percussionist—very similar to most non-Cuban Latin-jazz groups.

The American jazz, funk, and fusion styles and players have had a great impact and influence on Cuban music and musicians as well as their drum set playing. The integration of this influence with the Cuban percussive approach to the drum set often results in a very unique drum set style. The wealth of percussion parts and the myriad of Afro-Cuban rhythms live very well and in a very interesting and new way on the drum set. The application of one instrument's parts (from one particular style) to the drum set is quite common and results in very different drum set parts. The application of small pieces from a variety of instruments' parts results in practically an ensemble sound all its own.

The Cuban drum set adaptation of many of its folkloric and popular rhythms often consists of a variety of parts from a variety of percussion instruments of a particular style's instrumentation, and while the actual timbre of a style cannot be reproduced exactly on the set, another new and different texture develops.

Another approach that offers endless possibilities is that of mounting percussion instruments around the drum set. With resourceful planning of the placement of the instruments and the development of good technique and good coordination between all four limbs, a single player can create a monstrous groove and in some cases an entire percussion section sound. When a set player with this approach pairs up with a percussionist with a similar approach, not only can much of the standard percussion repertoire be reproduced quite fully, but the sky is the limit as far as what can be invented and improvised.

Of course all of these drum set scenarios—as impressive as they may sound— have a couple of prerequisites that must be met if one is going to perform this music on drum set, fulfill the necessary musical roles in ensembles, and realize the endless possibilities that exist in this relatively new territory.

The first of these has already been mentioned numerous times thus far in the book. You must have a thorough knowledge and at least a basic technique on all of the percussion instruments. Second, you must have a thorough knowledge of all of the musical styles and as many versions of each of them you can possibly absorb. Everything you can learn about a style from the simplest cliches to the most detailed intricacies will enhance your interpretations on the drum set. Third, you must know what to play on each of the instruments in each part of the arrangement in each of the styles. Last and most important, you must be able to adapt parts in whatever manner necessary to fulfill the role required by the music and the ensemble in which you happen to be playing the drum set. Because the role of the drum set is not clearly defined in traditional Afro-Cuban musical styles and ensembles—with the exception of ensembles that have incorporated the set and arranged it into its format—what has to be played is not always totally clear.

You may find yourself in many scenarios where you have no idea what to do on the set. One very common scenario is you end up playing drum set and there is already someone playing timbales and also a conguero and bongocero. What do you do? Or, the bongo player moves to the campana and that's the bell you were going to move to. Or, there are only two of you and the particular piece really needs not only the timbale, conga, and bongo parts but also the second bell parts as well as some guiro and maracas in certain parts. Obviously two people are not going to play every nuance of every part, and the fact is that the hihat is not a maraca no matter how you play it. But if you know your stuff, you can simulate all of the parts and give the music and the ensemble the textures and the feel that these instruments provide.

The only thing that will keep you together in these situations is having the prerequisites together. Then it becomes easy to either find a part to complement the section or to play a part one of the other players dictates to you. The key factors that will determine what you play on drum set in a given situation are the music you are playing and what other percussion is present or missing. With this as the basis we'll take each style and establish what to play on drum set with a variety of percussion accompaniments. These situations will

have the drummer playing the role of the percussionist, and playing some or all of the missing percussion parts and not really drum set parts. We'll also examine what to do if all the parts seem to be covered by the other percussionists in the ensemble. Through examining hypothetical situations and combinations of all sorts, you'll gradually become adept at finding the right part to complement the music.

From this we'll work towards functioning as the only drummer/percussionist in an ensemble and examine how to cover a variety of parts. In most traditional situations you won't generally find yourself being the only drummer because most styles call for at least two (really three) percussionists, but you may find yourself in a nontraditional situation trying to emulate the sounds and textures of a full section. We'll examine how to achieve this.

It is also increasingly common—especially in contemporary jazz and fusion and Latin-jazz settings—for there to be a drummer and a percussionist. This is where I find things can get really interesting and great grooves and textures can be achieved if both players have the right mindset about the combination of the drum set and percussion. Keep in mind that though you may be physically sitting behind the drum set you are still one of the percussionists and, provided you know the percussion instruments and parts, you can and should incorporate a variety of them into your drum set setup. *Even though this section is directed at the drum set it means drum set/percussion setup.*

You also must keep in mind the timbre and volume power of the drum set. The Afro-Cuban percussion instruments all have a unique timbral register that allow them to blend and complement a Latin ensemble. In some scenarios the true sound of the drum set will also blend and may even be called for and will work quite well, but in others, where the drum set isn't really a part of the sound, you have to find not only the rhythm pattern to add but the timbral or tonal blend with the percussion section as well as the ensemble. Review all of the percussion parts to each of these styles before continuing on.

Situation I

We'll begin with the scenario that you are the drum set player and you also have three other percussionists. This is not a common occurrence and would be the most limiting of circumstances, but I've been in this situation and there are plenty of things to play. This situation can happen if the group plays a variety of styles and now happens to be playing a Cha-Cha and you're on drum set, or if there are guest artists or people sitting in, and consequently more percussion than normal. The timbalero is playing the small bell and the left hand tumbaó on the low drum. The conguero is playing the tumbaó and the bongocero plays martillo and will go to the Campana in the higher dynamic sections.

You play the following pattern: the guiro pattern in one hand on the closed hihat and the clave in the other hand on the rim of the snare. The bass drum plays the bombo rhythm. You could also mount a guiro and a woodblock for the guiro and clave parts and place a set of timbales to one side and play parts on them as well.

1.

If the timbalero is playing the clave on the woodblock then you play the left hand tumbaó from the low timbal part *softly* either on a tom using your hand or a stick—playing the closed stroke on beat two and the open stroke on beat four—or using a stick playing a rim click on the snare on beat two and an open tone on the tom on beat four.

If there were to be a guiro player you could also play a maraca variation on the hihat as follows. The first example is the basic eighth note pattern, the second and third are common articulations. The sixteenths and sixteenth triplets must be slurred to sound correct.

When the bongocero goes to the campana you move to the cymbal with the left hand playing either the left hand tumbaó with rim click and tom or with the left hand playing the clave on the rim or a mounted woodblock.

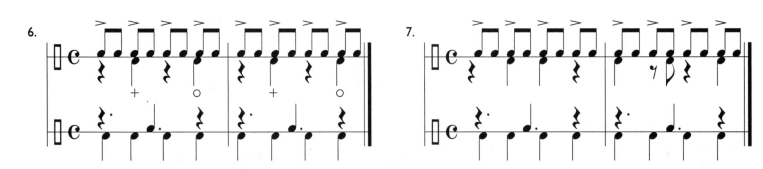

If there are three percussionists and three singers playing the maracas, guiro and clave, then go to the bar or the dressing room and get yourself a drink or go find someone to dance with.

If the ensemble is somewhat contemporary then you have one other option. You can play a Cha-Cha-funk style pattern with a backbeat. Here are a couple of combinations.

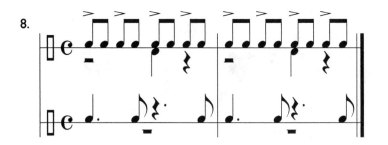
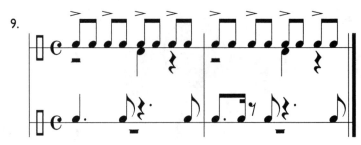

Situation 2

The second scenario involves you, the drum set player, with two other percussionists—one playing congas and the other playing bongos and campana. Some of these patterns would also be what you'd use if there were only one other percussionist playing congas.

In this situation you function as the timbalero with the added layer of the feet playing bass drum and hihat. You can add whatever other colors (drum set colors) the music calls for but if the ensemble is at all traditional you need to function like the timbalero first.

Ideally this scenario would have you playing a full drum set with a set of timbales to the left of your hihat as well as (at least) all of the usual timbale bells mounted around your setup comfortably. Following are some possibilities.

The first two patterns are the standard timbale parts with the addition of the feet. The first example has the standard timbale left hand tumbaó and the second has the clave which you'd play on the rim of the snare or on a mounted woodblock.

1.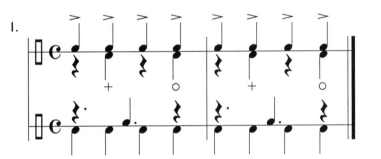

2.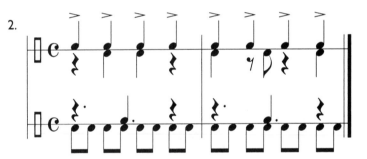

The next two variations function the same as the previous two but have a different cowbell pattern. Although this pattern is also common for the Cha-Cha, the music has to call for it. The first pattern is the most common.

3.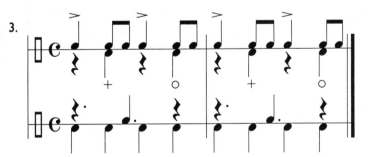

4.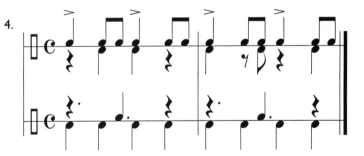

When the bongocero moves to the campana, you can move to the ride cymbal and play clave in the left hand or move to the cymbal and keep the quarter note Cha-Cha bell in the other hand. The music will dictate which.

These patterns can also be played on the cowbell and used as you'd use any of the previous four patterns, and you could still use it on the cymbal in a different section of the arrangement.

5.

6.

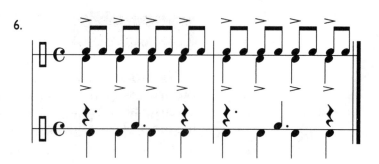

Situation 3

This scenario involves the drum set/ percussion setup with only one other percussionist playing congas. In this situation you will probably, as mentioned in the previous section, employ some of those patterns. One of the key differences here is that there is no bongo player to play the campana, so you must play that part when the music calls for it.

You are basically free to play any of the percussion parts except those of the conga player. Here is an additional possibility. The first is a basic timbale comp but playing the guiro part on the closed hihat. Remember that all the patterns from the previous section might apply here also.

1.

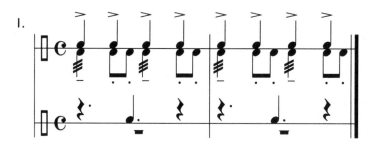

When the campana is called for you can add it along with keeping the small cowbell with either of the following

patterns. The first has the standard campana pattern. The second puts the campana part into clave (2-3).

2.

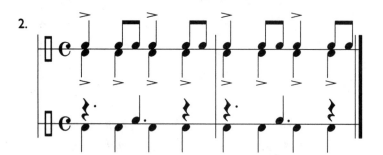

3.

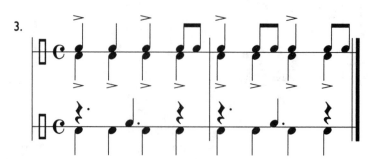

Situation 4

This final scenario involves the drum set/percussion setup alone. While it might seem that this situation would afford you the most freedom—and in some cases it might—it is the last situation that really affords the greatest variety of possibilities.

In this music certain parts, sounds, and textures, need to be there for the music to sound right and when too many components are missing it can also start to sound empty. Nonetheless, here are some possibilities for the drum set without percussion.

These first two examples are the basic timbale/bell pattern with the other hand playing some conga parts. The examples show the two basic bell patterns. The third and fourth examples are essentially the same as the first two but with a slight variation in the bass drum. In this situation you are free to play all of the variations that any of the instruments might play, but remember that you have to provide the whole groove plus provide all the right textures so don't go nuts just because you can.

Note: The circled note on the snare line indicates a rim click. The X notes indicate the hihat with the foot.

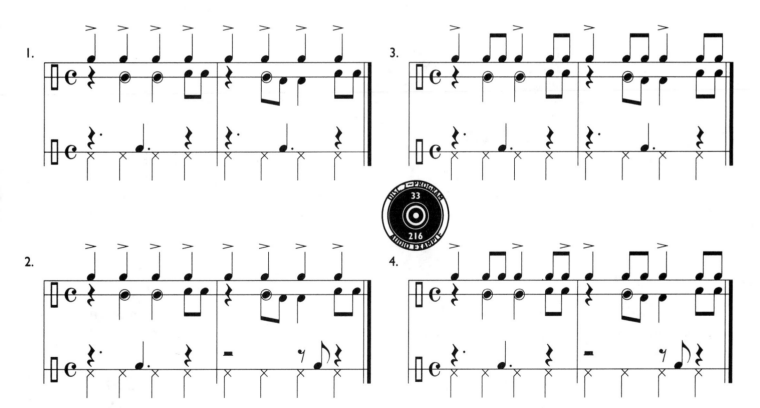

Another possibility is to play the funk style grooves but now adding the cowbell since no one else is playing it. These two patterns are the same as the previous backbeat patterns but with the ride on the cowbell and the hihat playing with the foot. You can also play eights with the left foot on hihat.

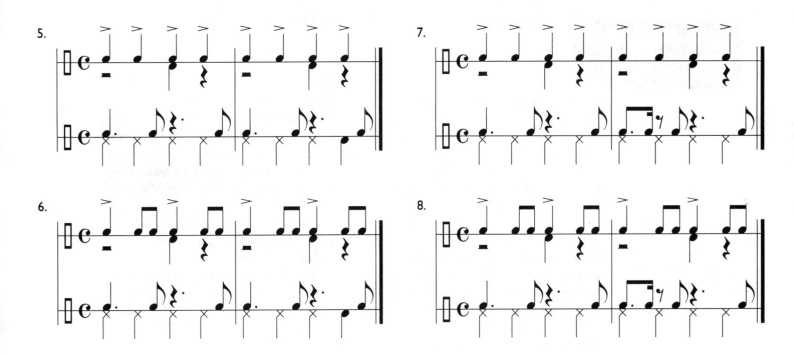

These last two patterns incorporate the backbeat as well as some conga stuff on the rim and toms. Since these are a little busier you have to be careful when you use them and make sure you can play them without disrupting the groove.

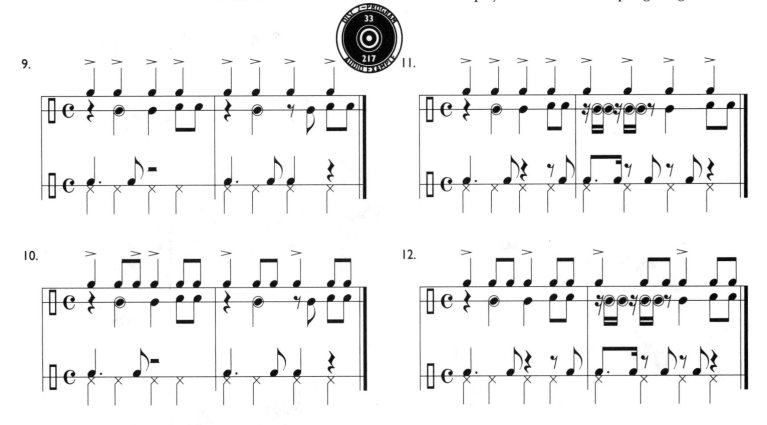

GUAJIRA

FOR THE GUAJIRA WE WILL EMPLOY MANY OF THE SAME PATTERNS AND APPROACHES AS FOR THE CHA-CHA. MANY TIMES THE DIFFERENCE BETWEEN ONE STYLE AND ANOTHER is based on lyric or harmonic content or song form or perhaps even just varying regions of origin. When certain parts of the ensemble are examined purely from a rhythmic perspective they are often identical. This is the case with the conga tumbaó in the Son styles, as well as with many of the timbale parts, bongo parts and bass parts.

Such is the case with the Guajira in that it is very similar rhythmically in the percussion to the Cha-Cha. Of course certain nuances and feels will be different because the songstyle is different, but the bottom line is you are still playing some parts identically.

Again, look at what other percussion is present and then pick your parts. The tempos will vary from song to song and will generally be slower than the Cha-Cha.

1.

2.
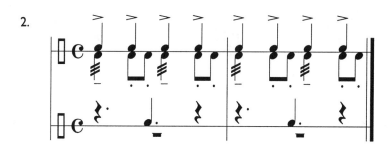

3.
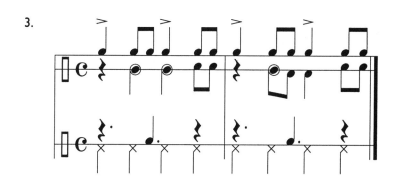

BOLERO

THE BOLERO IS A LATIN BALLAD FORM. IT IS IN THE PRETTY SLOW TEMPO RANGE BUT CAN SOMETIMES HAVE OPEN VAMPS FOR IMPROVISATION THAT PICK UP IN ENERGY QUITE A BIT—such as in a Bolero-Son. It has some unique rhythmic patterns in the congas, bongos, and timbales and those have to be incorporated onto the drum set.

Also, even though it is quite a different songstyle than the Cha-Cha or Guajira, rhythmically some of the same parts will cross over, especially in an open vamp section.

Here are examples for all of the situations presented in the Cha-Cha section. Check out what percussion there is and develop your part.

These first two patterns have you functioning as the timbalero, playing the paila pattern on the hihat along with the bass drum pattern.

There are two common variations. These patterns will work if you are working with two other percussionists that are covering the congas and bongos.

You can also play more of a standard drum set groove along with the two other percussionists' parts. You're still covering the signature paila sound as well as filling it up a bit. Here is a very common pattern for this approach.

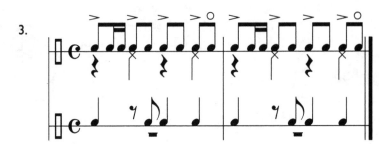

If you are playing a Bolero with no percussionists then you have a variety of possibilities to choose from—including some from the Cha-Cha section—and you'll probably end up playing a few different ones throughout the course of a given piece.

The following example is basically the last groove beefed up a little with the addition of the tom-toms playing the signature conga/bongo notes of this style. Which of the following you choose depends on the music and the ensemble.

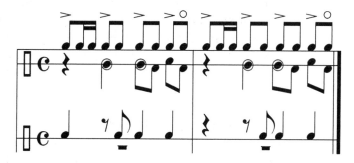

The next groove is a combination of the paila rhythm and the conga or bongo part. The middle line is played with muted strokes on the snare drum with the snares turned off. The left hand plays cross-stick but with the stick hitting the snare head not a rim click. The right plays muted and light rim shots as variations.

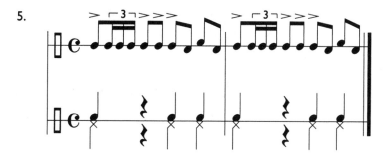

For the Son you have to keep in mind that the original, traditional percussion instrumentation was bongo, maracas and clave. If you happen to be in an ensemble that is trying to capture the flavor of the original Son then one percussionist will have to play bongos and the drummer can play the maraca rhythm on the hihat or a paila variation on the hihat and the clave in the other hand, along with the basic bombo notes on the bass drum. Note that these are the same patterns presented in the Cha-Cha section. Remember that all of these styles came to exist from the Son tradition.

1.
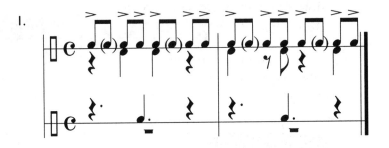

2.
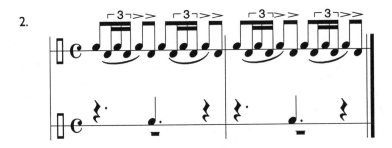

3.

SON-MONTUNO

WITH THE SON-MONTUNO THERE IS ANOTHER CONSIDERATION IN ADDITION TO THE ISSUE OF HOW MANY OTHER PERCUSSIONISTS THERE ARE AND WHAT THEY ARE PLAYING. It is that of tempo. Basically a Son-Montuno—still a descendant of the Son family—is played with a similar vocabulary but is generally felt in ¢ time. It is brighter than a Cha-Cha but slower than the Guaracha or Mambo (which is generally even faster).

The patterns here are presented in ¢ time. If you encounter a situation where the piece is played slow enough that the groove feels better articulated in C rather than ¢, then instead of playing the 2 and 4 on the hihat play quarter notes. If it's really slow you can use one of the two bar cascara patterns or use one of the patterns from the Cha-Cha section instead of these two bar phrases.

In this style you also have to keep in mind the section changes that occur within the arrangement. Refer back to the score to review what each instrument does at each part. Now we move on to a variety of situations and examine what to play on the set for each of them.

Situation 1

We'll move quickly through this scenario since what to do in this situation has already been established in the Cha-Cha section. You on the drum set along with the full percussion section means you look for guiro, maraca, clave or alternate cascara, cowbell and woodblock patterns to orchestrate on the set along with the bass drum and hihat. You basically have to find parts that are not already being played or you may have to invent something based on a combination of parts. Again, this is a rare situation so anything musical and supportive of the ensemble will work.

Situation 2

In this situation—drum set along with two other percussionists covering the congas and bongos and campana— you are functioning as the timbalero/drummer/percussionist .

Note: This entire section is presented in 3-2 clave. Remember to practice all of the patterns starting on the second bar so you'll have them down in the 2-3 position also.

These first two examples are the basic cascara pattern played with one hand on either the side of your floor tom, or some other wood sound or on the closed hihat. The wood sound is very traditional but heavier sounding than the hihat and may not be appropriate for all vocal oriented situations but may be preferable in others. If you play cascara on the closed hihat then you obviously wouldn't play the 2 and 4 with your foot. If you play on the side of a drum you can add the left foot. You can play beats 1 and 3 on the hihat instead. I use the 2 and 4 more often and feel it swings better but there will be times you'll need both.

The first example shows the left hand playing the standard tumbaó and the second has the left hand playing the

clave. You could play this on the rim of your snare or on a mounted woodblock. These parts are taken directly from the timbales and have the feet playing very common standard parts. These patterns are for the low dynamic sections—vocals and piano solos.

1.
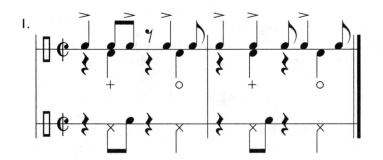

2.
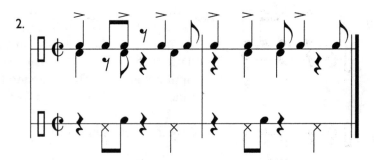

The next set of examples show alternatives to the previous two, employing the two-handed cascara patterns

along with the bass drum (and hihat). Again, if you play this on closed hihat don't play the left foot part.

3.
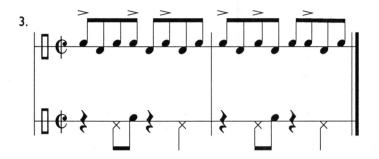

5.
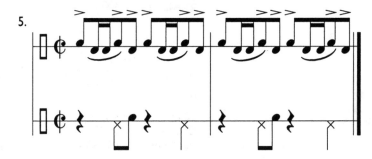

4.
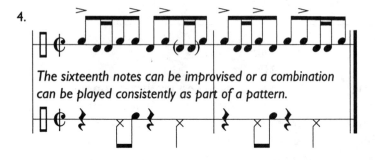

The sixteenth notes can be improvised or a combination can be played consistently as part of a pattern.

6.
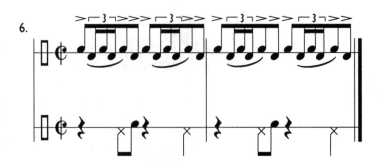

7.
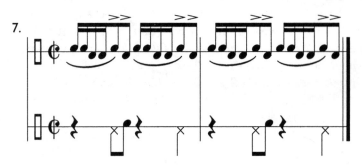

The following patterns would work for the higher dynamic sections—the montuno, Mambo and any other section of an arrangement where the bongo player would go up the campana. Here you play either of these patterns on the timbale bell you have in your drum setup along with the left hand tumbaó played with a rim click and an open note on the tom along with the bass drum and hihat. Also take these examples and substitute the clave for the tumbaó in the left hand. You would also move these patterns up to the cymbal for certain sections of a piece or to shift dynamic levels.

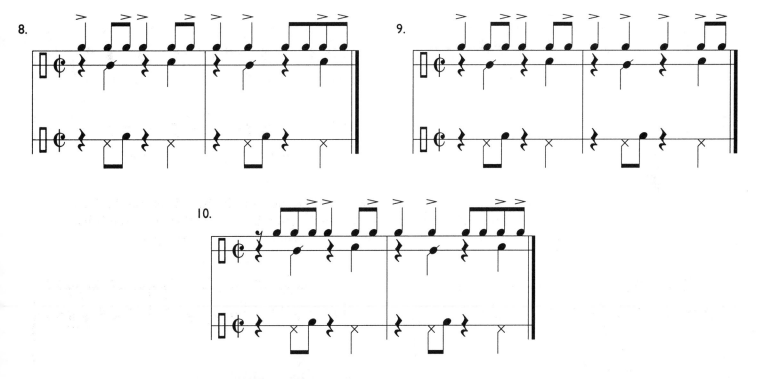

Situation 3

In this situation—drummer/percussionist with only one other percussionist playing the congas—you would employ all of the previous examples as needed throughout the various sections of a piece. Unfortunately, the missing bongos cannot easily be duplicated on the drum set.

One option is to have bongos mounted and play occasional riffs on them in order to provide the color but you still have to keep the other stuff going as the main groove. Aside from this option, the low dynamic sections would take all of the previous examples while trying to keep the sound full.

At the higher dynamic sections you would play your timbale bell part along with the bongocero's campana part as follows. This would be the only major additional pattern. Also remember that the campana can be played in a variety of ways—single notes, the basic one bar pattern and the two bar pattern in clave—among others. Of the following examples, the first one is shown with the timbale bell and the one bar campana pattern, and the second shows the timbale bell with the two bar campana pattern outlining the clave.

One other way you could beef this up would be to play the Son clave in the left foot on the hihat or on a woodblock mounted on a pedal. More on this in the next section.

1.

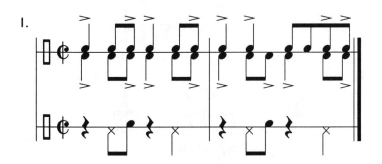

2.

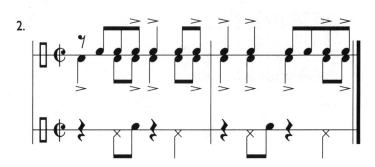

Situation 4

With the drum set alone you have to incorporate some of the hand drum parts into your patterns. For the lower dynamic sections the following pattern would work best—cascara with the basic conga tumbaó between the snare rim and the tom, along with the bass drum and hihat.

1.

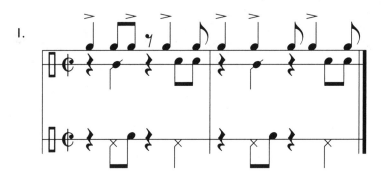

When the arrangement goes to the montuno or higher dynamic section— the timbalero would go up to the large cowbell and the bongocero would go to the campana—you move to the same bell on the set and basically keep the rest of the pattern the same but building in intensity. At another part of the arrangement you might move the same pattern to the cymbal.

Following are three variations. The first pattern has the basic bell pattern with the basic left hand tumbaó.

2.

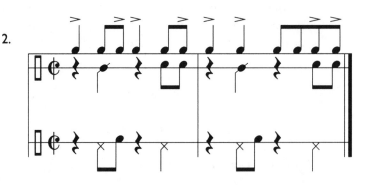

This pattern uses another bell variation along with a couple of more notes from the conga patterns. These are the key tones from the conga's two drum tumbaó split up between the rim of the snare and the low and high toms.

3.

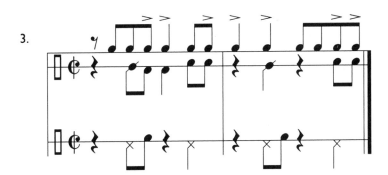

The next pattern is a variation of the last pattern but now playing the conga tumbaó notes split between the tom and bass drum instead of the low and high toms.

4.

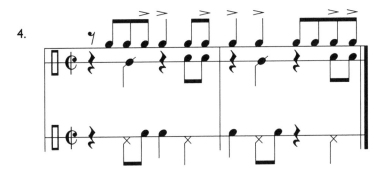

At certain sections of an arrangement—the highest in dynamic and intensity—you need the two bell patterns (the timbale and the campana) plus, since you are the only percussionist you need to keep some of the conga /drum set stuff going or it will sound empty.

The following is a pattern you can work with and then expand upon as you get comfortable. Basically you play the campana in one hand and then split up the other bell pattern between the timbale bell and keep the conga notes. (In the lower line of the top system the triangled notes indicate the cowbell and the regular noteheads the toms). You can also improvise variations around the drums and the bell as individual percussionists playing each instrument separately would do as the piece builds and gets looser.

You can also incorporate the bass drum into this dialogue, as well as play the Son clave rhythm on the hihat or on a woodblock mounted on a pedal. Many variations of this sort for all of the limbs will be presented in the Mambo and Songo sections, and these could be applied here in the Son Montuno section as well.

5.

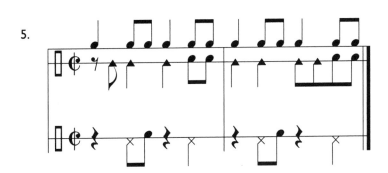

MAMBO

THE MAMBO, ALSO BEING FROM THE SON (AND DANZÓN) TRADITION, WILL USE MANY OF THE PATTERNS ALREADY ESTABLISHED IN THE PREVIOUS SECTIONS. THE KEY DIFFERENCE in terms of the percussion parts is that of tempo. The Mambo is generally considerably faster than the Son-Montuno and

similar Guaracha style. *Note: For the sake of variety and showing rhythms in both of the ways in which you'll see them, this entire Mambo section will be presented in 2-3 clave unless noted otherwise at a specific example. The previous Son-Montuno section was presented in 3-2. Don't forget to practice starting all patterns from either bar.*

Situation 1

For this scenario all of the Son-Montuno parts will apply. If there is a full percussion section plus drum set, then find something to play from an alternate cascara or bell pattern or guiro or maraca or clave part. Refer to the previous sections for the specific parts.

Note: In a contemporary ensemble it is quite possible to have the drum set as a regular part of the ensemble along with the three other percussionists. In

this case parts for the drum set (and each member of the section) are created by the section or leader or composer. In many instances these parts would be those that are already written or might be Songo style drum set parts—presented later in this section. The following patterns (already presented in the previous sections) are primary choices if no one else is playing them and if no specific drum set part is developed by the ensemble.

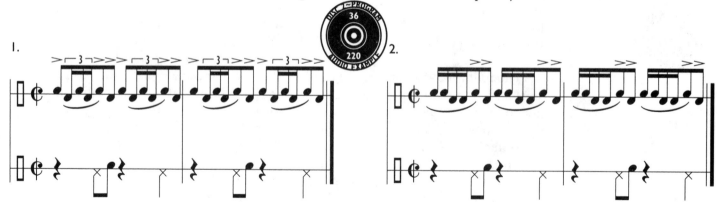

The following three examples are also possibilities. The first is a variation of the previous example but using an open hihat note on the last partial of each beat. (Remember that you're now in ¢ time.) The second is another variation with the hihat opening right off of each downbeat. The third is a standard hihat ride pattern commonly

played in the Songo styles. This pattern uses clave in the left hand along with the bass drum.

The benefit of using patterns like these is that no one else in the ensemble has a hihat so your part is not likely to clash with anyone else's and will complement the ensemble correctly.

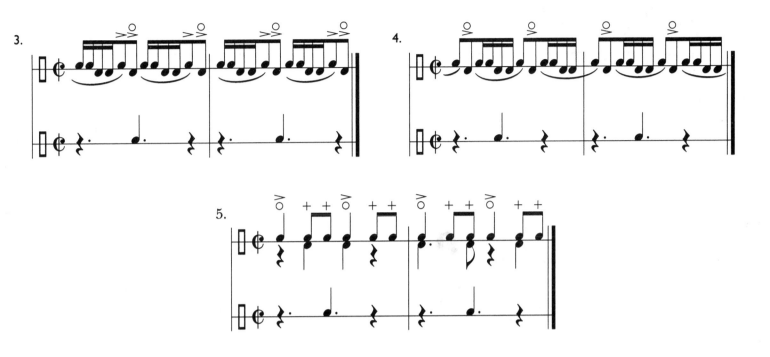

Situation 2

In this scenario—drum set and two other percussionists playing congas and bongos— you're functioning primarily as the timbalero, then drummer/ percussionist. All of the material from the Son Montuno section will pretty much apply here as will a few other alternate possibilities. During all of the low dynamic sections—vocals, piano solo—where the timbalero would normally play paila, you could play any of the following patterns. The first two examples show the standard timbale comp with cascara and either the left hand tumbaó or clave, along with the bass drum and hihat. Play this cascara pattern on the hihat (in which case you wouldn't play the left foot part on 2 and 4), or on a wood sound such as the side of your floor tom or rim of a tom.

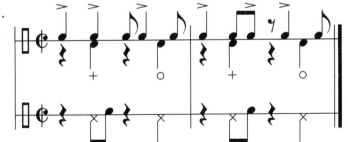

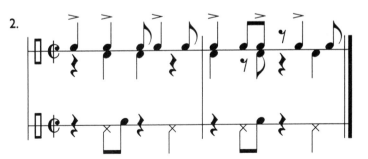

The next six examples are all paila variations taken from the standard cascara pattern or from maraca parts.

The last two include some open note variations on the hihat.

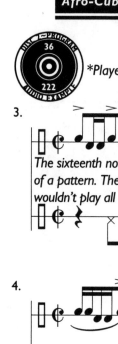

Played in 3-2 Clave on the audio recording.

3.
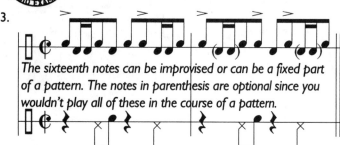

The sixteenth notes can be improvised or can be a fixed part of a pattern. The notes in parenthesis are optional since you wouldn't play all of these in the course of a pattern.

6.
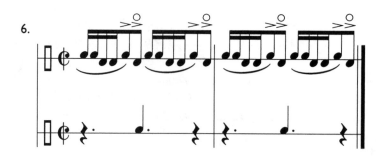

4.
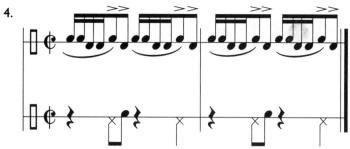

7.
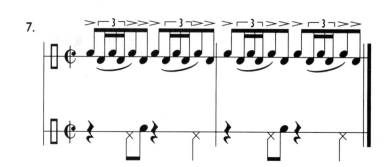

5.
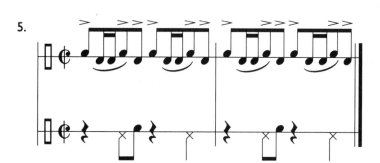

8.
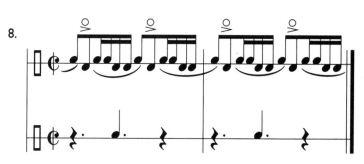

In the higher dynamic sections you would play this or a similar pattern. This is taken from the timbalero's part—ride pattern on large timbale bell along with the left hand tumbaó and the bass drum and hihat. Many variations of the bell pattern will be presented later in this section.

9.
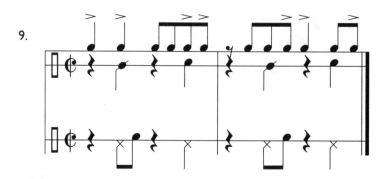

Situation 3

Here we move to the drum set along with only one other percussionist playing the congas. As with this scenario in the previous section—the Son

Montuno style—you function primarily from the timbale parts but now adding any additional percussion parts you can, as well as playing the campana pattern (from the missing bongo player) anytime the arrangement calls for it. You can work with incorporating bongos into your setup as mentioned in the Son Montuno section but aside from this you basically would use any of the six patterns from Situation 2 above as well as the following pattern for the higher dynamic sections. This pattern consists of the most common timbale bell pattern along with the campana part playing its two bar version (outlining clave) over the bass drum and hihat.

1.
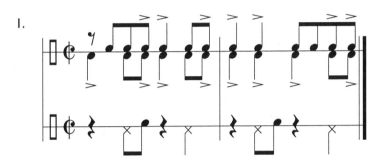

Another very common combination is the following. Here the timbalero would be riding on the cymbal (with the same rhythmic pattern for now). When this happens in an arrangement the bongocero, now playing the campana, could either keep the same pattern or switch to the following pattern. This would be another possible combination for the higher dynamic sections or for a conga solo.

2.
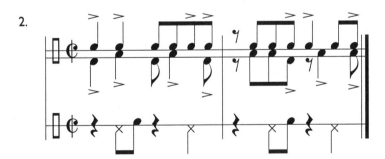

Situation 4

In this scenario you are playing drum set with no other players on percussion. Here your patterns will be very similar to those presented in the Son Montuno section. You are incorporating timbale parts on the bells, as well as some of the key conga notes on the drums, the campana part where needed, the bass drum and hihat and any other percussion colors you can add. Following are some basic patterns. The first example is the basic cascara pattern with the conga tumbaó on the rim of the snare and the tom. The cascara can be played on a hihat, side of floor tom, rim of tom or on a cowbell depending on the section of the arrangement or the piece you are playing.

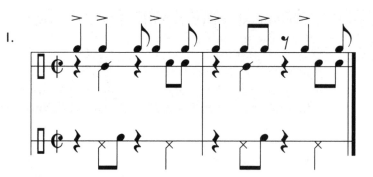

The next two examples have the Mambo bell pattern with parts of the two drum conga tumbaó. The first has the notes played between a high and low tom and the second has the pattern played between the bass drum and the high tom.

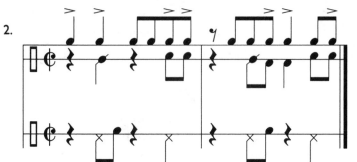

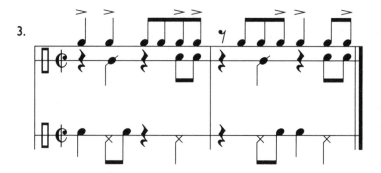

This last pattern incorporates the campana pattern in the right hand while the left plays pieces of the timbales bell and the conga's tumbaó notes. The left hand part can be split up between the cowbells, cymbals, toms and any other percussion instruments you mount around your drum setup. Even though this left hand part is written based on the mambo bell pattern of the timbales, this type of pattern is often improvised.

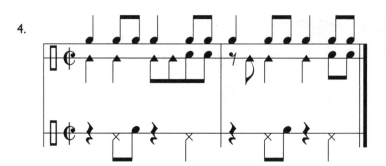

DRUM SET WORKOUT FOR MAMBO

ADDITIONAL VARIATIONS AND COMBINATIONS

THIS SECTION IS THE FIRST OF THE HEAVY DRUM SET WORKOUTS PRESENTED FOR SOME OF THE STYLES. SIMILAR WORKOUTS ARE PRESENTED LATER IN THE BOOK FOR THE SONGO, RUMBA, AND some other styles. Presented here are additional patterns, variations, and combinations for each of the voices of the percussion section applied to each of the voices on the drum set. We'll take each limb (voice on the drum set) and show a variety of patterns for it individually.

You must then take every combination from each of these sections and practice it with every combination from each of the other sections until you have exhausted all possibilities. Having done this you should have both the rhythmic vocabulary as well as the technical facility necessary to play standard parts as well as improvised parts. You'll also have enough vocabulary and facility to come up with a part "on the fly"—something you have to do quite often when playing these styles on the drum set.

This is a key area of this section and a significant section for the drum set. It presents a vast amount of material and you'll be undertaking a pretty serious workout. Take your time and do it right. There's no shortcut through this material.

You must develop a methodical system for getting through all of this in a thorough manner. Specific example/instructions for a thorough approach are presented after all of the patterns. If you can't devise one that works better for you that achieves the same end, then just follow tthe ones provided here.

Look through this section and study all of the patterns presented. They are all based on material that was presented in the percussion section for each of these instruments. The only new material here are the orchestrations written specifically for the drum set—bass drum and hihat and the left hand combinations. If necessary, review the percussion section. Specific instructions follow all of the patterns.

HIHAT VARIATIONS

Following are the hihat patterns that can be played in this style. They consist of beats 1 and 3, 2 and 4, all four beats, the Son clave, and the Rumba clave. They won't all work with every musical situation. Some arrangements or ensemble settings will groove better with certain patterns more than others.

The key is to play the variations the music calls for and never force anything into a piece of music or ensemble. The two clave variations can also be played on a woodblock mounted on a bass drum pedal. Several companies make brackets specifically for this, or you can make your own.

I.

2.

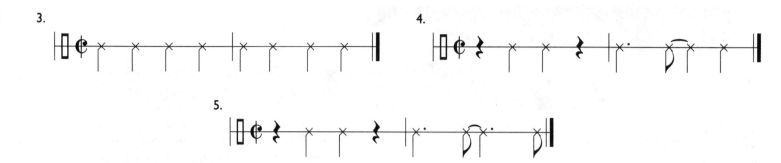

BASS DRUM VARIATIONS

Following are the bass drum combinations for this style. These are the most common in descending order from the first through the ninth. Others are also possible. You can make up all that you want with these as a model.

A note regarding some of these bass drum patterns: the eighth works in this style in traditional settings but works best when arranged into the music and when the bass player (and the rhythm section) is either duplicating this rhythm or playing something that complements it. This is also the case with the fifth and sixth ones, but these generally work okay with a standard bass tumbaó. The ninth is almost never

used in traditional settings. It is presented here because it seems to work better in nontraditional settings where players are not familiar with this idiom, and this is the way many drummers learn these grooves for the first time. Keep in mind that this is not the correct pattern. It does work well in that it seems to help an ensemble that is more rooted in American pop styles—where the bass drum often duplicates the bass part—get this groove happening. Just don't use it when you are with other percussionists, or with an ensemble that plays this music. As always, the rule is to play what the music (and the leader) calls for. (Remember that this whole section is in 2-3 clave.)

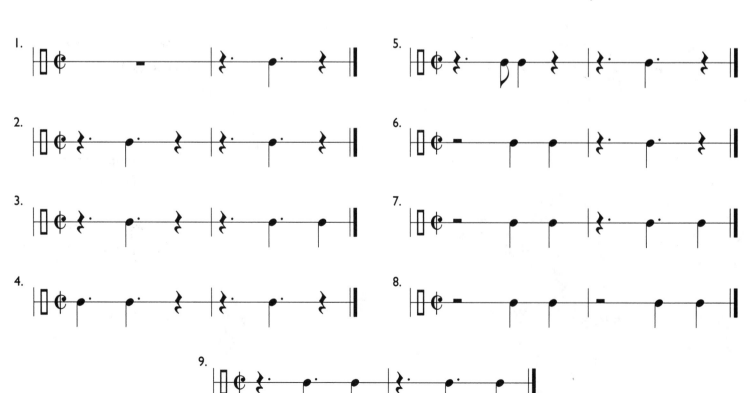

Mambo/Timbale Bell Variations

Following are a number of variations for the timbale bell. Note the articulation markings—the accents—and notes that are played nearer to the neck (marked with a staccato dot for a shorter sound) and those played closer to the mouth (marked with an "o" for a more open or longer ringing note).

It is very important that you review the Timbales section from Part I to refresh your memory on this material.

1.

8.

2.

9.

3.
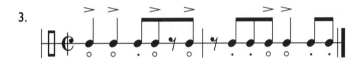

10.

4.
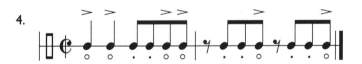

11.

5.
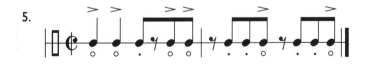

12.
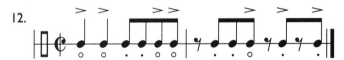

6.

13.
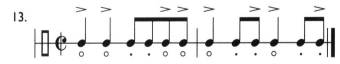

7.

14.

15.

TUMBAÓ & CLAVE (LEFT HAND) COMPING VARIATIONS

The variations below are those that you will play around the drums while your other (right hand) plays the bell patterns. If you are left handed you will probably reverse this. There is no rule here. Do what is most comfortable. Some right handed players ride with their left hand or either hand depending on the situation. Ideally you should be able to play these patterns both ways as this will afford you the most possibilities in any musical situation you may encounter.

I'm presenting the way I do it but your physical drum setup may be different. It doesn't matter as long as what you're playing sounds right.

You'll sometimes need to rearrange your setup or create a new setup to deal with a specific situation. This can involve moving a bell from one side of the set to the other or mounting another percussion instrument to cover a part.

If you practice all of these combinations methodically, any new situation should simply be a small time investment in getting the mechanics of it together.

The first two patterns presented are the Son and Rumba Clave. (Again, remember this whole section is written in 2-3 so practice everything in 3-2 also.) This means that every combination in this section will be played with each of these clave rhythms as your left hand pattern. You can play this on the rim of your snare or on a mounted woodblock.

The following patterns are taken from the key notes, usually the accented—slap—tones and the open—melody—tones, of the conga parts. These are usually played on the set as rim clicks for the slap tones and tom toms for the open tones, and that's how they are presented here. You can of course find other ways but get these down first.

The first pattern is a rim click on beat 2 and an open tone on the high tom on beat 4. This is from a conga tumbaó as well as from the left hand tumbaó part of the timbalero.

The second pattern is probably the most common variation used on drum set in this style. It is basically the key notes of the one bar conga tumbaó.

The third pattern is taken from the two bar conga tumbaó.

CAMPANA/CENCERRO/BONGO BELL VARIATIONS

The following patterns are the three most common campana patterns in this style. The first pattern is the most basic and represents the pulse. (All of the notes of the first pattern are played on the mouth of the bell. The second and third patterns use the neck and mouth of the bell for two different sounds.) The second pattern is a one bar (really one beat) pattern. This pattern does not outline the clave by

itself so make sure your clave phrasing is straight with your other patterns. The third pattern is the basic two bar campana pattern. This pattern does outline the clave and is written here in 2-3.

These patterns are to be combined with all of the timbale bell patterns until each of the timbale bell patterns are played with each of these as an ostinato.

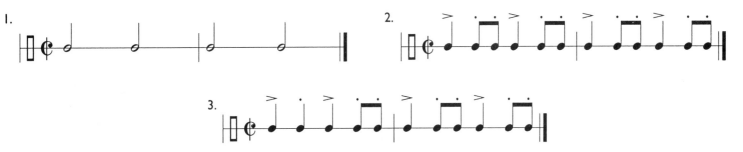

INSTRUCTIONS FOR THE MAMBO DRUM SET SYSTEMS & WORKOUT

Here are the specific instructions for attacking all of this. This is my approach and it works. So if you can't devise something that works better for you, just go through everything exactly as it's presented here and you'll exhaust every possibility.

We'll use the concept of *systems* and *exercises* to go through the workouts. *A system is a set of up to three ostinatos*—repeating patterns that remain constant. Over these systems you will vary one voice as you work through all of the patterns of each particular section. The systems can have major differences or can change only by virtue of changing one ostinato—such as the

hihat. Regardless of how small the change may seem, you still have to go through the entire sequence with each system because even a small change in one voice will affect the feel and can affect the coordination between all of the limbs. A *workout* is the playing of the varying patterns in the fourth, or third and fourth limbs.

It would take a vast amount of space to actually notate each possible combination and it really isn't necessary. Just set up a system with three voices/limbs and work out the fourth voice/limb. Here are the systems and specific instructions for the workouts.

System 1~Workout 1

In this first system you have the basic orchestration for the Mambo on the

drum set. You have the basic cascara pattern in the right hand, the basic tumbaó from the conga part in the left hand, basic bass drum playing the bombo on each bar and hihat playing beats 2 and 4.

You're going to address the right hand and work on the timbale cowbell you have mounted on your drum set. Get this pattern going and when you

have it grooving go to the section called *Mambo/Timbale Bell Variations* and substitute each of those patterns for the basic cascara in the right hand. Go down the list playing each pattern at least four times each at a variety of tempos and dynamics. Pay attention to your articulation on the bell—accents, ghosted notes, etc.

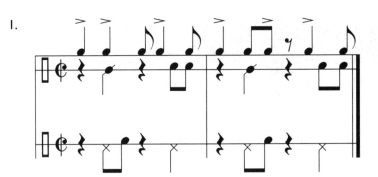

When you have finished going through all of the patterns with this combination (system) go back and do the same thing with the right hand playing the bell patterns on the side of

the floor tom, then on the ride cymbal and also on the closed hihat. These are all orchestrations you'll use when playing this style.

Systems 2 through 5~Workout I

We continue by changing the left hand comping pattern to the other four variations presented in the *Tumbaó and Clave left hand Variations*. Your basic systems would be the following. The first example—system 2—shows the basic left hand tumbaó from the timbale part. The second example—system

3—shows the two bar conga tumbaó. The last two examples—systems 4 and 5—show the left hand playing the Son and Rumba clave rhythms. Go through each of systems substituting the timbale bell variations as you did for system 1, exercise 1.

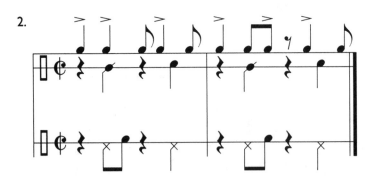

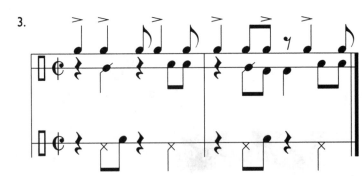

4.
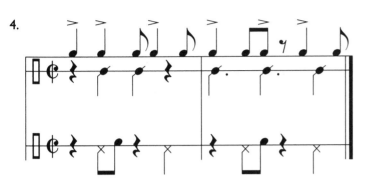

5.
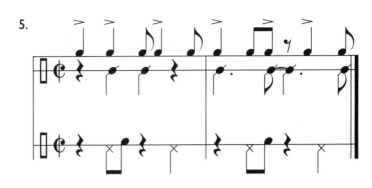

Systems 6 through 9~Workout 1

These three systems have the remaining four hihat ostinatos (or left foot if you are playing the clave rhythm on a mounted woodblock). You already played the fifth hihat variation—beats 2 and 4—in the previous systems. They

are presented first with the other basic parts from system 1.

Go through and substitute all of the timbale bell parts with these four systems.

6.
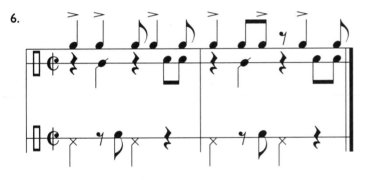

8.
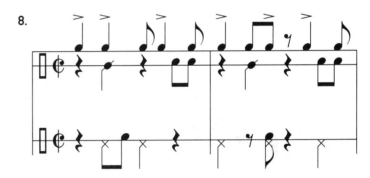

7.
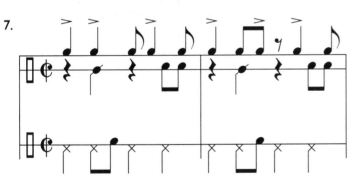

9.
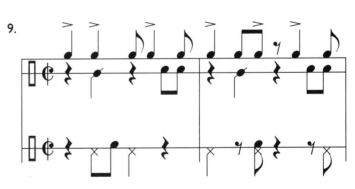

Continuing with the left foot ostinatos, now take these remaining four hihat ostinatos and put them with each of systems 2 through 5. You end up with sixteen systems—four variations for each of the four systems 2 through 5. Now take all of the timbale bell patterns and play them over all of these systems.

All of this repetition serves three purposes. First, the constant repetition of all of these ostinatos and variations should get you to memorize all of this quickly. Try to memorize, this is not material to be read. You will never read it on a gig. Second, the repetition will help build your chops by playing material for long periods of time.

Third and probably most important, rhythms groove by virtue of repetition. This is the case in all styles. Patterns that are constantly varying don't tend to have as serious a pocket as those that just sit on a rhythm. These are the rhythms that make you dance. Just think about a Blakey shuffle or a serious funk pocket. Even a rumba, which seems to have a lot of varying material in the voices and quinto and dialogue between the salidor and tres golpes still has the clave and palitos and the bombo and shekeré which rarely move. They just sit there and create the serious pocket. Repeating all of this material over and over should make you able to create the same effect. Here are the sixteen systems. Time to go to work.

Systems 10 through 13~Workout 1

This is system 2 with the other four hihat variations.

Systems 14 through 17~Workout 1

This is system 3 with the other four hihat variations.

 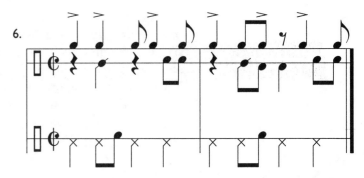

5.
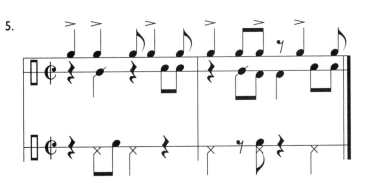

6.
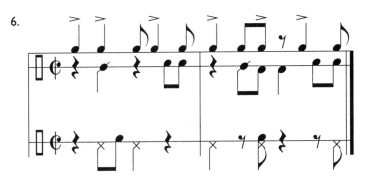

Systems 18 and 19~Workout 1

This is system 4 with the other two hihat variations. Since system 4 has the Son clave rhythm in the left hand you don't double it with the left foot.

1.
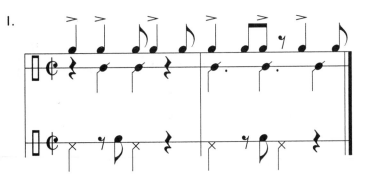

2.
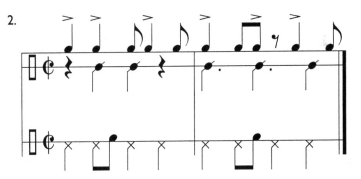

Systems 20 and 21~Workout 1

This is system 5 with the other two hihat variations. Since system 5 has the Rumba Clave rhythm in the left hand you don't double it with the left foot.

3.
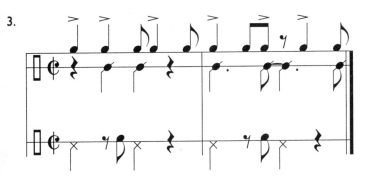

4.
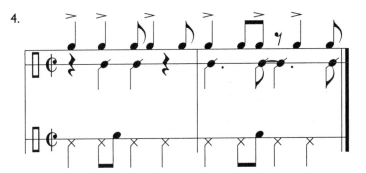

Systems 22 through 189~Workout 1

The last set of systems consists of taking systems 1 through 21 and applying each of the remaining eight bass drum variations. You have 8 of these and 21 variations already presented that account for all of the left hand and hihat patterns for a total of 189 systems. Start by taking any of the bass drum variations and plugging it in to all of the first 21 systems, and play through all of the timbale bell variations with each of these. You have 21 system variations for each of the bass drum variations. These are not written out here because it would take too much paper and because it should be obvious at this point what to do. If you need to, write out a couple to get started. From then on it should be pretty straight ahead to do it by memory.

You may be shaking your head at this point and saying "...this is ridiculous," among other bits of swearing and throwing your sticks around, so let me put this into another perspective to lighten the load. You have 21 systems, each of which is 2 bars long. You have 15 timbale bell variations that you'll play over each of these systems. Each of these is also two bars long. If you play each timbale bell variation 8 times that is a total of 120 bars of music—roughly four times through a 32 bar standard. If your metronome tempo is 120—a nice moderate tempo for a Mambo—this workout will take you exactly 3 minutes and 58 seconds—call it 4 minutes. This is shorter than most arrangements in this idiom unless they were created strictly for commercial airplay. Lets say you do each one twice—8 minutes and you do five of the systems at each practice session—40 minutes—and then you spend 20 minutes improvising and working the material into other stuff you already play—or listening to some stuff. This is one hour and really not that much when you consider the following.

If you want to play this music well and do pro level gigs this should account for about one eighth to one tenth of your practice session for about the first five to seven years of your development. And if you want to be a free-lance pro you need this type of technical facility in all styles. If you

don't have this under your belt you're not even a contender. Ask anyone who plays at a high level and they'll tell you they put in this kind of time—if not more—at first. All other things being equal, this determines the heavies from the lightweights and who does the good gigs and who does the not so good gigs. Of course we know that all other things are not equal and what determines how you get the good gigs is not by your musical skills alone. It's determined by who you know, who knows you and a whole other set of undefinable circumstances that are baffling, surprising, depressing, joyful and confusing—sometimes all at the same time. But the fact remains that without the musical skills you can't even get remotely involved with all of these other elements. The high level artists assume that if you're vying for those gigs your musical skills are incidental. If you do manage to get a gig and they're not, you'll soon be history and you'll have a much harder time recovering from that than if you'd never played a note to begin with. Also consider that compared to all of the other things that you may have to do to get the hot gigs, this is probably the easy part.

This should put the tackling of all of this material in a little easier light. With all this said, continue with the following exercises. Just budget a group of them into your practice schedule and you'll systematically get through everything in due time. There are no shortcuts. Just nail it a little at a time. With each group you get down it becomes easier to get the rest down.

This concludes the exercises with the first set of systems—1 through 21—and the timbale bell variations—workout 1. All of these workouts have addressed playing varying patterns in the right hand while the other three limbs remain constant within each of the given systems.

Systems 190 through 324~Workout II

We now move on to the second set of systems—190 through 324—and workout 2. This workout consists of playing all of the timbale bell variations in the left hand—either on the timbale cowbell, snare rim, snare, or cymbal bell (you must do all of these eventually but do them on the cowbell first)—while the right plays one of the campana patterns from the bongo players part. The systems consist of three different campana variations combined with all of the possible bass drum and hihat combinations. There are a total of 5 hihat (left foot if you play clave on a mounted woodblock) variations, and a total of nine bass drum variations to be done with each of the three campana patterns. This gives you a total of 135 systems. Following are the first 15 systems written out to get you going. Write out the rest if you need to but it's best to do it by memory.

Systems 190 through 194~Workout II

These first five systems consist of the first campana pattern with bass drum pattern 2 and the five hihat variations.

Substitute the fifteen timbale bell variations in the left hand part.

Systems 195 through 199~Workout II

The next five systems consist of the second campana pattern with bass drum pattern 2 and the five hihat variations. Substitute the fifteen timbale bell variations in the left hand part.

Systems 200 through 204~Workout II

The next five systems consist of the third campana pattern with bass drum pattern 2 and the five hihat variations.

Substitute the fifteen timbale bell variations in the left hand part.

You now only have a little over three hundred systems to go. Approach them methodically and you'll get through them all in no time. This concludes the section on the Mambo.

RUMBA GUAGUANCÓ

THE RUMBA GUAGUANCÓ IS A STYLE THAT TODAY HAS MANY INTERPRETATIONS. IT IS PLAYED BY FOLKLORIC ENSEMBLES IN TRADITIONAL FASHION AS WELL AS IN TYPICAL SALSA-oriented arrangements and has also been used quite extensively in fusion or instrumental type Latin jazz styles. When not played in the traditional folkloric settings, this style is often mixed with other rhythms or arranged and played in sometimes very non-traditional ways. Consequently this style has to be approached from the perspective of what type of ensemble it's being played in and what other percussion is present. This is also true in the other styles, but the drum set parts (as well as every percussion part) in styles like the Danzón or some Son styles, are much more defined because they are generally not subjected to many interpretations and settings outside of the *Tipico* approach. The Guaguancó's conga drum melody is so familiar that it has found it's way into numerous settings, thus requiring you to be that much more adaptive with the parts you come up with.

We'll work by looking at situations where both various or no percussion is present. In a traditional situation there won't be a drum set. If you ever are in this situation you will play strictly from the percussion parts. Refer to the percussion section for these parts. They will more than likely be a bombo, palitos, clave, or bell part. If this rhythm is used in a Salsa or dance-type ensemble and played during some part of an arrangement, generally there will be at least congas and probably other percussion, so here you'd play some combination of parts—probably cascara/palitos, bell, clave, and bombo.

The two situations we'll focus on are those in which the combination is drum set with congas (and possibly another percussionist or two) and that of playing the rhythm by yourself.

Situation I

This first situation shows what to play on the drum set when you are playing with a conga drummer playing all three drums—salidor, tres golpes, and quinto. Your part would basically consist of the following, palitos rhythm, clave, and bombo. The hihat can vary between playing only the downbeat of each bar and playing on the half notes—beats 1 and 2 (remember you're in ¢ time). This doubles the rhythmic attacks of the shekeré and could be played even if the shekeré is present.

If there is other percussion present, it is going to be either a quinto player—which does not change your role—or other players on accessory percussion. Whatever it is, you play some part that is not being played. If they play clave then don't play it; play a two-handed palito rhythm instead. If someone plays the bombo then don't play it, or play something that complements it.

The only other consideration is that if it is you and one other player on three congas, then the quinto playing is going to be more limited than if one player was playing that drum alone. The ideal here would be to have both the drum set player and conga drummer create the improvised dialogue that the traditional Rumba drummers create.

This first example shows the palitos played in one hand (on a wood sound—representing the guagua, but also on a bell during higher intensity sections), the clave, and the bombo.

The hihat is playing the downbeats of each bar representing one rhythmic attack of the shekeré (the other being both beats of the bar).

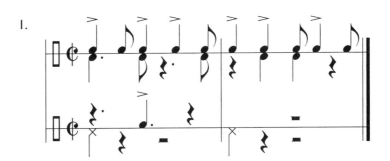

The next two examples follow along the same lines but now have both hands playing the palito rhythm, along with the bombo (illustrated here in both bars) and the clave in the left foot.

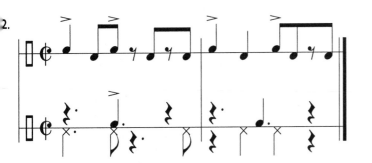
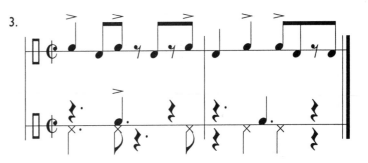

Next are the specific patterns that can be played in the feet. Shown are two bass drum and five hihat patterns. Play all of these combinations with the examples above just as you did with all the previous workouts. Take the first example and apply all of the left foot patterns to it as well as the second bass drum pattern. Then do the same for the second and third examples. Also keep in mind that none of these patterns account for improvisational

phrases that you may play with any of your limbs should the musical situation allow. The Rumba styles are improvisational so make sure you can get in and out of these patterns as well as go from one to the other without disrupting the groove. This is what you'll do when improvising variations.

The first two examples are for the bass drum and the last five for the hihat.

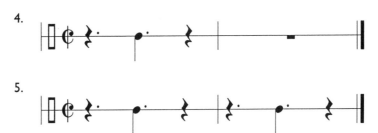

6.

8.

7.

9.

10.

Systems 1 through 5~Workout 1

Next you will do a set of workouts just as you did with all the Mambo examples. Systems 1 through 5 consist of bass drum pattern 1 with the 5 hihat variations. Over these five systems you will play all of the palito pattern variations from the following page. The first five systems are written below. Systems 6 through 10 follow the palito variations. Do the same workout with both sets.

1.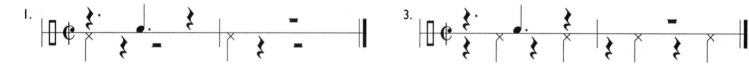

3.

2.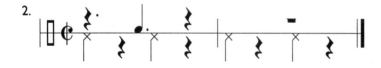

4.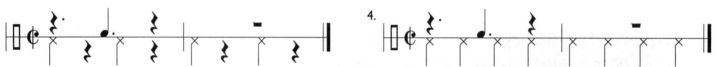

5.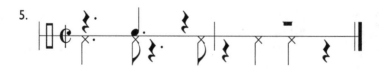

Palito Pattern Variations for Workout 1

1.

2.

3.
RH
LH

9.
RH
LH
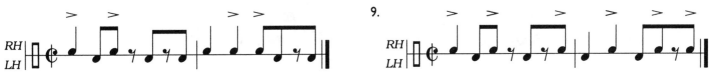

4.
RH
LH

10.
RH
LH
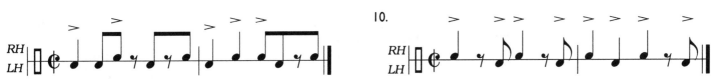

5.
RH
LH

11.
RH
LH
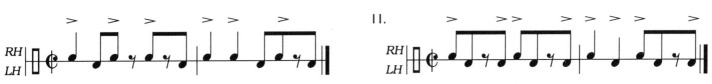

6.
RH
LH

12.
RH
LH
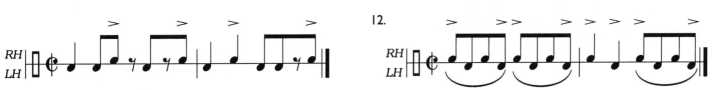

7.
RH
LH

13.
RH
LH

8.
RH
LH

14.
RH
LH
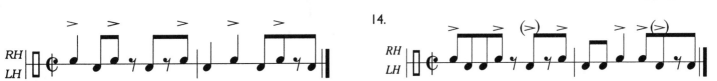

Systems 6 through 10~Workout I

6.
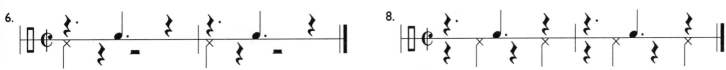

8.
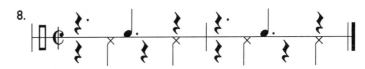

Used to accompany above patterns in audio examples.

7.
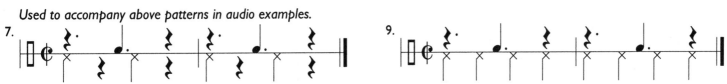

9.
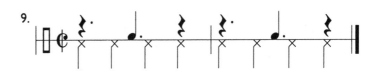

10.
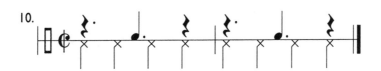

Situation 2~Solo Drums~ Approach I

In this scenario you are playing drum set with no other percussion present. Here you need to play all of the parts from the previous section— clave, palitos, bombo—which provide the accompaniment to the Guaguancó, as well as all of the conga drum parts. The salidor and tres golpes parts become part of your patterns. The quinto, as well as the improvisational parts of the salidor and tres golpes are played within the patterns, "in the cracks," as would a conguero playing all three drum parts. The improvisation on the quinto is worked within and around the more fixed patterns.

We'll begin with some standard approaches to the salidor and tres golpes patterns played along with clave in one hand and the foot patterns. Remember that you have five hihat/left foot variations and two bass drum variations to apply and work with all of these combinations. The first and most

basic example is the Guaguancó melody in the right hand on the toms with the clave in the left hand (either on the rim of the snare or a mounted woodblock). Some patterns also include the bombo in the hands. (It is also being played in the bass drum.)

These examples are written with the second bass drum variation and the second hihat variation. You must do them all with all of the foot variations.

The objective here is to begin with the basic pattern and play variations— both as fixed patterns and improvised dialogue—between the salidor and tres golpes as is done when played on the congas by individual players. Following are a few examples to use as patterns and then improvise variations and come back to them. Eventually you'll include other parts as well as the feet into all of your variations.

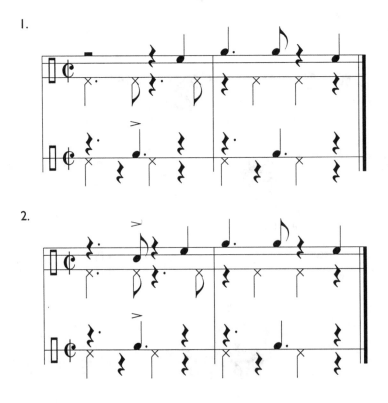

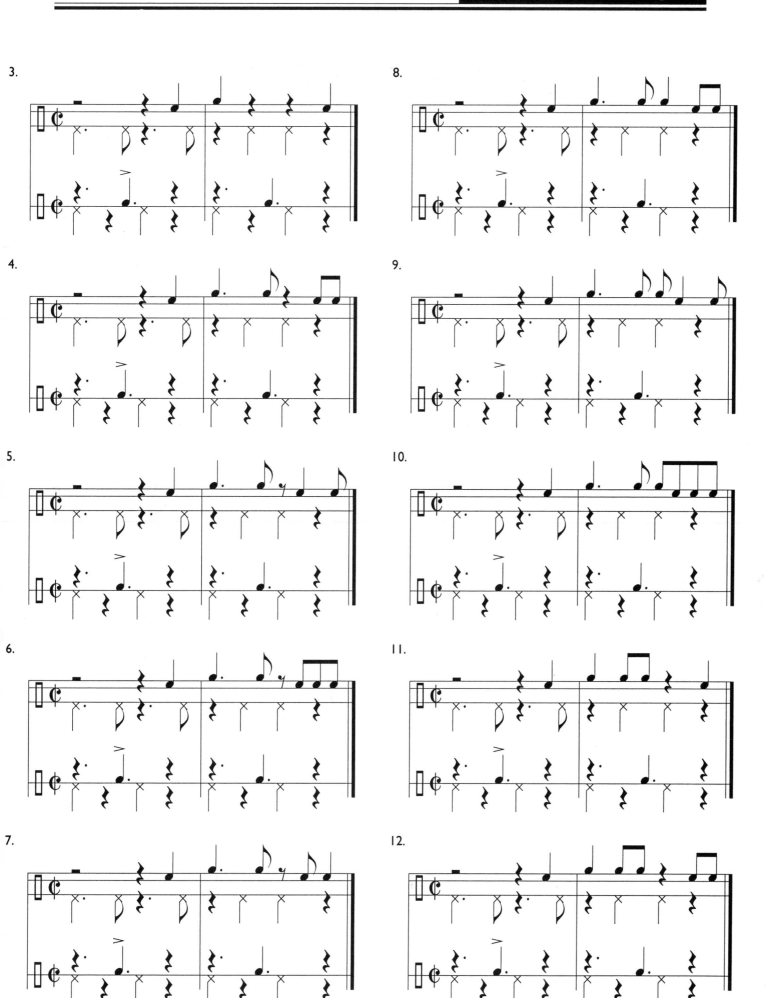

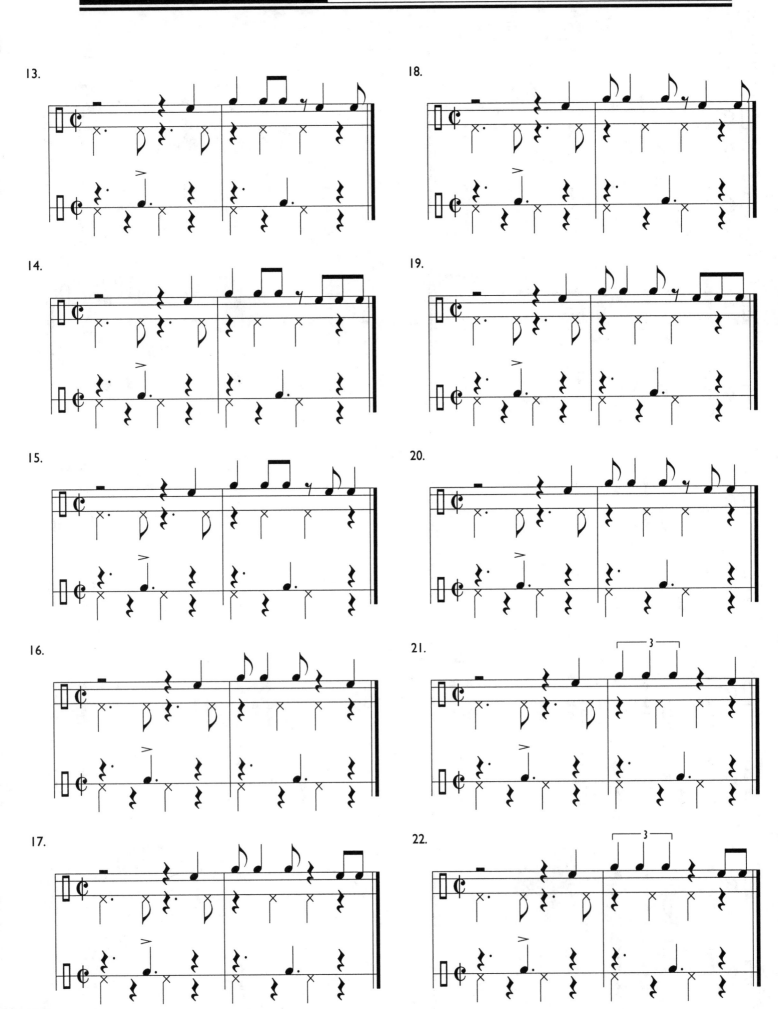

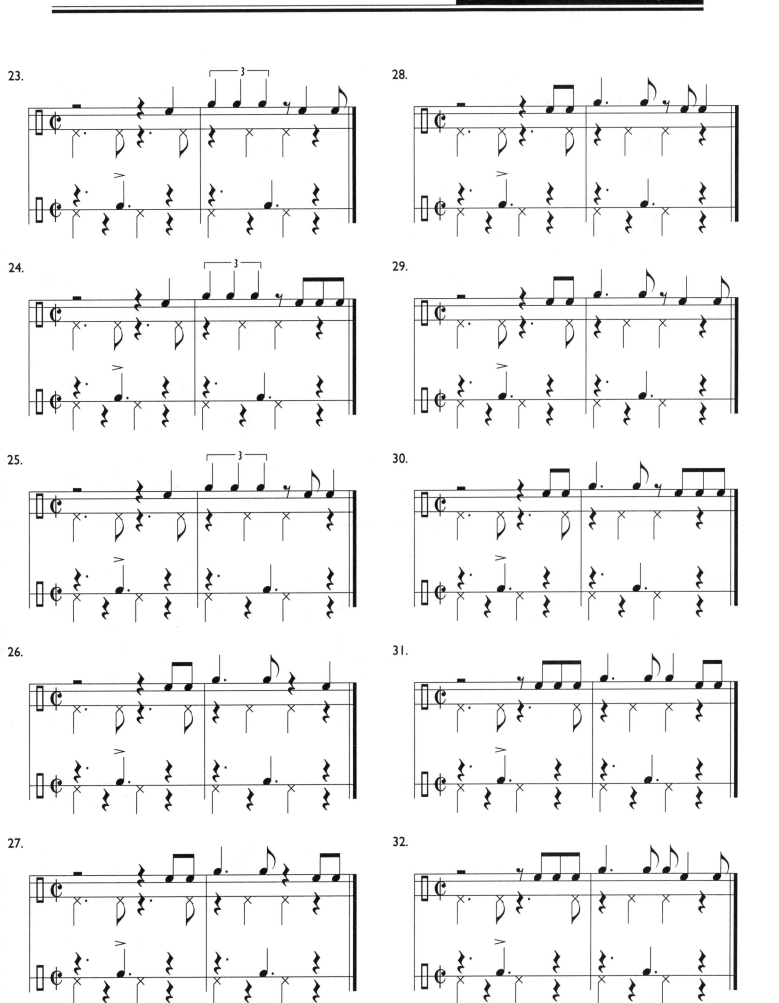

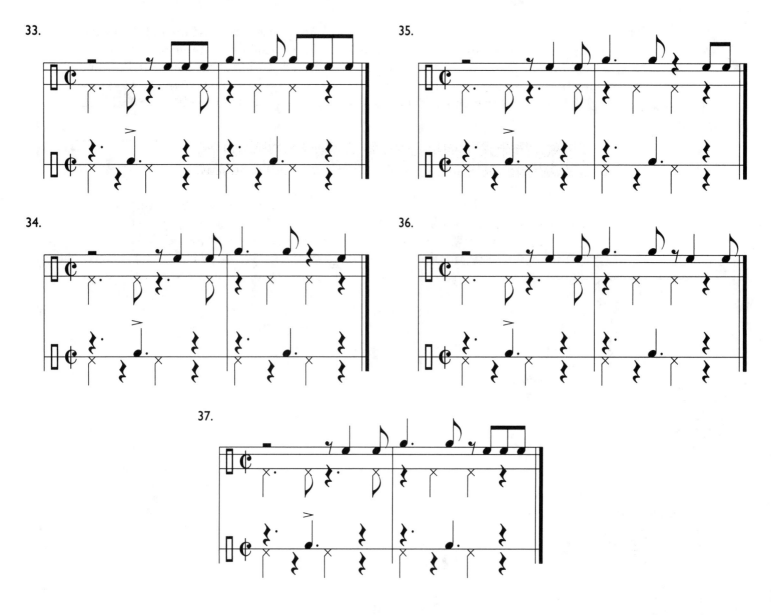

These last two examples of this section add a note on the low tom (the salidor) right off of beat one. This note should be played as a dead-sticked (dampened) note with the tip of the stick in the center of the drum. It is often played as a tapado stroke on the tres golpes or the quinto.

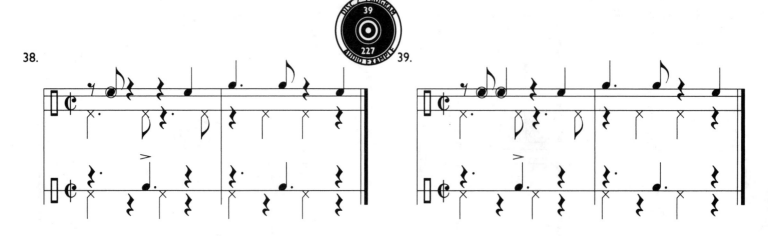

Continue on in this way by combining all of these systems with the other bass drum pattern as well as with the other hihat/left foot patterns. Eventually you should be able to simply improvise phrases like this and add the other voices or other rhythmic parts to your overall playing. That is essentially how the Rumba Guaguancó works when played by a full ensemble.

Situation 2~Solo Drums~ Approach 2

With these systems we have yet another approach to the Guaguancó. This entails playing the palitos rhythm in the right hand, (either on a wood sound like the side or rim of your floor tom, or on a cowbell, or your cymbal bell), and playing the conga drum parts in the left hand. This approach should also eventually become one in which you can improvise variations with all of your limbs, and go in and out of patterns "on the fly."

All of these patterns are also presented with one bass drum and hihat pattern. It is up to you to run the patterns with all of the other foot variations. We'll use bass drum pattern 2 and left foot pattern 5—the Rumba clave. You don't have to start with these foot patterns. You can start with any combination you want as long as you eventually play them all.

You can use all of the melody combinations from the 37 patterns in the previous section. Following are 24 combinations based on the previous 37 patterns.

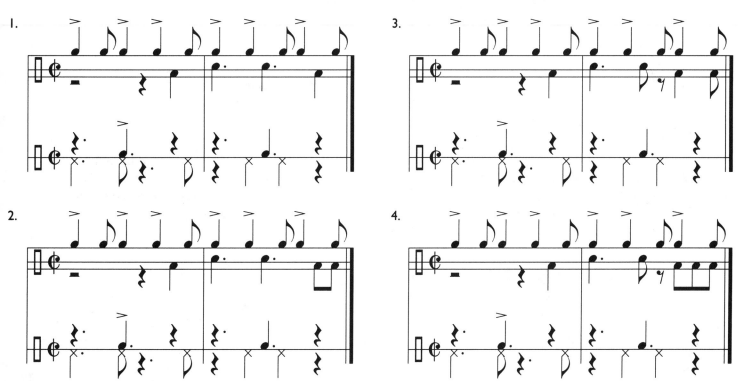

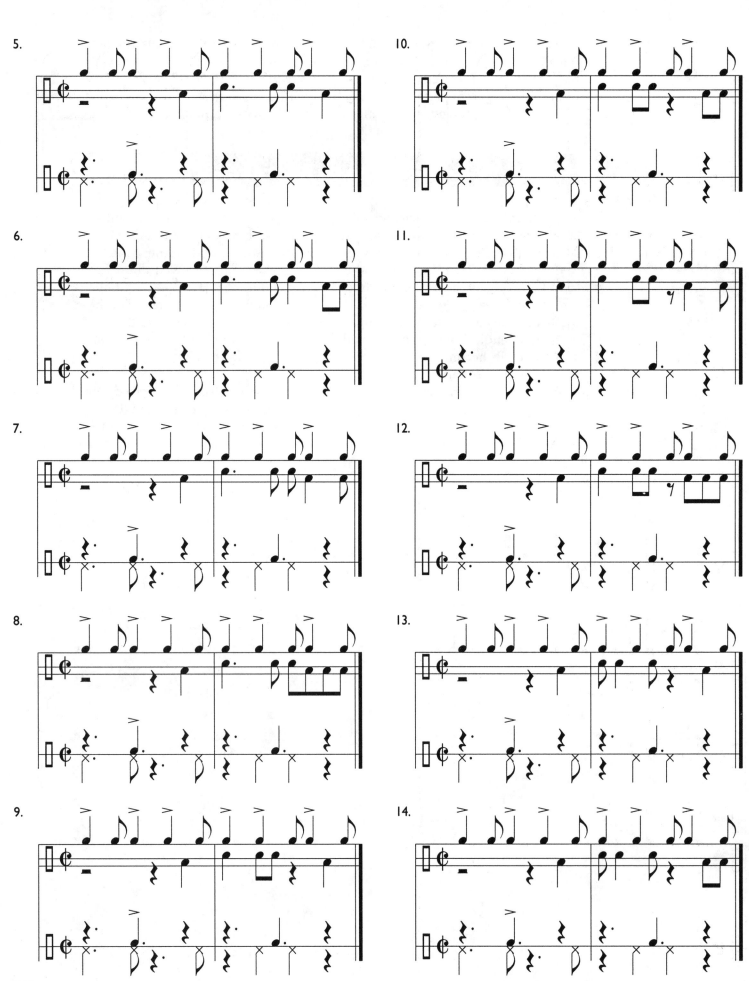

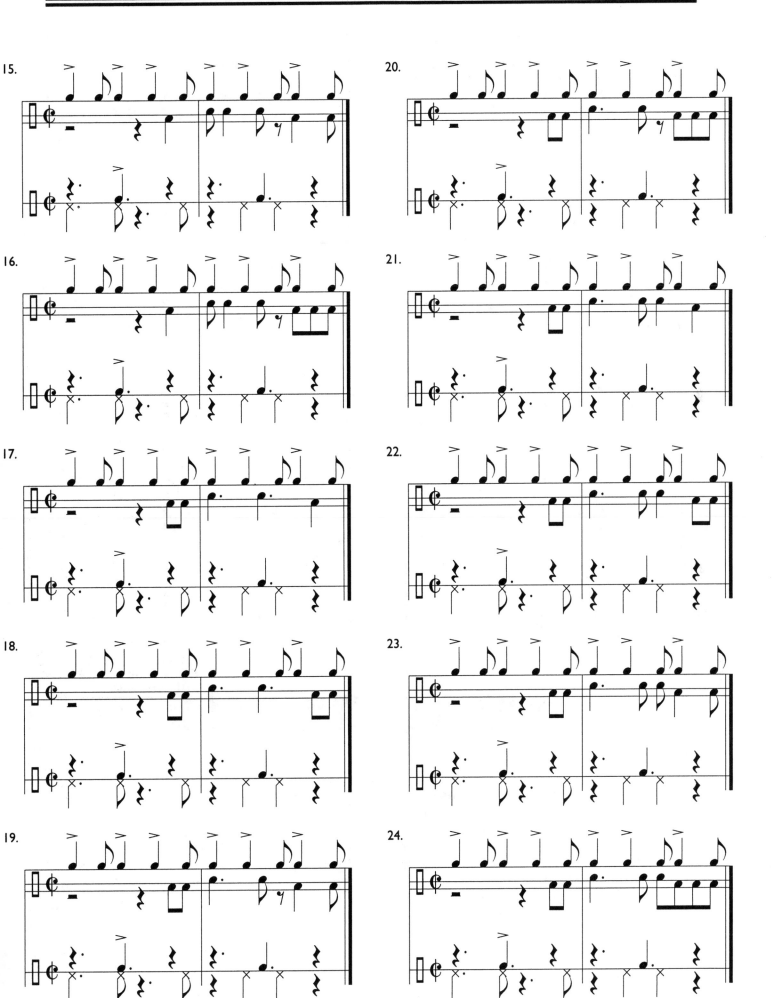

Situation 2~Solo Drums~ Approach 3

These systems are the same as in the previous section. The three ostinatos are the palitos in the right hand, the bass drum, and the left foot patterns. The only difference here are some notes on the rim of the snare that also come from the conga drum parts. These can be played cross-sticked on the rim of the snare or as rim shots if a more pronounced sound is sought.

1.
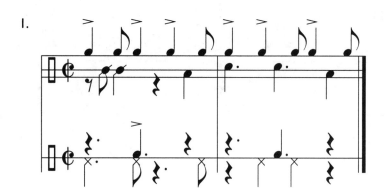

3.

2.

4.
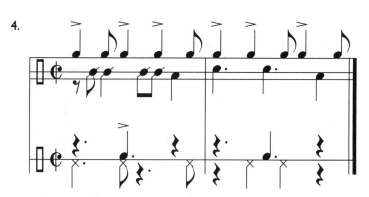

Situation 2~Solo Drums~ Approach 4

These systems are also basically the same as in the previous section but really only have two ostinatos—the palitos in the right hand and the left foot clave pattern. The big difference here is that now the bass drum is also involved in the varying rhythmic line. If you have a coordination problem with this while playing clave in the left foot then play a simpler left foot ostinato or even eliminate the left foot altogether until you have the rest of the pattern. Then slide the left foot in with beats 1 and 3 or 2 and 4.

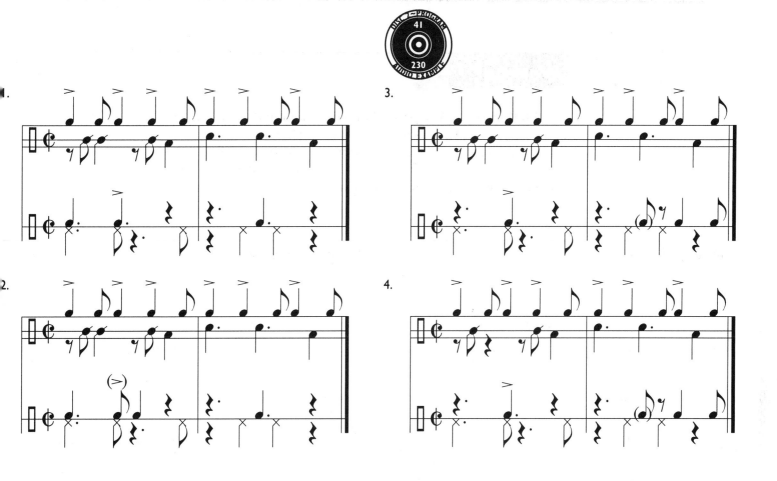

Situation 2~Solo Drums~ Approach 5

This last approach to the Rumba Guaguancó entails duplicating the parts of the three conga drums—salidor, tres golpes and quinto—for one player. The patterns in the hands are basically duplications of the sticking of the conga drum parts. Even though it's written as two separate lines it should be perceived and executed as one rhythmic line. The rim click notes can also be played directly on the snare as rim shots or a variety of strokes. The idea here is to start playing and to take off from this pattern and improvise dialogue between all three drums along with soloistic variations imitating the quinto while maintaining the Guaguancó, as a player on the three congas does. Get the pattern down first over the foot ostinato and then gradually add variations based on all of the previously presented material. Gradually you should just be able to play a full solo from something like this.

RUMBA COLUMBIA

FOR THE RUMBA COLUMBIA WE TAKE THE SAME APPROACH. THE FIRST SITUATION SHOWS PATTERNS FOR THE DRUM SET COMPING THE PERCUSSION PARTS FOR THE TUMBADORAS. This scenario could also have other percussion present. The second situation shows combinations for the drum set playing alone. Review the percussion sections for this style, particularly the congas, bell and palito sections.

Situation I

These patterns can be used to accompany the congas and any other percussion that may be present. If there is a second or third percussionist find the parts that are not being played.

Ideally another player would play shekeré since this would not be possible from the set. If someone plays the palitos then play the bell and clave or vice-versa if that is the case.

Note: The previous rhythm is really played with this inflection.

Situation 2

These are possible combinations for capturing this feel with only the drum set. They also work very well if you arrange parts with other percussionists.

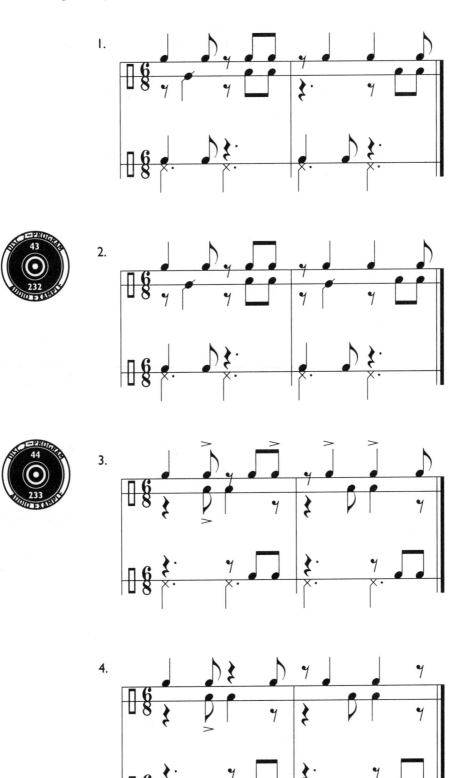

DANZÓN

THE DANZÓN IS RARELY PERFORMED AS A DRUM SET STYLE. THE PLAYING OF THIS RHYTHM FOR DRUM SET BASICALLY ENTAILS PLAYING THE BAQUETEO PATTERNS FROM THE TIMBALES. Go back to that section and play all of those combinations on your snare with the snares off. The open notes can be played lightly on the low or floor tom. The two basic baqueteos are written below. The second can be played with the left hand as rim clicks or as muted strokes crosssticked directly on the head.

There is no specific bass drum pattern. If the tempo is slow then an occasional "beat 1" for emphasis works well, as do various carefully placed improvised strokes. If the tempo is on the bright side then the bombo note (beat 2-and) works well too.

The two hihat patterns listed are for the slower and faster tempos. The quarters are for slow and the 2 and 4 for faster. (The style is never fast. We're talking medium here.)

The last pattern presented is what you could play if you're functioning as the timbalero during the Nuevo Ritmo or Mambo section.

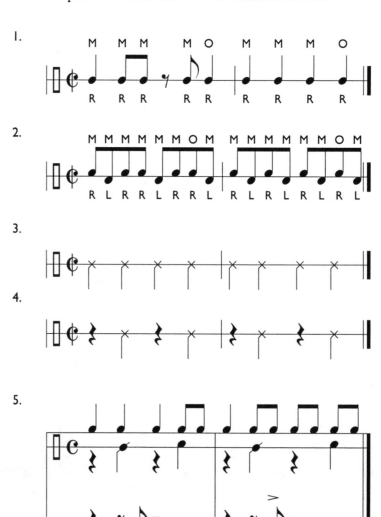

CHARANGA

THE CHARANGA STYLE ON THE DRUM SET IS GOING TO BE VERY MUCH LIKE OTHER SON STYLES BOTH IN SITUATIONS WITH AND WITHOUT PERCUSSION. IF YOU ARE PLAYING SET AND there is another percussionist or two playing congas and Bongos or other accessory percussion, then you find parts from the timbales (cascara with the left-hand tumbaó or clave), or you can play any of the cascara variations, or maraca or guiro style rhythms on the closed hihat. Refer to the Son-Montuno section for all of these patterns. Below is a rhythm you could play during the higher dynamic sections. This would work both with and without congas but if there are congas, your left hand is like the left hand tumbaó of the timbales. If you are the only drummer, then you can be more active with variations on the toms.

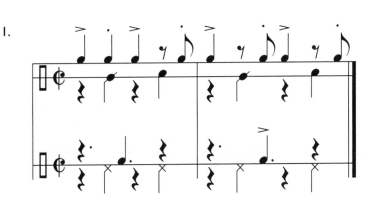

THE SONGO (ALONG WITH SOME
GENERIC VERSIONS OF THE MOZAM-
BIQUE) IS PROBABLY THE MOST WELL
KNOWN AND IMITATED CUBAN RHYTHM
THROUGHOUT THE WORLD TODAY. IT
ENJOYS MORE POPULARITY AND INTE-
GRATION WITH other musical genres
than any of the earlier Cuban/Latin
music crazes of the Mambo and the
Cha-Cha in the earlier part of this
century. It is a unique blend of Rumba
and Son styles integrated with funk/
fusion and jazz style improvisation. The
patterns of all of the instrumentalists
are generally much more syncopated
and more significantly, much freer
from repetition than the tumbaó
approach of the Son styles.

While emanating from very long-
standing musical and instrumental
traditions, where specific patterns are
associated with specific instruments in
specific styles, this rhythm and style is so
open that it allows the player to draw
from any one of a vast number of
traditions to bring to the musical
situation at hand. Consequently the
style can be used to play the Son dance
style as well as a totally open full blown
instrumental improvisation and everything in between. The performances
would all be Songo but they each would
be as different as the players interpreting them. This is its strongest similarity
with Jazz.

Presented here is a very methodical
approach to learning this rhythm and to

learning how to apply it and stretch out
on it while adhering to the traditions it
comes from—this is to say, play it correctly. This means that since the Songo
is a derivative of a number of other
Cuban styles—along with its influences
from the funk and jazz arenas—your
technique and vocabulary in all of these
styles needs to be in control. If not you
will merely be executing some type of
Songo *pattern*. It must also be noted here
that if you are going to stretch out and
"funk out" a Songo, your funk techniques and vocabulary must also be
together. If you really want to play this
style in a convincing way you have to
bear in mind the importance of your
knowing all of the styles and vocabulary
you're trying to mix up with the Songo.
If you simply play memorized patterns
over and over with no regard for feel,
clave, or the rhythmic vocabulary associated with this tradition, you aren't even
beginning to scratch the surface of what
playing this really is. While it's certainly
okay to play patterns in some musical
situations, you'll have many more possibilities if you really learn the style instead
of only the specific combinations.

We'll first begin by looking at the
basic skeleton pattern in 3-2 clave. It is
very important that you play all of these
patterns and workouts starting on
either bar so you are comfortable
phrasing with the clave regardless of
which direction the tune put the clave
rhythm in. *This entire section is presented
in 3-2 unless noted otherwise.*

Start with the *right hand on the closed
hihat, left hand on rim of snare and the bass
drum.* When you have this together

move the left hand to the snare. When
you have this under control move on to
the next paragraph.

I.

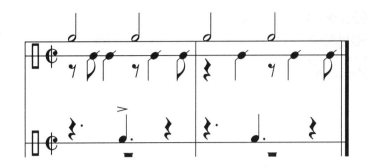

Now take this basic pattern and play it the following ways. Notice that you are not changing the pattern at all. You are orchestrating the same pattern to different voices on the drum set.

Once you move away from the closed hihat you can use beats 2 and 4 in the left foot as in the following

pattern. Other left foot patterns will follow. Now work with the following.

Right hand on either the side of the floor tom, cowbell or cymbal bell, left hand moves around the set playing on the hihat, rim of snare, snare and toms. Make repeating phrases. Also vary the accent patterns left hand rhythm.

2.

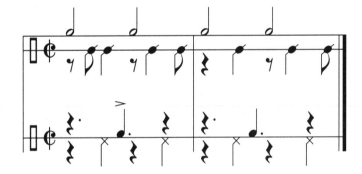

Improvisation based on audio examples 236

Next we look at variations for all of the voices. The playing of the Songo is basically an improvisation based on the above skeleton rhythm with the addition of the basic variations to be presented in the next section. These basic rhythms and the vast rhythmic vocabulary of the Son and Rumba traditions are what you draw on for your accompaniments and solos. Obviously what variations you improvised are determined by the particular music you are

playing and the type of ensemble you happen to be playing in at the time. Following is a common combination with a couple of extra variations added to the above skeleton rhythm. The cowbell ride changed, a note was added to the rim, and a note was added to the bass drum. These are very simple changes but they really change the pattern. Practice this then move to all of the variations for each voice in the next section.

3.

Note: The audio track has the basic bass drum pattern in first example in order to emphasize the hand patterns, and this pattern as written in the second example.

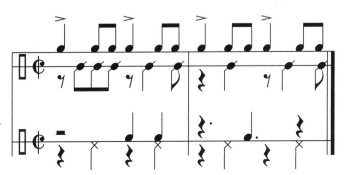

Cowbell (Ride Pattern) Variations

The following are the three ride patterns for the Songo. Do all of the combinations in this section with all three of the ride patterns. The first is the basic half-note pulse. The second is the one-beat, one-bar Campana phrase, and the third is the same phrase but made into a two bar phrase in clave—3-2 clave in this case. Remember to play all of the combinations starting on either bar. *Eventually you'll also need to be able to start all the combinations not only on* *either bar but on any beat of any bar.*

Even though these are primarily cowbell patterns, you must practice these on a wood sound (like the side of the floor tom), and on the cymbal bell. You should also do them on the closed hihat as well as doing patterns 2 and 3 on the hihat and opening the notes on beat 1 and 3. All of these sounds are played in the course of playing the Songo style in an ensemble.

HiHat Variations

Following are the four main hihat/left foot variations you'll play in this style. They are beats 1 and 3, beats 2 and 4, all four quarter notes (this is probably most useful in a more fusion or nontraditional style), and the rumba clave, (this can be played on the hihat or on a woodblock mounted on a bass drum pedal). Play all of the combinations in this section with all of these patterns.

When you're first starting, pick one simple pattern (i.e. the first or second pattern) that is most comfortable to you and get all of the basic playing down with that. You don't have to start with

the clave in the left foot. Save that for later. It makes no sense to have the feel falling apart because you're trying to play the clave with your foot. If your feel is great and you can't play clave in the left foot no one really cares. If you can, then it's icing on the cake. But if you're playing clave in one foot and a bunch of other syncopated stuff in your other limbs and nothing is locked in, then your playing is of no use to anyone. The people you're playing with won't know whether to follow your feet or your hands. So be practical and get the basic stuff feeling real good first and you'll be out there playing. Then you can add everything else.

1.

2.

3.

4.

Bass Drum Variations

These are the most common bass drum variations. Again, do all of the combinations in this section with all of these patterns.

The bass drum, unlike the hihat patterns, not only functions as an ostinato part but also plays an improvisational role. It can be part of a dialogue with the left hand and also plays its usual role of playing big accented parts. This means you have to address not only the ostinato bass drum parts but also do exercises that will free up your right foot to be able to improvise rhythmic lines along with your left hand. For now get these combinations down. Other technical exercises for improvisation are presented later in this section.

1.

2.

3.

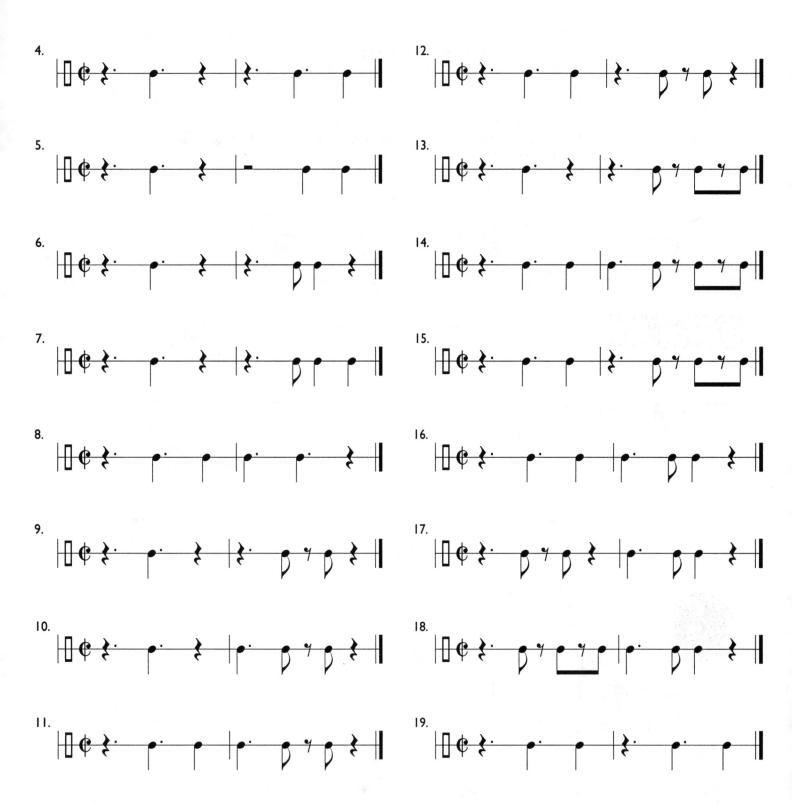

The combinations that you can come up with here are endless. Read down all of the previous combinations at least four or eight times each then move on to the next one without stopping. After you can go from any one to any other one without disrupting the flow then put them together into longer phrases by using one pattern as a repeating groove and introducing some others every eight or sixteen bars as variations.

Next we move on to a couple of specific approaches for developing grooves, variations and soloing.

Here we start creating the systems for the workouts as we did in the previous sections. The most involved so far has been the workout for the Mambo. This will be similar in approach. Basically you will take each combination (ostinato) just presented for each of the three limbs—right hand ride, hihat and bass drum—and combine them with every combination for every other limb.

Just as with the Mambo workouts, you'll end up with several hundred systems over which you'll play varying lines in the left hand around the set. All of the systems will not be written out here since it would needlessly take a large amount of paper. Some are presented and the rest is up to you. Just be methodical and you'll get through them all.

The approach you take to attacking these workouts is up to you as long as you eventually get through all of the possible combinations. More specific instructions are in each of the following sections.

Approach I

This approach deals with playing ostinatos in three of the limbs—the right hand ride pattern, the left foot, playing one of the hihat variations, and the bass drum playing one of its variations. Over this three voice ostinato you'll work on playing *thematic* combinations that include the toms and snare.

Following are some examples. They are presented here with right hand pattern #2—which can be played on the cowbell or on the side of your floor tom or cymbal bell—hihat pattern #4—the Rumba clave—and bass drum pattern #2.

A methodical approach for working through this section is to take each of the following examples and play them as written, then change the right hand pattern and play through them all again; then play the other right hand pattern and go through them yet again. Next go through them using the remaining three hihat combinations (with each of the three right hand patterns). Then do the same thing again with the bass drum combinations. Here are some two bar examples. *The notes in parenthesis are optional or can be played ghosted. These examples are in the 2-3 clave position.*

1.

2.
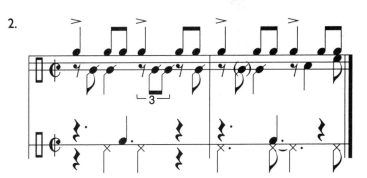

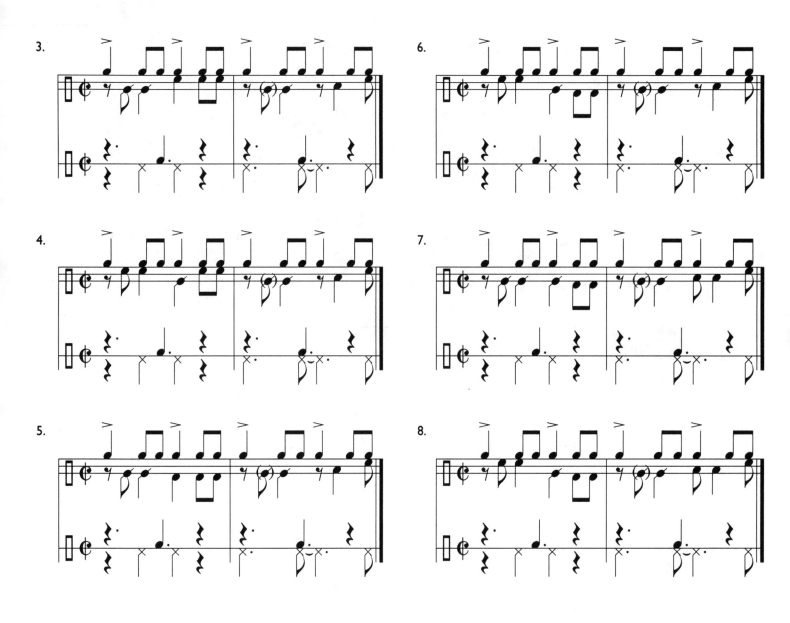

Following are some four bar examples. These are created by combining the two bar phrases as well as adding other variations. *The notes in parenthesis are optional. They can be played ghosted or not at all or every other time through the pattern. These examples are presented in the 2-3 clave position.*

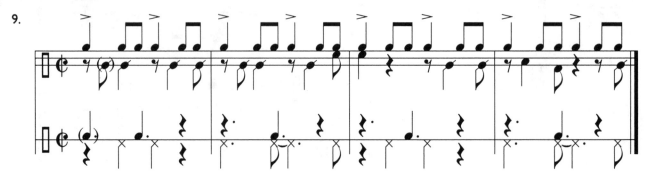

Keep in mind that though these are improvised patterns they are thematic in nature. They have easily identifiable tom-tom melodies. Also, how you apply accents and ghosted notes will greatly enhance as well as change the patterns. In addition to using these as time feels you can also use them as themes for building solos. The possibilities here are infinite.

Next go back and play all of the previous patterns with all of the different cowbell/ride, hihat and bass drum patterns. This is essential for you to get a lot of vocabulary as well as technical facility with the style. You have three cowbell ride patterns, four hihat patterns and four basic bass drum patterns (you really have nineteen bass drum variations but four basic ones) for a total of forty eight systems to work with. If you make systems using all of the bass drum variations you have two-hundred twenty-

eight systems to work with.

Also think about adding the bass drum not only as an ostinato line but as part of the varying pattern. In the end your playing in this style will be much like a jazz approach on the drum set, one where all of the limbs are playing both ostinato patterns as well as improvised variations.

Following are a couple of patterns written to include the bass drum playing variations based on the two bar ostinato patterns. *You'll get all of these patterns as you play through the examples in Approach 1 with all of the bass drum variations.* The more you work with combining all of the ostinato patterns for each limb, the more facility you'll have to develop patterns like this on the fly, and this is where you want to be with this material. *These examples are also in the 2-3 clave position.*

17.

Approach 2

Next we move on to an approach for developing facility for improvising freely with the left hand over the three-part ostinato system (right hand, bass drum, and hihat). Again, it is very important that you focus on the feel of all of these technical exercises and play them as if you were playing in an ensemble, as if you are playing music, not exercises. It is also very important that you play all of these exercises over *all* of the variations for all of the limbs. That is, combine all of the cowbell/ride, bass drum and hihat/left foot variations with each other into three-part ostinato systems and then play all of the following exercises in the left hand.

Remember to do all of these workouts over all of the pattern variations combined into

the 228 systems. You need to eventually get them all down but to get started you must have all of this material down with at least the first 48 basic systems.

As an example the following system is shown. It consists of cowbell variation #2, bass drum variation #2 and hihat variation #4—the clave rhythm. This now is the ostinato system for all of the workouts. You don't have to start here. You can start with any combination you want as long as you can play them all in the end. If your technical facility and familiarity with this style is limited, you should start with a simpler system. Take your first system and play all of the following workouts in the left hand on the snare, snare rim or on any of the sound sources on your drum set.

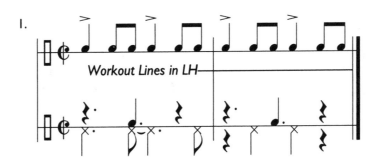

1.

Workout Lines in LH

Workout I

This first workout consists of playing one note per two bars (the clave phrase is two bars long) in the left hand over the particular three-part ostinato system. Make sure it is "in the pocket" and that the whole feel is grooving. There are sixteen rhythms—two bars of eighth notes—one note from each of the two bars for each of the exercises.

1.

2.

3.

4.

5.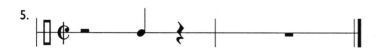

6.

7.

8.

9.

10.

11.

12.

13.

14.

15.

16.

Workout 2

This workout consists of playing one note per bar for each of the two bars of the clave patterns. Make sure it is "in the pocket" and that the whole feel is grooving. There are eight rhythms—two bars of eighth notes—one note from each bar for each of the exercises.

1.

5.

2.

6.

3.

7.

4.

8.

Workout 3

This workout consists of playing two notes per half note pulse. Each pulse—half note—is divided into four eighth notes so there are four exercises.

Although this workout seems very simple, these are rhythms that are used all of the time so you have to be able to play them "in the pocket."

1.

3.

2.

4.

Workout 5

This workout uses every possibility of a half note subdivision and spreads it out "per beat" over the two bars. You are playing one of the possible subdivisions for the two bars per example.

Once you can knock this out over all of the systems you are pretty much technically ready to play practically anything. Everything else is up to your knowledge of the style and your imagination.

Approach 3

This approach also employs the three-part ostinato system but introduces two new rhythms for the right hand ride. These are the Rumba clave rhythm and the basic palito pattern.

Create three part systems with all of the bass drum and hihat variations using these two ride patterns and go back and play Workouts 1 through 4 in the left hand. (When you play the clave in the right hand as the ride pattern you don't duplicate it with the hihat; no need to do hihat variation #4 with this ride pattern). These ride patterns can be played on a cowbell, wood block or other wood sound like the side of your floor tom or the cymbal bell.

Illustrated below are two systems, one with each of the ride patterns. The first uses bass drum variation #2—the bombo note on both bars, and hihat variation #2—beats 2 and 4. The second uses the same bass drum variation and hihat variation #4—the Rumba clave.

Approach 4

For this final approach take all of the previous three part systems you've created—remember there are 228 possibilities to exhaust—and play *pages 16 to 25* of the *Modern Reading Text in $\frac{4}{4}$* by *Louis Bellson* and *Gil Breines* with your free (left) hand in ¢ time. (You can use any book you like with single rhythm lines written out but I like the Bellson book best for this type of thing.) Play all the lines first on the snare and then move them around the set. Remember to use the correct phrasing and feel in reading the lines. Make them groove and make them sound like music. Use a variety of stroke types, accents, ghosted notes, rim shots, buzz strokes, and a variety of dynamics. Beyond all of these workouts what's left is for you to listen to and go see people play this style and play as much of it yourself.

The Pilón is a predecessor to the Songo, having evolved and developed as a culmination of Rumba and Son styles, and having specific conga and timbale parts which give it its identity. It has also ended up on the drum set with a character similar to the Songo—that of the funk-Latin flavor or combination. In practice (as an accompaniment in a musical group) it provides a similar base as the Songo style. Following are several drum set combinations taken primarily from the timbale parts.

Situation I

These first twelve patterns have timbale type variations orchestrated on the drum set.

This is what you'd play if another percussionist is playing the conga parts.

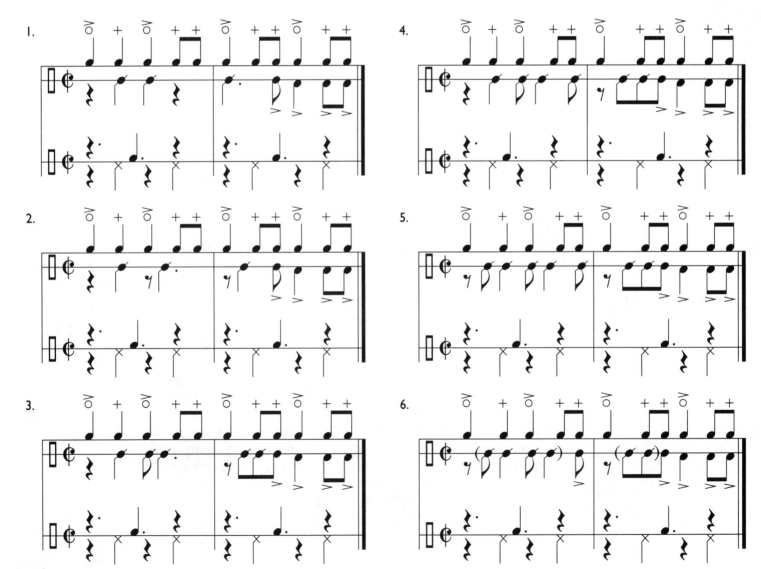

Situation 2

The following are examples of what to play if there is no one playing the conga parts and you want to capture those parts in your feel also. You might also try playing the following patterns combined with some of the patterns above to create four-bar phrases .

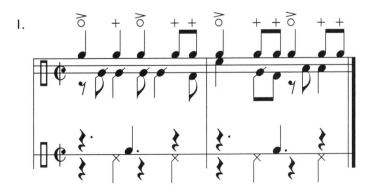

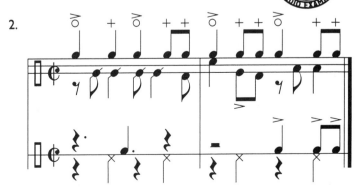

CONGA DE COMPARSA

THE CONGA RHYTHM IS SELDOM PLAYED ON THE DRUM SET—AT LEAST NOT IN ANY TRADITIONAL SETTINGS LIKE THE COMPARSA CARNAVAL PARADES—BUT THE SONGSTYLE ACTUALLY FITS THE DRUM SET QUITE NICELY. As in the previous sections, if you are going for the traditional ensemble sound and there are conga drummers and/or other percussionists present then you draw from the traditional percussion parts and orchestrate them on the drum set. There are a variety of these you could play and these patterns are presented first. These range from any of the multiple cowbell parts, to clave, snare drum, or bass drum (either on the bass drum or on the floor tom), imitating the way it is played traditionally in a Comparsa.

The second set of patterns presented are adaptations of this rhythm on the drum set for nontraditional ensemble settings. Basically this leaves you wide open for interpretation and the more you can combine the sound of the full ensemble into your solo drum set parts the better. You can also combine these parts with material from any other style as well, in order to create new rhythms, or to adapt the conga rhythm to a particular ensemble.

Situation 1

The following are patterns you can play if you're on the drum set and there are other percussionists playing. If this is the case then the other percussionists are probably conga drummers and you can play any or as many of the other ensemble parts—bell, snare drum, bass drum, clave—as possible. Of course if there are other percussion instruments being played by these percussionists then substitute a different part on the set. You wouldn't double parts already being played.

This first group of examples uses the clave in one hand and the main bell pattern in the other. You can choose which hand plays which. The bell part can either be played on one bell by using the neck and mouth of the bell for the low and high parts or better yet, played on two cowbells—a high and a low. The bass drum plays the standard bombo accented notes only—beats *2-and* of each bar—and the hihat is playing beats 1 and 3.

Notice that all of the parts in this section stay away from using parts from the conga drums since this section assumes the other percussionist(s) will be covering those parts.

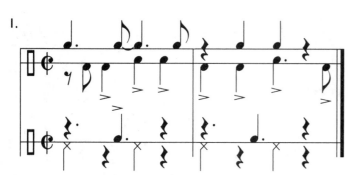

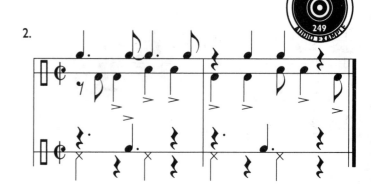

3.
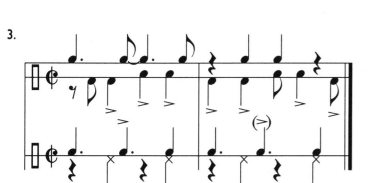

4.
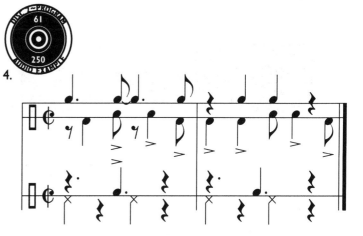

The following group uses the patterns usually played on the *Sartenes* (frying pans) and is a two-handed pattern. These are played over the standard foot pattern.

5.
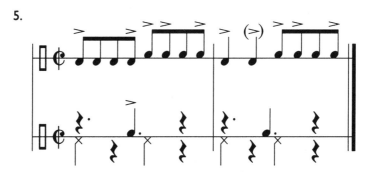

6.
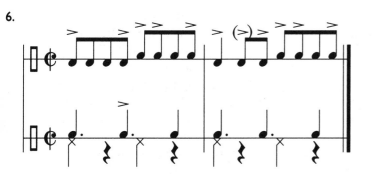

7.
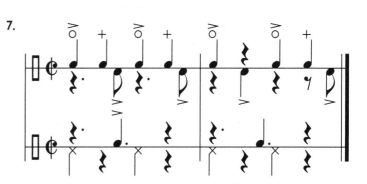

Continuing along these same lines, the following patterns are four other bell variations that can be played along with the basic patterns (the very first three examples presented), and the patterns for the sartenes, when a full ensemble is playing and there are many players. All of these bell parts put together create quite an intense ensemble all on their own.

8.

9.

10.

11.

271

The following examples take a slightly different approach. The clave is now played by the hihat foot with the bass drum playing either the rhythm presented in the last set of examples, or the one written here (which is the full basic rhythm, but on the bombo all notes but the accented *2-and* are muted tones, so don't play all the notes with the same emphasis). One hand plays the basic bell pattern and the other hand now plays a very simplified version of the snare part that is sometimes used in sections of a Comparsa performance, quite often in medium tempo intros where a vocalist may be speaking over the ensemble's vamp. (Listen to recordings of Pello El Afrokan for examples of this.) Alternately, the snare drum part below can be substituted.

Remember to practice all of the examples with both versions of the bass drum pattern.

These examples have the traditional full snare drum part over the feet playing the bombo and clave. Note the different stickings and accents.

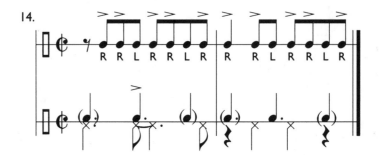

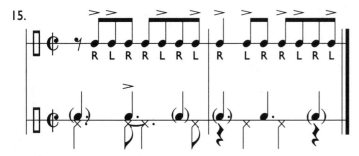

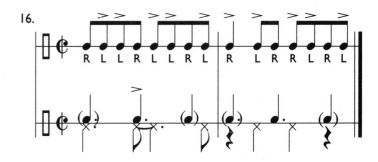

This example transitions us into the next section. It contains the traditional snare part along with the open bombo accent on the floor tom. Again, remember to play this with both bass drum patterns.

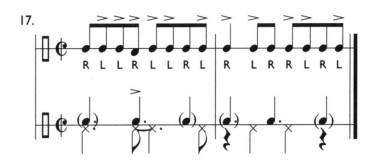

Situation 2

Here the examples focus on the drummer playing solo with the parts played mostly on the tom toms and snare (and snare rim). They either have elements of the cowbell rhythms from the previous section orchestrated on the toms, or have the conga drum patterns orchestrated around the drum set. These would work if you're playing alone and want to capture the sound of this style, but they could also work well with other percussionists as long as all are familiar with the style and each player's part is predetermined to create an ensemble sound. Observe the accents but keep in mind that the accent possibilities vary and can be improvised, as well as being a fixed part of a combination.

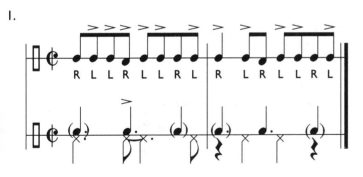

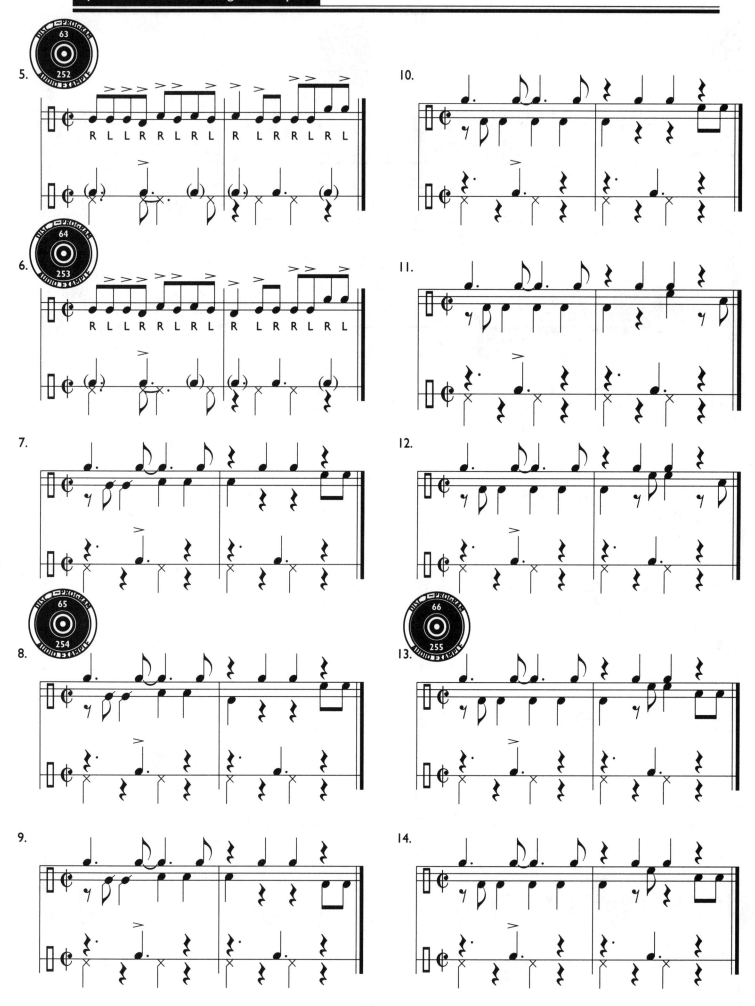

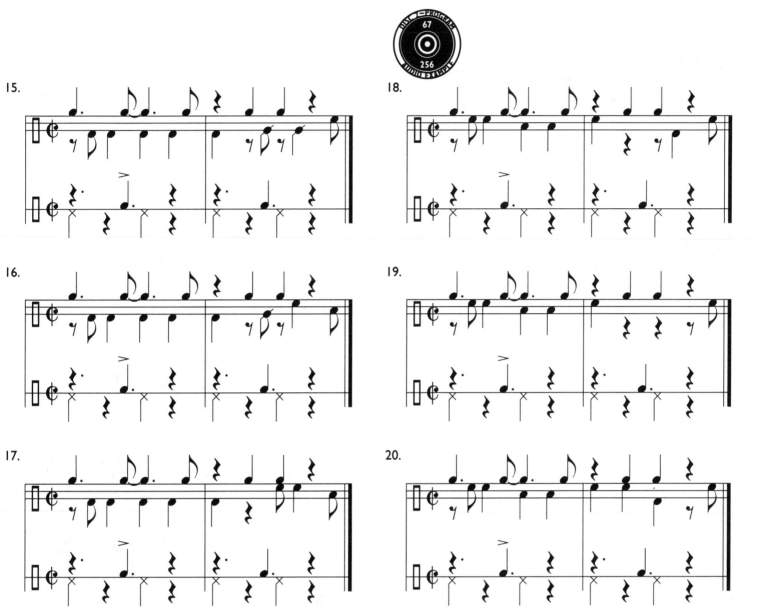

MOZAMBIQUE

THE MOZAMBIQUE DESCENDED FROM THE CONGA STYLES AND, AS MENTIONED EARLIER IN THIS TEXT, WAS GREATLY DEVELOPED AND BROUGHT TO THE FOREFRONT OF CUBAN styles by Pedro Izquierdo—Pello El Afrokan. This style was also brought to the forefront of American drumming through its adaptations by fusion drummers in the '70s and '80s, particularly Steve Gadd's interpretations. His popularity and his frequent use of this style brought it to the attention of a lot of drummers who otherwise may never have heard it or been interested. At this point though, most of these drummers were merely copying a hip pattern and weren't really aware of where the rhythm itself came from and how much traditional rhythmic material there is to draw on. We'll look at some of those hybrids here too, but we'll also focus on more traditional parts.

We'll examine both adaptations for accompanying on the set with other percussionists as well as combinations for solo drums.

Situation I

These examples are accompaniment parts to be played along with other percussionists playing conga drums and other percussion. They would work on unaccompanied drum set and, since the cowbell patterns are a signature sound of the Mozambique, you would definitely sound like you're playing the style; but without some congas or tom tom parts it might sound a little empty. (We'll examine more complex parts later in this section.)

These first three examples show the three basic and most common cowbell patterns played in this style along with the clave pattern. You can decide which hand plays which. The feet are playing the basic bombo note on 2 and 4 on the hihat. The bell part can be played on two bells—a high and a low—or on one large bell using the neck and mouth for the high and low pitches. This is a common accompaniment part for one percussionist or drummer.

All three of these patterns are fundamental and integral to this style and having them under control is essential in playing the other patterns in this section as well as to stretching out and improvising with the Mozambique.

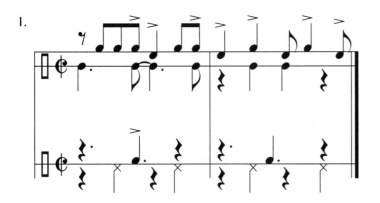

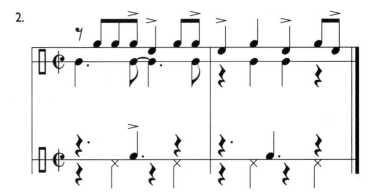

Next we look at another fundamental accompaniment pattern, the bombo (bass drum) pattern. The next two examples show the two most fundamental bombo patterns along with the clave rhythm and basic foot patterns.

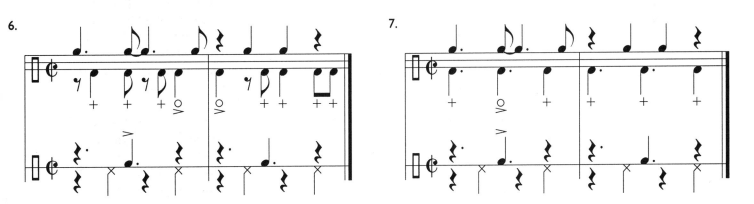

The bombo rhythms can also be combined with a cowbell pattern and the clave played by one of the feet. This combination starts to sound much fuller. These two examples show the first of the two bombo patterns above (with one note omitted), combined with two of the three basic cowbell rhythms. *These two examples are presented in the 2-3 clave position. Remember that you* *have to be able to play all patterns starting on either bar and really from any point of either bar.*

These examples also show the basic bombo rhythm broken up between two toms. You can practice the rhythm on one tom first in order to learn the pattern and then break it up over two or more drums.

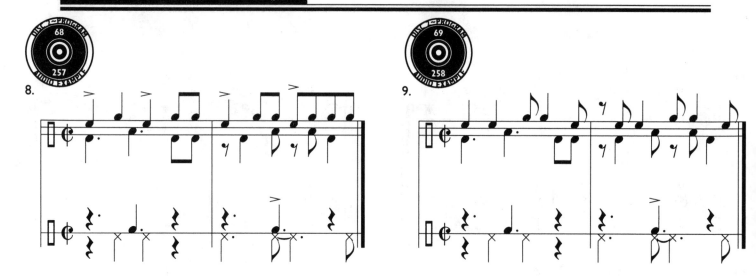

8.

9.

The next example is actually two bell parts—a high and a low—and one hand plays each part. You can play clave with your left foot if you like, or else just play 2 and 4. It is not as common as the last two examples but is heard quite often on recordings of Pello El Afrokan. *The accents in parenthesis show one possibility. The accents could also be on the downbeats of those groups of notes.*

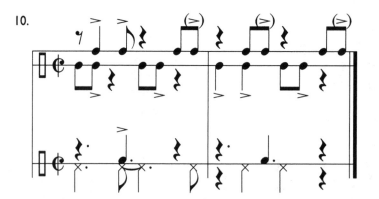

10.

Now that we've looked at some fundamental approaches to comping in this style, let's look at a number of variations based on the already established concepts.

The next set of examples consists of the clave-bombo approach. They have the clave in one hand with a variety of bombo patterns in the other hand. The "+" and "o" designate muted and open tones. These markings must be observed for the patterns to sound right. Again you can choose which hand plays which.

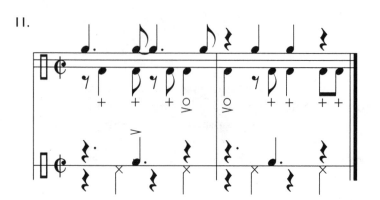

11.

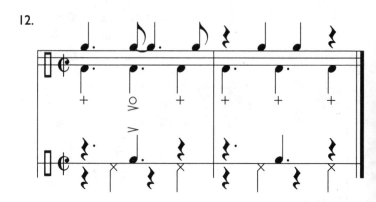

12.

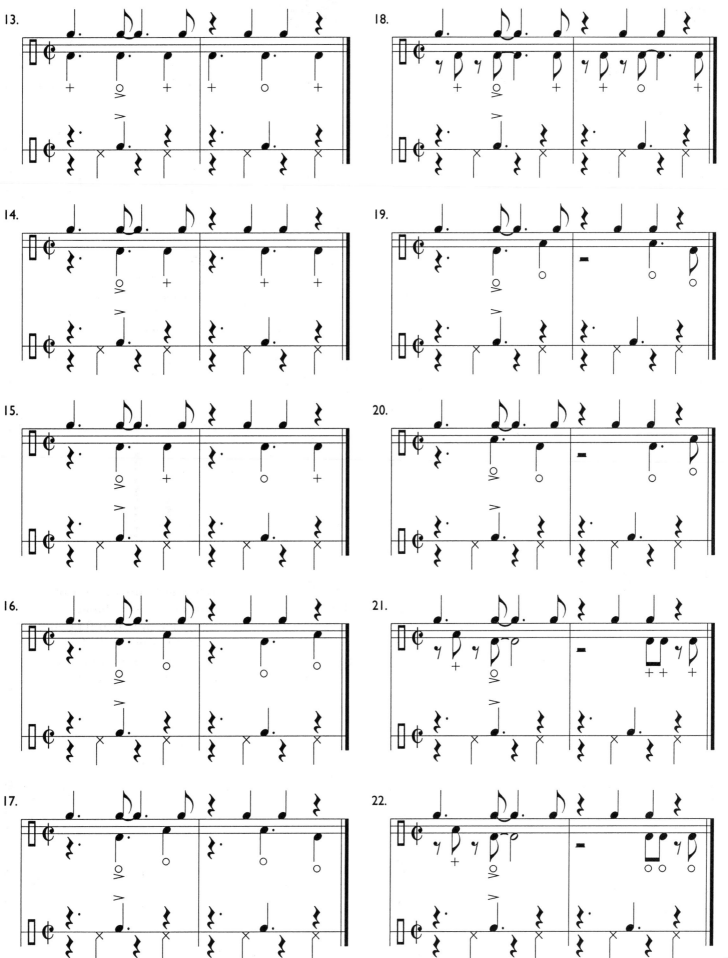

The next group of patterns follow the cowbell-bombo approach and have bell pattern #2 (from the very first patterns presented in this section), along with the previous twelve bombo patterns. The choice is yours as to which hand plays which part.

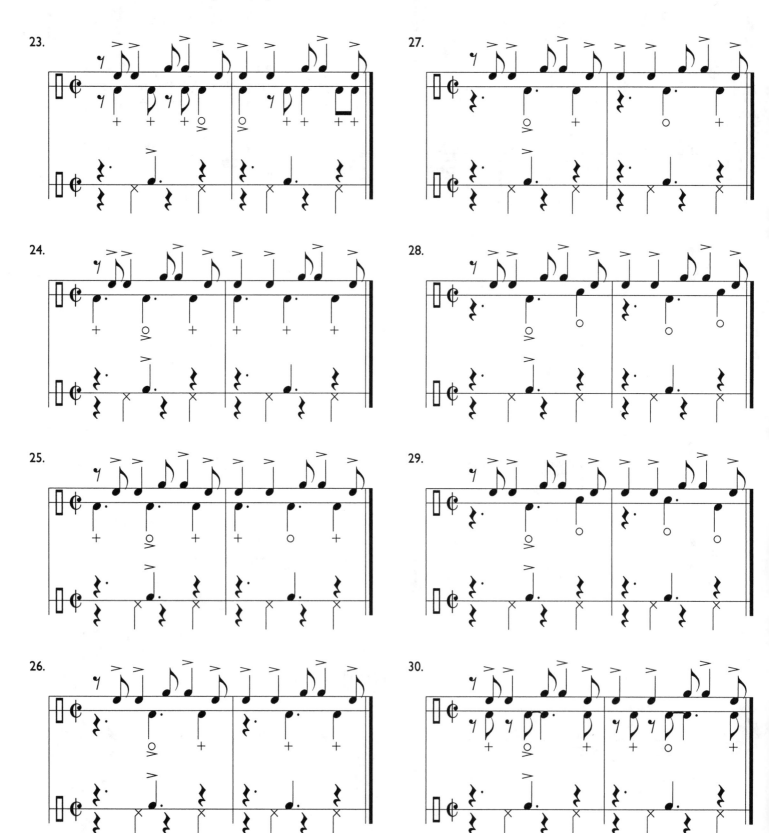

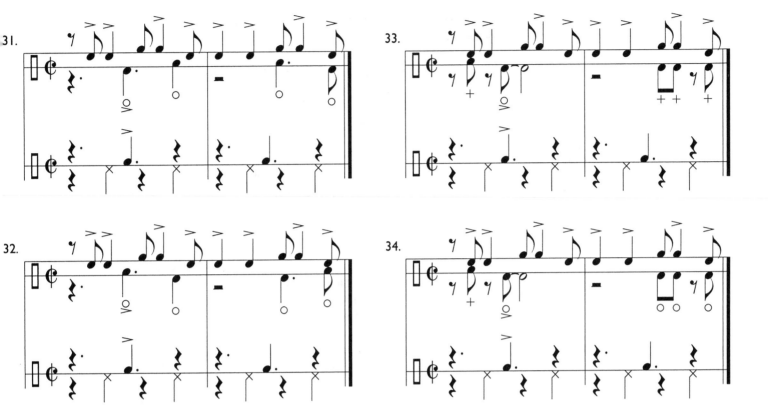

For the next group of patterns play the bombo rhythms from the previous twelve examples with the following bell combination. If you need to see where the hands fall together and apart then write out the twelve examples.

This pattern can be played on two bells with the lower and higher lines playing the low and high bells respectively, or on one large timbale bell with the low notes towards the mouth and the high notes towards the neck. You must make this distinction and observe the accents for the patterns to sound right. The low notes should feel long and the high notes short.

Finally, take the same twelve bombo patterns and combine them with this bell pattern. With this you should now have combined all of the twelve bombo variations with the clave as well as with all three cowbell patterns. You've also combined all three cowbell patterns with the clave. Go back and repeat the exercises but this time change the foot patterns you were using. Remember that the more variations you have under you're belt the more you'll be able to stretch out.

Situation 2

This section focuses on playing the style on the drum set with no other percussionist present. There are more parts from the conga drums combined with the percussion parts.

Although these patterns work well alone, they work even better with another percussionist or two when all the players parts are predetermined.

The first group of rhythms has the first (of the two) traditional bell parts, along with a new part for the other hand that is taken from the full four bar phrase of the congas. The first example shows only the rhythm of the second part. Learn this rhythm on one sound source—i.e. the snare drum or rim or another bell—until you can play both parts smoothly *and with the correct articulations on the bell part and the second line (neck and mouth strokes and accents).* After you have that down move on to the other patterns. The combinations presented here are a few of the many possibilities for orchestrating this rhythm around the set.

Again, you can play the second line on the snare, rim, woodblock, a second cowbell, or any combination of sounds that you come up with. First use only one sound source to get the parts down, then start moving the line around the set.

In this final section we focus on using the Mozambique parts to create hybrid drum set patterns, combining it with elements of funk style playing to create contemporary drum set patterns.

What you can come up with here is endless and basically up to you or whatever your musical situations call for. Here are some examples of what you can do. Don't memorize and then regurgitate these patterns. These are meant as examples of what can be done with this, and they are basically licks off the top of my head and represent nothing more. The idea is to know the traditional material well enough that you can use it to come up with different things in a variety of musical applica-

tions. Don't get locked into patterns. Learn the style and the patterns will come out of your knowledge and the music you're playing. I've seen entire books dedicated to presenting merely patterns with no basis or connection to the style they represent. When you go through those books and learn all the patterns you basically have nothing except a bunch of patterns, many of which probably won't really work in any real musical situations. They quickly sound dated and, more importantly, they are really someone else's patterns. The key is to take the material from the previous Mozambique sections and work it into new sounding orchestrations around the drum set while giving it a funk—or nontraditional—style inflection.

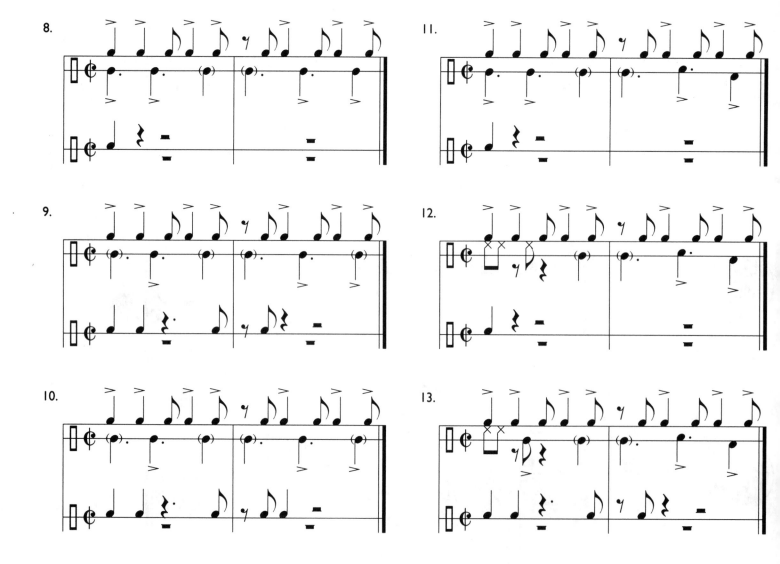

14.
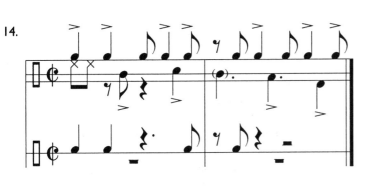

17.

15.
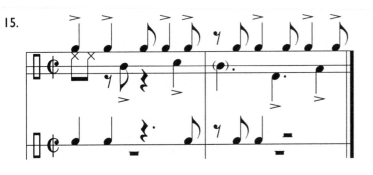

18.

16.
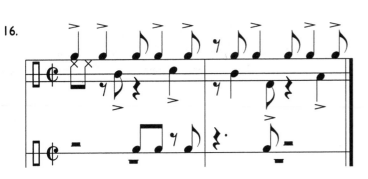

19.
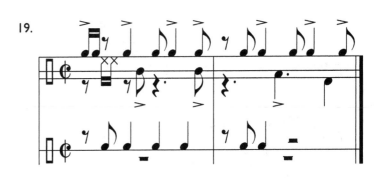

BOMBA & PLENA

THE BOMBA AND PLENA ARE FOLK-LORIC RHYTHMS FROM PUERTO RICO. THE BOMBA IS TRADITIONALLY PLAYED ON CONGA DRUMS CALLED BULEADOR AND REQUINTO. THE DRUMS ARE larger (fatter) than regular conga drums and are indigenous to this style. The other instruments are *cuá* which functions as a clave or palito part and the *guicharo*—scraper or guiro. The Plena is traditionally played on tambourines called *panderetas*. Although both rhythms are folkloric and are still performed that way they also are used in contemporary arranging and ensembles.

The drum set really has no connection to these rhythms—not even in their contemporary adaptations, but as you can see from the following examples, some interesting patterns can be got from adapting the Bomba on the drum set. Here are several two bar as well as four bar phrases.

The last example is an adaptation of the Plena.

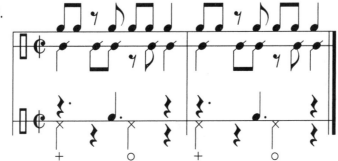

Here is an adaptation of the Plena rhythm.

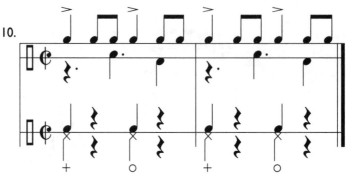

ERENGUE

THE MERENGUE IS A RHYTHM AND DANCE FROM THE DOMINICAN REPUBLIC BUT HAS EARLIER HISTORICAL ROOTS IN HAITI FROM THE INTEGRATION OF THE FRENCH COLONISTS and the Angolan slaves. It made its way into Cuba and then into other Caribbean regions after the Haitian revolution of 1791.

It is probably one of the most popular Latin dance rhythms through-out the world and is consequently played by a wealth of different types of ensembles, both traditional and nontraditional. Since it is played by so many dance style ensembles it has come to have a variety of drum set adaptations all taken from the percussion parts.

The key to what you play on drum set is, once again, if and what percussion is present. We'll examine both situations.

Situation 1

In this situation you are playing drum set but there is a tambora player or someone playing the tambora parts on the conga drums. In this case you draw from the other percussion parts. If no one is playing the guira then you definitely will play that on the hihat as that is a critical part. Otherwise you draw from other percussion or create nonconflicting parts around the set.

Remember, don't be afraid to sit out a number if you can't find something to play. This is always preferable to getting in the way with bad parts.

The first example has the bass drum and the guira part. The second has a common hihat part along with an adaptation of a simple conga part.

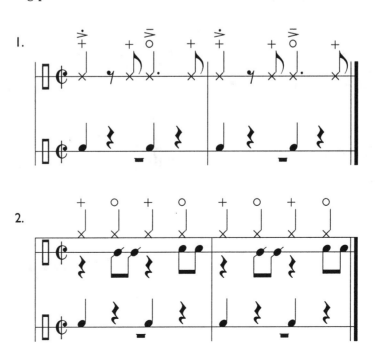

Situation 2

In this situation you are the only drummer/percussionist so you have to play the tambora parts as well as anything else you can slide in. Following are some possibilities. You can also go back to the section on the tambora and orchestrate any of those patterns onto the set as these were. These are basically a duplication of those patterns but orchestrated for drum set. Also remember to review the section on the style itself (Songstyles section) so you know which of these patterns to play during which section of the arrangement—verse, chorus, Jaleo, Pambiche, Apanpichao, etc.

1.
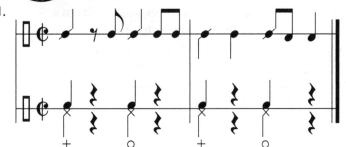

4.
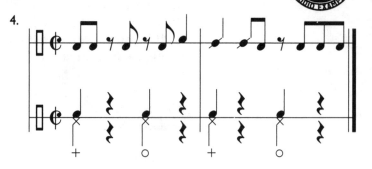

2.
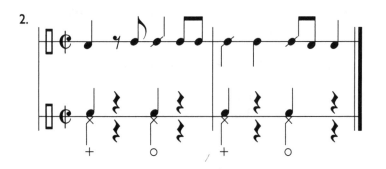

5.
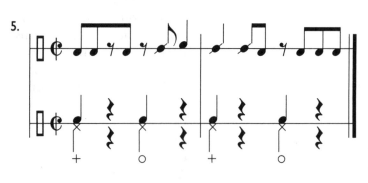

3.
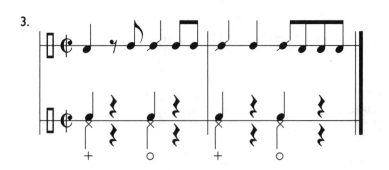

6.
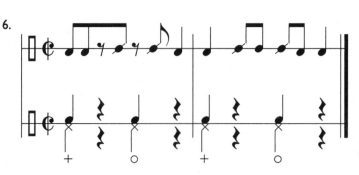

7.
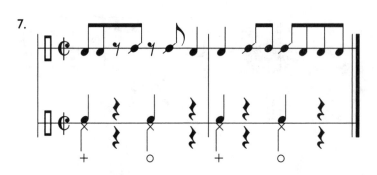

A NOTE ABOUT $\frac{6}{8}$ STYLES

WHEN EXAMINING SOME $\frac{6}{8}$ STYLES FOR THE DRUM SET IT IS NECESSARY TO KEEP THE FOLLOWING IN MIND: MOST OF THESE STYLES SHARE MANY OF THE SAME CLAVE, COWBELL, GUAGUA, and even some hand drum patterns. Regardless of the hand drum patterns that they may share, the style is often *defined* by the rhythmic patterns of the congas or batá drums. Other aspects defining the styles may include the geographic region a particular style emanates from, lyric content, dances, arrangements and what particular event a style may be performed for. (Much the same takes place with many Son and even Rumba styles when transferred to the drum set—the patterns played on the set for many of them are exactly the same). Consequently, your playing a $\frac{6}{8}$ cowbell pattern on the set along with $\frac{6}{8}$ clave, the downbeats on the hihat and a generic bass drum pattern will *not define a specific style,* and the same patterns may be used to accompany a number of them. For example, you are playing the following cowbell pattern: $\frac{6}{8}$| ♩ ♪ ♪ ♫ | ♪ ♩ ♩. ||. Are you playing Rumba Columbia, Guiro, Bembé, an Afro $\frac{6}{8}$ funk feel or what? Would you play this in Abakuá? Hopefully not if you're trying to play it traditionally. That style uses other cowbell patterns in its folkloric settings.

This situation requires your knowing these styles in that much greater detail because your including or omitting one small detail in your drum set part may be all that you can do (or that is required) to define or play a particular style correctly. This is particularly true if the parts you are playing on the drum set are accompanying parts for other percussionists playing conga or batá drums. Of course if you are playing the style by yourself and employing the conga drum parts onto the drum set this is not as much the case as you will be drawing on all the specific parts from a particular style and then orchestrating it onto the set.

Another area to consider is that of names of styles when referring to playing $\frac{6}{8}$ on the set. The terminology used to describe styles is often used incorrectly—or at least very generically by many people. For example, I have often heard the term Bembé to describe or to tell someone or a group to play a $\frac{6}{8}$ style and ended up hearing a Rumba Columbia or elements of Abakuá or a generic $\frac{6}{8}$ style with conga drum and bell parts not really associated with Bembé. Traditionally a Bembé is a folkloric performance with bells and shekeré accompanying vocals and dance. There is one conga drummer playing the role of a quinto player in a Rumba group—that is soloing or interacting with the vocalists and dancers—but the drum played is not a quinto but a large tumbadora. There is no conga pattern for two or three congas in Bembé as there is for the Rumba Columbia or Abakuá. I have also quite often been given charts by jazz oriented composers or arrangers with an indication for a $\frac{12}{8}$ Nañigo when what was being sought was an Elvin Jones $\frac{12}{8}$ feel. Any and all of this is okay if you are not playing in a traditional setting or trying to perform a specific style. If you are, this generic mixing of patterns does not work. You must know the specific parts. Go back to the percussion section and learn all of the specific parts to each style. Then you have many options when playing these rhythms on the set.

Since these issues arise with these styles, I have grouped them in the following way for this drum set section.

Hopefully this will put them in enough separate categories for you to see the distinctions necessary to play them on the set. *When I have grouped styles together it does not mean they are the same. It means they share similar patterns and would be comped the same way on the set. It is the rest of what's going on that will define the specific style being played. This presentation applies only in regards to the drum set. When examined in their full traditional settings, these styles are all very distinct.*

All of the 6/8 styles for the drum set are presented in this part of the book except for the *Rumba Columbia* which is presented with the Rumba Guaguancó and Rumba Yambú. Even though it is a 6/8 style and it also uses some of the patterns presented in this section, it is clearly and unequivocally part of the Rumba family and traditionally (in folkloric settings) performed almost exclusively by Rumba groups who have defined the approach to this style.

The *Abakuá* is presented in its own section because it contains enough different parts that its interpretation on the set—if done correctly—clearly spells out that you are playing or drawing from the Abakuá rhythm. This is also the case with the Guajira in 6/8—not to be confused with the Guajira from the Son tradition. This rhythm, when played on the drum set is distinct enough that it would not be confused with any other.

I have grouped the Guiro and Bembé together since orchestrations I present for the drum set would work for either approach when the 6/8 style is approached generically. I've made a couple of small distinctions with regard to the Bembé in that section. Remember that these are not the same styles but outside of the traditional Bembé folkloric presentation, the drum set parts cross over.

The Cha Cha Lokua Fun could almost have been included with the Guiro and Bembé, as it has the same drum set pattern except for the placement of the tom toms. But this, when coupled with its conga rhythm, is distinct enough to be presented separately.

The final section is called Afro 6/8 with Backbeat. This section is separate because it is truly a generic section. These patterns are basically drum set patterns using the traditional 6/8 cowbell and playing bass drum and snare drum combinations with it. These may or may not work with any of the other styles. If you're performing traditionally, you wouldn't play these patterns, but if you're in a Latin jazz band, and a particular piece calls for this type of feel (even though the percussionist may happen to be playing a folkloric rhythm on batá drums or other percussion), then it's still okay. These rhythms are basically made up and can be used anywhere they work.

ABAKUÁ

THIS STYLE TRADITIONALLY EMANATES FROM THE ABAKUÁ SOCIETIES. GO BACK TO THE PERCUSSION AND SONG-STYLES SECTIONS FOR MORE SPECIFICS. ONE OF THE VERY UNIQUE characteristics of the Abakuá is its simultaneous use of duple and triple rhythms between the hand drums and the cowbells. Although many rhythms of the Afro-Cuban tradition have this inflection in the playing, the Abakuá has it built into some of its patterns.

As with the other styles we look at situations for playing on drum set with and without other percussion.

Situation 1

These first two patterns show the two main cowbell parts played in one hand with the clave in the other. The hihat plays the downbeats and the bass drum plays a basic bombo pattern.

Traditionally, the Abakuá does not have this bombo part in all sections, but if you're playing this style on drum set you aren't really in a totally traditional setting anyway, so this pattern will work.

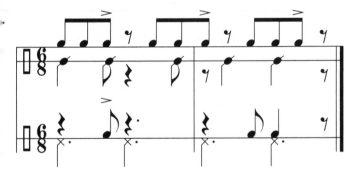

2.

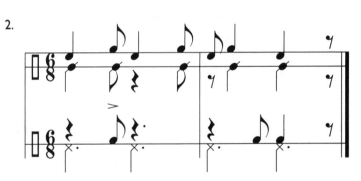

Situation 2

In this situation you are playing drum set alone so you're trying to play some of the hand drum parts in your patterns. These first two patterns use the clave in one hand and a couple of adaptations of extracted conga or batá parts for the drums. These would also work well along with other percussionists as long as you arrange all the players' parts.

1.
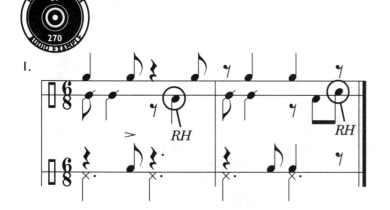

2.

The next two patterns show an adaptation for the drum set of the three conga parts when played by one player. The "+" and "o" markings indicate open and dampened strokes. Both patterns are the same except for the left foot pattern.

3.
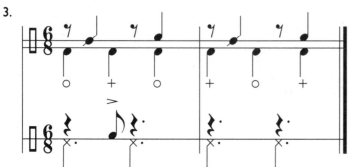

4.
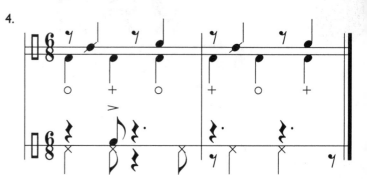

These last three patterns show an adaptation of another three-conga pattern for one player approach. The patterns are all the same with regard to the hands, but the feet change in each. Notice how changing the foot pattern really changes the overall feel. The snare note with a circle around it indicates a rim shot. This is a slap stroke when played on congas. The notes with slashes are rim clicks. These are HT (Heel-Toe) strokes when played on the congas. *Use all alternate strokes starting with the right hand.*

5.
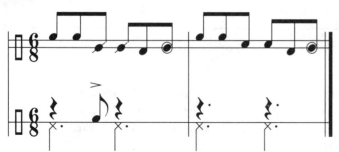

6.
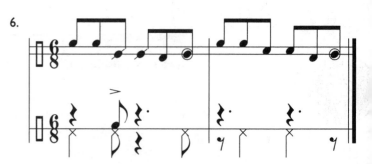

7.
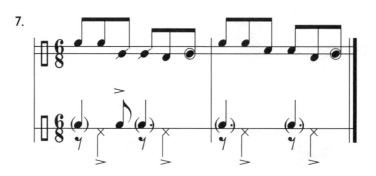

GUIRO & BEMBÉ

THE FOLLOWING COMBINATIONS WILL WORK FOR BOTH OF THESE STYLES IF YOU ARE PLAYING DRUM SET WITH OR WITHOUT OTHER PERCUSSIONISTS. IF YOU WERE IN A TOTALLY traditional setting you would not be playing drum set so that is a non-issue; so for practically any situation where the drum set would be present this would work. All of these patterns have the cowbell pattern along with some combination of the hand drum parts orchestrated around the snare, rim and toms. There are also some bass drum variations in some of the patterns.

The first six patterns are commonly played as Guiro patterns and can also work as accompaniments for a Bembé that is not totally traditional.

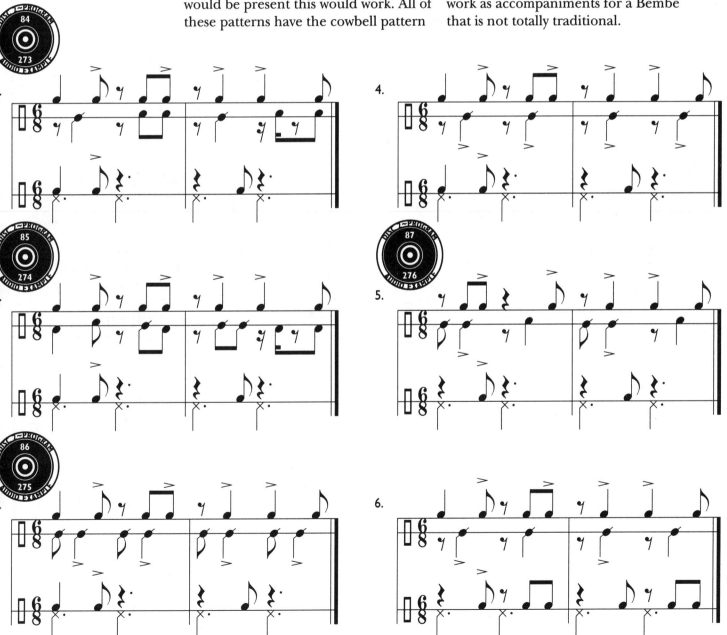

These three patterns are commonly played as Bembé for the drum set but would also work as Guiro patterns. Again, the specific musical situation is going to be the determining factor in what works and what doesn't.

The "+" and "o" denote open and dampened strokes.

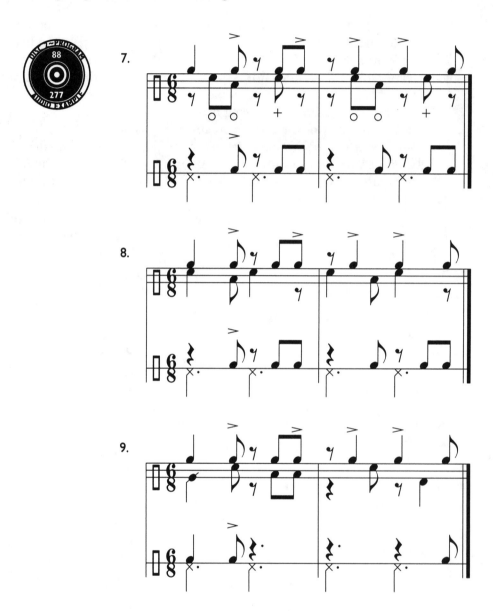

CHA CHA LOKUA FUN

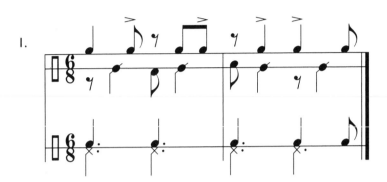

GUAJIRA IN $\frac{6}{8}$

AFRO ⅝ WITH BACKBEAT

FOLLOWING ARE SOME TWO BAR PHRASES WITH BASS DRUM AND SNARE COMBINATIONS UNDER THE COWBELL PATTERN. THE NOTES IN PARENTHESIS ARE GHOSTED NOTES and must be observed for the pattern to sound right. Use one inch or less of stick height for the ghosted notes and eight to ten inches for the accented back beats.

1.
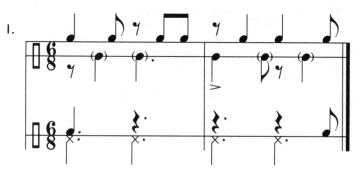

4.
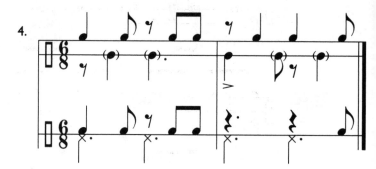

2.
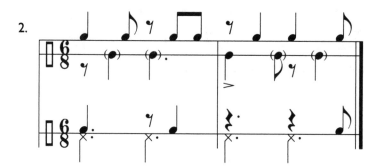

5.
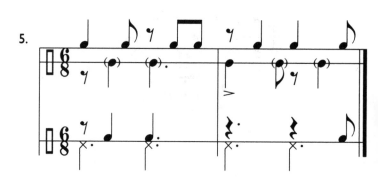

3.
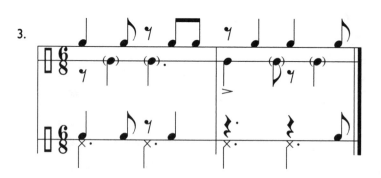

6.
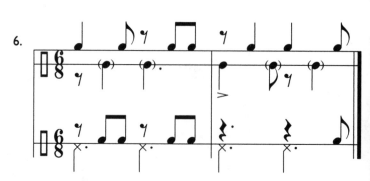

Here is a sixteen bar phrase using the previous two bar phrases. Again, remember to play the ghosted notes correctly.

7.

ADDITIONAL TECHNICAL EXERCISES

THE FOLLOWING SECTION ADDRESSES TECHNICAL ISSUES RELEVANT TO PLAYING THESE STYLES. WHILE HAVING A GREAT AMOUNT OF TECHNIQUE IS NEVER A SUBSTITUTE FOR HAVING great knowledge of a style and great feel and groove, these exercises present fundamental techniques necessary for playing these styles, and particularly for playing variations to the feels and for stretching out and improvising. To do any of this at an advanced level of playing you pretty much *have* to be able to execute the technical material on these pages. None of these exercises are merely for technique's sake. They address fundamental issues of coordination and endurance that are essential to playing these styles.

The exercises are divided into two sections. The first is for duple-meter feels ($\frac{4}{4}$ and $\frac{2}{2}$ time), and the second is for triple-meter feels (feels in $\frac{6}{8}$). The exercises consist of a group of *ostinatos*. The duple-meter ostinatos consist of seven essential cowbell ride patterns, four essential bass drum patterns, and five essential hihat patterns. The triple-meter ostinatos consist of four essential cowbell ride patterns, six essential bass drum patterns and six essential hihat patterns. (The two hihat patterns that are the Son and Rumba clave patterns can be played on a woodblock mounted for a foot pedal).

The cowbell patterns should be practiced on the corresponding cowbells, ride cymbal, hihat and wood sound—like the side of your floor tom or a mounted woodblock. The grooves will all feel and sound different when played on these different sound sources so you should practice them that way. Additionally, these are all sounds you'll use when performing these styles so you

need to have facility with them all.

The ostinatos are combined into *three-part systems*. The systems consist of three ostinatos—one cowbell pattern, one bass drum pattern, and one hihat pattern. This three-voice *system* now becomes an ostinato itself, and is repeated without variation while playing the *workouts* in the fourth limb—which is your left or right hand (depending on which hand is playing the cowbell ride pattern). You should ideally practice all of this material first riding with your strong hand—what you usually do—right if right-handed and left if left-handed. You should then ride with your weak hand and do all the workouts with the strong hand. This way you'll be able to play all of this stuff both ways, affording you that much more flexibility.

The workouts consist of single line rhythms to be played first on one sound source—i.e. the snare drum, and later can be moved all around the drum set or percussion setup. There are five sets of workouts. More specifics on each of the sets of workouts appear with each workout group.

All of the systems are not written out. You can write them out if you need to. Seven cowbell rides combined with four bass drum patterns equals twenty-eight patterns. Of those twenty-eight we combine twenty of them with the five hihat patterns. (We only combine twenty because cowbell rides #7 & #8 are the Rumba and Son clave patterns. If you play these as your ride pattern you don't double it with the hihat and vice-versa.) This equals one-hundred *systems* you have to do the workouts with. Everything is written in 3-2. You must also do it all in 2-3—the whole section again—two-hundred systems. I have included three systems as examples. It doesn't matter what order you take them in as long as you are methodical and you get through them all. Don't cheat (yourself) on this and don't hurry through it. If you can play all of this stuff and you learn the patterns presented in this book and listen to a lot of music so you have the feel down, you will be able to burn in this idiom, and that I hope is what you want to do.

¢ Ostinato Groups

Cowbell Ride Patterns: Following are the three groups of ostinatos for the cowbell, bass drum, and hihat. The first group are the seven patterns for the cowbell ride. Combine each of these with the bass drum and hihat combinations.

Bass Drum Patterns: Here are the four bass drum ostinato patterns.

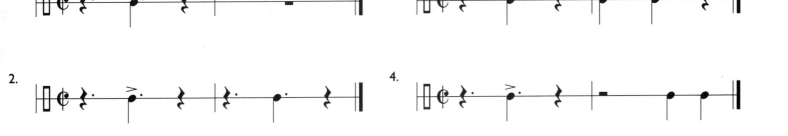

HiHat Patterns: Here are the five hihat ostinato patterns.

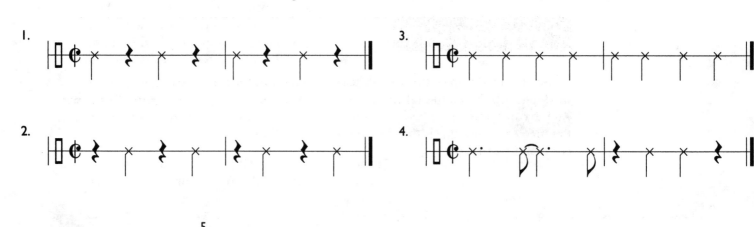

System Examples: The following are three examples of the systems created by combining the ostinatos. The first is cowbell pattern #1 with bass drum pattern #2 and hihat pattern #4. The second is cowbell pattern #4 with the same bass drum and hihat, and the third is cowbell ride pattern #7 with bass drum pattern #2 and hihat pattern #2. Again, you can approach this in any order you want as long as you create a method for yourself. This makes it easier to practice as well as easier to gauge what you've accomplished and what remains to be addressed.

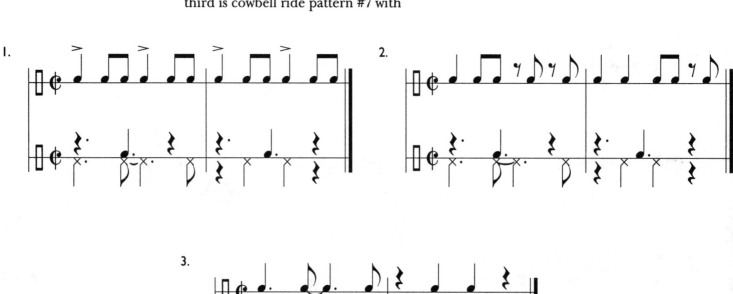

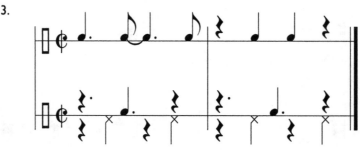

¢ Workout Sets 1 through 5

¢ Workout Set 1

Set 1 is made up of two bar phrases working with the eight eighth notes of each bar playing *one note per two bars* . Practice each one until you get it under control then practice going down the exercises four times each, eight times each, and then practice going from any one to any other one without disrupting your time feel.

1.

9.

2.

10.

3.

11.

4.

12.

5.

13.

6.

14.

7.

15.

8.

16.

¢ Workout Set 2

Set 2 continues with the method of Set 1 but employs playing *one note per bar*. Practice each one until you get it under control then practice going down the exercises four times each, eight times each, and then practice going from any one to any other one without disrupting your time feel.

1.

5.

2.

6.

3.

7.

4.

8.

¢ Workout Set 3

Set 3 continues with the method of Set 1 but employs playing *every possible even subdivision* of each of the two main beats of each bar. Practice each one until you get it under control then practice going down the exercises four times each, eight times each, and sixteen times each. Then practice going from any one to any other one without disrupting your time feel. Do it at a tempo that you can get through them all without slowing down to play the busier figures. Speed will come from repetition.

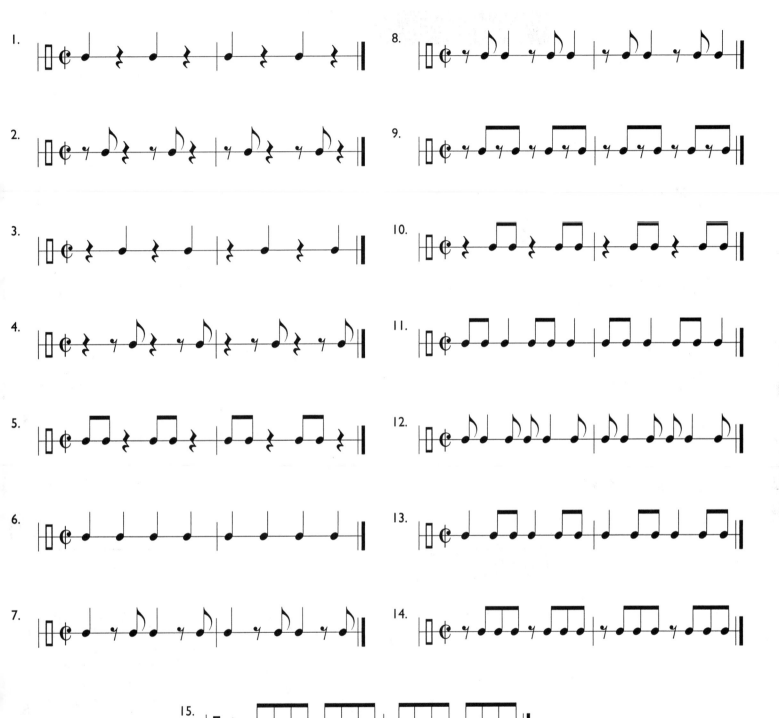

¢ Workout Set 4

Set 4 consists of taking a book with single line rhythms—I recommend the *Modern Reading Text in ⁴⁄₄* by *Louis Bellson and Gil Breines* pages 16 through 25. Play a system and read the lines from the book with the free hand (in ¢ time). Start first with the rhythmic line on the snare. After you have that down begin moving it around the set. Make sure your phrasing is in this style. Use accents, ghosted notes, buzz strokes and the like. Vary the inflection of the line. Don't just play it monotonically. Do this with all of the systems.

¢ Workout Set 5

Set 5 consists of two bar phrases of rhythmic vocabulary from this idiom. These are phrases that can be seen as riffs, licks or clichés that sound like you're phrasing in this style. In listening to and studying this style you will hear these types of phrases. Once you know these styles you should be able to come up with licks like these and many others right off the top of your head. For now, play all of these with all of the systems.

1.

7.

2.

8.

3.

9.

4.

10.

5.

11.

6.

12.

⁶⁄₈ Ostinato Groups

COWBELL RIDE PATTERNS: FOLLOWING ARE THE THREE GROUPS OF ⁶⁄₈ OSTINATOS FOR THE COWBELL, BASS DRUM AND HIHAT. THE FIRST GROUP ARE THE FOUR PATTERNS for the cowbell ride. Combine each of these with the bass drum and hihat patterns.

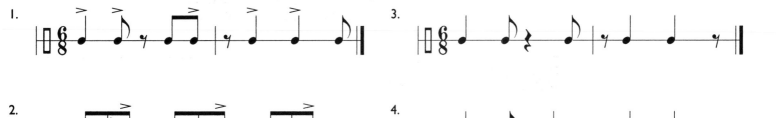

Bass Drum Patterns: Following are the six bass drum patterns.

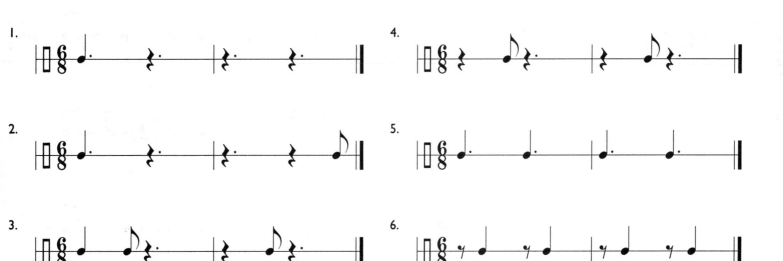

HiHat Patterns: Following are the six hihat patterns.

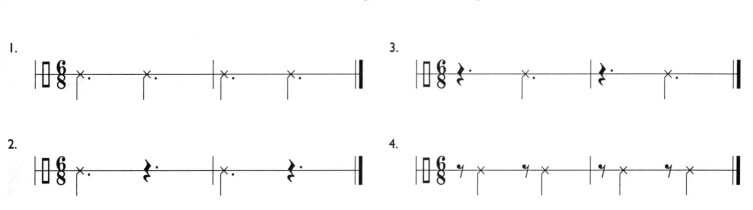

307

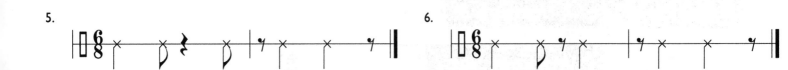

System Examples: Following are five examples of possible ostinato combinations put into systems. Apply the same approach and method you used for the duple meter systems here.

$\frac{6}{8}$ Workout Sets 1 through 8

$\frac{6}{8}$ Workout Set 1

1.
2.
3.
4.
5.
6.

7.
8.
9.
10.
11.
12.

$\frac{6}{8}$ Workout Set 2

1.
2.
3.

4.
5.
6.

$\frac{6}{8}$ Workout Set 3

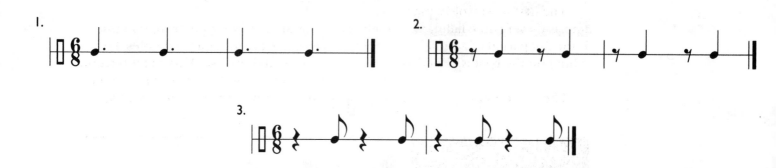

$\frac{6}{8}$ Workout Set 4

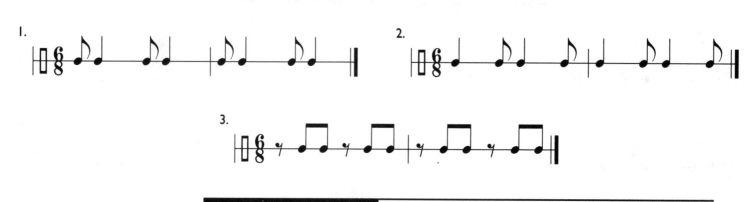

$\frac{6}{8}$ Workout Set 5

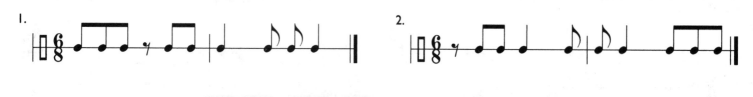

$\frac{6}{8}$ Workout Set 6

$\frac{6}{8}$ Workout Set 7

Set 7 consists of taking a book with single-line rhythms—I recommend the *Modern Reading Text in $\frac{4}{4}$* by *Louis Bellson* and *Gil Breines, pages 16-25.* Play a system and read the lines from the book with the free hand first on the snare only, and when you have that down move the line around the set in $\frac{4}{4}$ time.

Note: you must interpret the line as triplets in two different ways.

The first way involves playing the line as if every note falling on an offbeat is the *last* partial of a triplet. Every note falling on the beat is played as is.

The second way involves playing the line as if every note on an offbeat is the *second* partial of a triplet. Again, every note on the beat is played as is.

Make sure your phrasing is in this style. Use accents, ghosted notes, buzz strokes, and the like. Vary the inflection of the line. Don't just play it monotonically. Do this with all of the systems.

$\frac{6}{8}$ *Workout Set 8*

FOLLOWING ARE SOME IMPROVISED TWO BAR PHRASES. PRACTICE THESE and listen to music in this style. In time you should be able to play phrases like this on the fly.

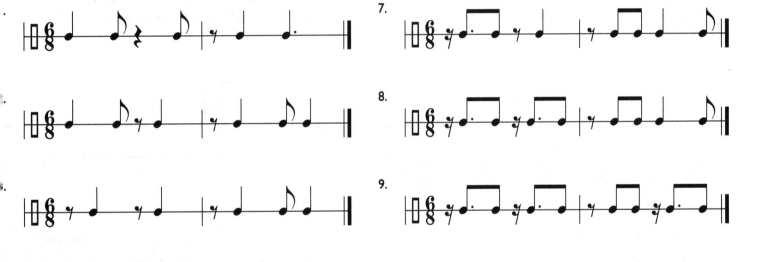

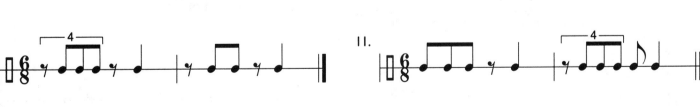

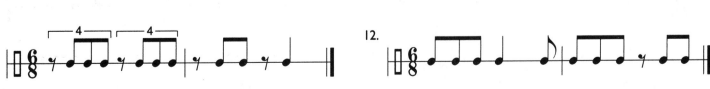

SIGNIFICANT ARTISTS AND ENSEMBLES

FOLLOWING IS A SMALL LIST OF SIGNIFICANT ARTISTS AND ENSEMBLES GROUPED BY INSTRUMENT AND BY STYLISTIC ORIENTATIONS. KEEP IN MIND THAT ALTHOUGH AN ARTIST might be listed under one instrument or style, chances are that many are more than adept at several, but are more well known as players of one particular instrument, or association or contributions to a specific style. This is frequently the case with percussionists and with composers and arrangers. I've listed individuals where they are most widely known. A book larger than this one could easily be written listing only the great players of these instruments and music and still not list them all. I apologize for the omission of many musicians but it is simply a matter of happenstance. There are texts with more complete reference sections. This list is meant to familiarize players first coming to this music with the names of key figures in order for them to get exposure to great instrumentalists and various musical forms. Listening to and studying these artists and ensembles will serve as the best reference for how the examples in this book should be played. It will also help in acquiring the musical vocabulary necessary to perform on these instruments and in these styles.

Timbaleros

Tito Puente
Jose Luis "Changuito" Quintana
Ubaldo Nieto
Humberto Morales
Endel Dueño
Orestes Vilató
Guillermo Barretto
Jimmy Delgado
Nicky Marrero
Manny Oquendo
Elio Revé
Jose Eladio
Marc Quiñones
Ralph Irrizary
Willie Bobo
Mike Collazo
Ray Romero
Carlos Montecino
Carlos Muñoz

Congueros

Ray Barretto
Francisco Aguabella
Milton Cardona
Candido

Tatá Guines
Giovanni Hidalgo
Eddie Montalvo
Bobby Allende
Papo Pepin
Armando Peraza
Daniel Ponce
Mongo Santamaria
Chano Pozo
Poncho Sanchez
Carlos "Patato" Valdez
Orlando "Puntilla" Rios

Bongoceros

Ray Romero
Armando Peraza
*Most of the artists listed in the Timbales and Congas section would be able to play Bongos, Bell and other percussion—guiro, maracas, clave. Also, in dance orchestras vocalists are usually playing the guiro and maracas.

Drum Set

Guillermo Barretto

Jose Luis "Changuito" Quintana
Jose Eladio
Steve Berrios
Horacio Hernandez
Ignacio Berroa
Enrique Plá
Jose Martinez

Pianists

Bebo Valdez
"Chucho" Valdez
Ernesto Lecuona
Antonio Roméu
Ché Belén Puig
Anselmo Sacasas
Pedro "Peruchín" Justiz
Lily Martinez
Frank Emilio
Papo Lucca
Clare Fischer
Larry Harlow
Oscar Hernandez
Eddie Martinez
Noro Morales
Charlie Palmieri
Eddie Palmieri
Pérez Prado

Gonzalo Rubalcaba
Emiliano Salvador
Jorge Dalto

___

Bassists

Israel "Cacháo" Lopez
Oscar D'León
Carlos Del Puerto
Juan Formell
Andy Gonzales
Ruben Rodriguez
Lincoln Goines
Sal Cuevas
Bobby Valentín

___

Tres, Cuatro

Isaac Oviedo (tres)
Yomo Toro (cuatro)
Arsenio Rodriguez (tres)
Papi Oviedo (tres)
El Niño Rivera (tres)

___

Folkloric Ensembles/Artists

Los Muñequitos de Matanzas
Los Papines
Papín y sus Rumberos
Orlando "Puntilla" Rios
Grupo Afro Cuba
Grupo Folklorico de Cuba
Totico y sus Rumberos
Carlos Embale
Conjunto Clave y Guaguancó
Pello El Afrokan/Los Afrokanes
Grupo Afro-Cubano
Milton Cardona
Carlos Embale
Grupo Afro-Cubano de Alberto
Zayas
Grupo Folklorico de Alberto Zayas

___

Popular Music Groups/Artists

Adalberto y su Son
Machito
Ray Barretto
Carlos Embale
Mario Bauzá
Tito Puente
Celia Cruz

Eddie Palmieri
Charlie Palmieri
Ruben Blades
Luis "Perico" Ortiz
Felix Chappottín y Conjuntos
Conjunto Afro Cuba
Willie Colón
Johnny Pacheco
Mongo Santamaria
Irakére
Oscar D'León
Orquesta Aragón
Jose Fajardo
Roberto Roena/Apollo Sound
Septeto Anacaona
Antonio Arcaño y sus Maravillas
Orquesta Batachanga
Batacumbele
Conjunto Clásico
Fania All Stars
Beny Moré
Jerry Gonzalez and Fort Apache
El Gran Combo
Havana Cuban Boys
440
Lecuona Cuban Boys
Sonora Matancera
Grupo Níche
Sonora Poncena
NG La Banda
Orquesta Original de Manzanillo
Orquesta Revé
Orquesta Ritmo Oriental
Conjunto Rumbavana
Sexteto Habanero
Sexteto Boloña
Septeto Nacional
Conjunto Son 14
Orquesta Típica '73
Los Van Van
Arsenio Rodriguez
Orquesta Broadway
Manny Oquendo y Conjunto Libre
Talking Drums

SUGGESTED LISTENING AND READING

FOLLOWING IS A LIST OF RECORDINGS FOR LISTENING TO AND STUDYING THE STYLES PRESENTED IN THIS BOOK. THIS IS ONLY A VERY SMALL SAMPLING OF what's available, but there are examples listed of music in every style presented here. Listening to any recordings of the groups and artists presented on the previous pages is highly recommended. Additionally, here are some names of specific recordings. Cuban releases are difficult to get in the States although more are becoming available, especially in the New York, Miami, and San Francisco areas. Most Cuban recordings are released in every other part of the world so if you tour or have friends abroad, they are quite easy to acquire in Europe, Japan, and most of Latin America. The same is the case for books, periodicals, and literature.

Conjunto de Clave y Guaguancó
Cantaremos y Bailaremos

Los Muñequitos de Matanzas
Rumba Caliente 88/77
Cantar Maravilloso
Guaguancó, Columbia, Yambú
Los Muñequitos de Matanzas
Folklore Matancero
Congo Yambumba
Vacunao

Conjunto Afro Cuba
Afro Cuba
Eclipse de Sol

Los Papines
Fantasia en Ritmo
Papín y sus Rumberos
Los Papines
Homenaje a Mis Colegas
El Retorno a La Semilla
Somos Del Caribe

Papín y sus Rumberos
Guaguancó—Conjunto...Matancero

Grupo Folklorico de Cuba
Toques y Cantos de Santos

Grupo Afro-Cubano
Congas y Comparsas—Carnaval...

Orlando "Puntilla" Rios

...from La Habana to New York

Milton Cardona
Bembé

Totico y sus Rumberos
Totico y sus Rumberos
Patato y Totico

Conjunto Guaguancó Matancero
Guaguancó

Carlos "Patato" Valdez
Patato y Totico

Carlos Embale
Carlos Embale
Los Roncos Chiquitos

Grupo Afro-Cubano de Alberto Zayas
Tambores de Cuba...

Grupo Folklorico de Alberto Zayas
Guaguancó Afro-Cubano: El Vive...

Pello El Afrokan/Los Afrokanes
Un Sabor Que Canta
Congas Del Barrio

Adalberto y su Son
Adalberto y su Son

Orquesta Aragón
Album de Oro Vol. I & II

Disco de Oro 50 Aniversario
Danzónes
Ultimos Exitos de Aragón
Charangas y Pachangas

Jose Fajardo
Saludos from Fajardo
Fajardo y sus Estrellas

Antonio Arcañó y sus Maravillas
Arcañó y sus Maravillas

Ray Barretto
Ricanstruction
La Cuna
The Message
Aqui Se Puede
Indestructible
Que Viva la Musica
Todo se Va a Poder
The Other Road
From the Beginning
Tomorrow: Barretto Live
Ritmo de la Vida
Handprints

Orquesta Batachanga
La Nueva Tradición

Batacumbele
Con Un Poco de Songo
En Aquellos Tiempos
Live at the University of Puerto Rico
Afro-Caribbean Jazz

Ruben Blades
Bohemio y Poeta
Caminando
Escenas
Buscando America
Live

Orquesta Broadway
Pasaporte
Esta Pegando

Felix Chappottín
Chappottín y sus Estrellas
Mi Son, Mi Son, Mi Son

Willie Colón
La Gran Fuga
El Juicio
El Malo
Lo Mato
There Goes the Neighborhood

Ruben Blades & Willie Colón
Metiendo Mano
Siembra

Orquesta Típica '73
Típica '73
Charangueando
Rumba Caliente

Celia Cruz
Canta Celia Cruz
Canciones Premiadas

Celia Cruz y Johnny Pacheco
Tremendo Caché

Celia Cruz y Sonora Matancera
Homenaje a los Santos

Celia Cruz y Tito Puente
Homenaje a Beny Moré
Cuba y Puerto Rico Son

Oscar D'León
Canta la Musica Cubana
Con Bajo y Todo
La Salsa yo Soy

Fania All Stars
Lo Que Pide la Gente
The Perfect Blend

Live at the Red Garter

Jerry Gonzales & Fort Apache
Rumba Para Monk
Obatalá
Ya Yo Me Curé
River is Deep
Earth Dance

El Gran Combo
De Punta a Punta
Mejor Que Nunca
25th Anniversary
Smile

Irakére
Bailando Así
Irakére
Chekeré Son
Irakére en Vivo
Misa Negra
Tierra en Trance
In London (Vol I & II)
Homenaje a Beny Moré

La 440
Ven, Sígueme

Israel "Cacháo" Lopez
Cuban Jam Sessions in Miniature
Descargas con El Ritmo de Cacháo
Dos
Maestro de Maestros
Cacháo '77
(also on "Patato y Totico")

Machito
Mucho Macho
Afro-Cuban Jazz
Machito and His Afro-Cubans
Greatest Hits
Tremendo Cumban
Machito Plays Mambo and Cha-Cha
At the Crescendo
Dance Date with Machito
Latin Soul Plus Jazz

Machito (on Dizzy Gillespie Record)
Afro-Cuban Jazz Moods

Sonora Matancera
Desfile de Estrellas
En Tu Busca

Ahí Viene La Sonora Matancera
Sus Grandes Exitos
50 Años de La Sonora Matancera

Noro Morales
His Piano and Rhythm
En Su Ambiente

Beny Moré
Asi Es Beny
El Inigualable
Sonero Mayor
Y Hoy Como Ayer
Beny Moré

NG La Banda
En La Calle
No Se Puede Tapar el Sol

Grupo Níche
Grandes Exitos
Cielo de Tambores
Grupo Níche

Orquesta Revé
Mi Salsa Tiene Sandinga
Suave Suave
Explosión Del Momento

Orquesta Ritmo Oriental
La Ritmo Te Está Llamando
Historia de la Ritmo (Vol I & II)
30 Años

Orquesta Original de Manzanillo
Yo Vengo de Allá Léjos
Luis Perico Ortiz
One of a Kind

Johnny Pacheco
El Maestro
Pacheco y su Charanga
Early Rhythms
Tres de Café y Dos de Azucar

Charlie Palmieri
Impulsos
A Giant Step

Eddie Palmieri
Azucar Pa' Ti
Sentido
Echando Pa'lante

Unfinished Masterpiece
El Molestoso
Justicia
La Verdad
Lo Que Traigo es Sabroso
Lucumi Macumba Voodoo
Palo Pa' Rumba
Mambo con Conga es Mozambique
The Sun of Latin Music
Echoes of an Era (Charanga Du-
boney)

Pedro Justiz/"Peruchín"
The Incendiary Piano of Peruchín
Piano and Rhythm

Daniel Ponce
New York Now

Tito Puente
El Rey
Dance Mania
Cuban Carnival
Goza Mi Timbal
Mambo Diablo
Pa'lante
Para Los Rumberos
Puente Goes Jazz
Top Percussion
Puente Now
Salsa Meets Jazz
Mamborama
Un Poco Loco
Homenaje a Beny Moré (Vol. I & II)
Ce' Magnifique (with Azuquita)
Carnival in Harlem
Puente in Percussion

Cal Tjader
Soul Sauce
Tjader Plays Mambo

Arsenio Rodriguez
Mano a Mano (with Antonio Arcañó)
Arsenio Rodriguez y su Conjunto
A Todos Los Barrios
Sabroso y Caliente
Exitos
Quindembo
Primitivo
(also on "Patato y Totico")

Gonzalo Rubalcaba

Live in Havana (Vol. I & II)
Grupo Proyecto de ...
Giraldilla

Conjunto Rumbavana
Déjale Que Baile Sola

Emiliano Salvador
Musica Contemporanea Cubana
2
Emiliano Salvador y su Grupo

Mongo Santamaria
Drums and Chants
Yambú
Afro Roots
Skins
Sabroso
Greatest Hits

**Septeto Nacional de Ignacio
Piñeiro**
Recordando al Septeto Nacional...
Bienvenida Grande Con el Septeto...

Sexteto Boloña
La Historia del Son Cubano-
The Roots of Salsa (Vol I)

Sexteto Habanero
La Historia del Son Cubano-
The Roots of Salsa (Vol II)
Colleccion de Óro

Conjunto Son 14
Ambassadors of Son
Y Sigue el Son

Jesus "Chucho" Valdez
Lucumi Piano Solo

Conjunto Casino
Conjunto Casino
Bailando Con El Conjunto Casino

Merceditas Valdez
Aché (I, II, III)

Los Van Van
Songo
Que Pista
De Cuba Los Van Van
Sandungera

El Son Del Caribe
Aqui el que Baila Gana
Anda Ven y Muévete

Tito Rodriguez
Esta Es Mi Historia
Tito, Tito, Tito

**Roberto Roena y su Apollo
Sound**
Roberto Roena y su Apollo Sound
El Progreso

**Manny Oquendo y Conjunto
Libre**
Sonido, Estilo y Ritmo
Con Salsa, Con Ritmo
Tiene Calidad

Series/Compilations/Anthologies
Cuba-Les Danses des Dieux
Cult Music of Cuba
Antologia de la Musica Afro-
Cubana (Various Volumes)
The Cuban Danzón: Its Ancestors
and Descendants
Cuban Jam Sessions Under the
direction of Julio Gutierrez (Vol. I & II)
Cuban Jam Sessions Under the
direction of Nino Rivera (Vol. III)
Cubanismo

FOLLOWING IS A SMALL LIST OF SUGGESTED READING MATERIALS FOR FURTHER RESEARCH followed by the names and addresses of several resource centers where recordings, literature, and other information can be obtained. (Some of these are Spanish language texts.)

La Africania de la Musica Folklorica de Cuba
Dr. Fernando Ortiz
2nd Ed. (Havana) Editora Universitaria

La Musica Afrocubana
Dr. Fernando Ortiz
(Madrid) Ediciones Júcar

Los Instrumentos de la Musica Afrocubana
Dr. Fernando Ortiz
(Havana) Ediciones del Ministerio de Educación de Cuba

African Rhythm and Sensibility
John Chernoff
University of Chicago Press

Diccionario de la Musica Cubana
Helio Orovio
(Havana) Editorial Letras Cubanas

El Libro de la Salsa: Cronica de la Musica del Caribe Urbano
César Miguel Rondón
(Caracas) Editorial Arte

La Musica, lo Cubano y la Inovación
Leo Brouwer
(Havana) Editorial Letras Cubanas

Musica Folklorica Cubana
Argeliers León
(Havana) Ediciones del Departamento de Musica de la Biblioteca Nacional Jose Martí

Del Canto y el Tiempo
Argeliers León
(Havana) Editorial Letras Cubanas

La Binarización de los Ritmos Ternarios Africanos en America Latina
Rolando Antonio Pérez Fernandez
(Havana) Casa de las Americas

La Musica en Cuba
Alejo Carpentier
(Havana) Editorial Letras Cubanas

Apuntes Para la Investigacion del Negro en Venezuela
Alejo Carpentier
(Caracas) Tipografía Garido

Sonido Urbano
Edgar Borges
(Caracas) Fondo Editorial Tropicos

Salsiology
Vernon Boggs
Excelsior Music Publishing

The Music of Santeria
John Amira & Steve Cornelius
White Cliffs Media

Salsa: The Rhythm of Latin Music
Charley Gerard with Marty Sheller
White Cliffs Media

To Be or Not To Bop
Dizzy Gillespie & Al Frazer
Doubleday

Del Tambor al Sintetizador
Leonardo Acosta
(Havana) Editorial Letras Cubanas

Resource centers for books, recordings, literature, videos and other information on Afro-Latin Music.

Subway Records
42nd St. Subway Station
New York, NY

Qbadisc
PO Box 1256
Old Chelsea Station
New York, NY 10011

Descarga Mail Order Catalogue
(800) 377-2647

Bate Records
140 Delancey St.
New York, NY 10002
(212) 677-3180

Tower Records
Some stores in the chain have good *World Music* sections with good Afro-Latin selections.

Center for Cuban Studies
124 West 23rd St.
New York, NY 10011
(212) 242-0559

World Music Institute
109 West 27th St.
New York, NY 10011
(212) 206-1050

Caribbean Cultural Center
408 West 58th St.
New York, NY 10019
(212) 307-7420

GLOSSARY

Abacuá/Abakuá/Abakwa—
1. A secret fraternal and initially all male society developed in Cuba by the African Carabalí people. 2. The musical styles of the Abacuá people and folkloric ensembles.

Abanico—
The Spanish word for fan, used to describe the Timbale figure (roll and accent) played to introduce or close sections and to set up various ensemble passages.

Acheré (Atcheré)—
A small rattle or shaker made of metal, or gourd used to play the standard bell patterns or other accompaniments in Batá ensembles.

Agbé—
The Yoruba name for the beaded calabash gourds, also called Shekeré/Chekeré or Guiro.

Agogo—
Pair of bells of Yoruban origin used in the Bembé and other ritual ceremonies.

Apanpichao—
The third section of a Merengue arrangement. Similar to the Montuno or Mambo sections of Salsa arrangements

Arará—
Dahomean ritual/ceremonial drums brought to the Oriente province of Cuba by the Haitian emigres after the Haitian slave rebellion of 1791.

Bantú—
The African Congolese people and culture.

Baqueteo—
The rhythmic pattern played by the timbalero in the Danzón.

Batá—
Sacred hourglass-shaped drums of Yoruban/Nigerian origin used in the Santeria religious ceremonies.

Bembé—
1. A religious gathering and festivity held to honor an Oricha. 2. A set of traditional drums made from hollowed palm tree logs used in the Bembé ceremonies.

Bomba—
1. A folkloric songstyle (rhythm and dance) of Puerto Rico with predominantly African influence. 2. Large barrel-shaped drums used in the Bomba style.

Bombo—
1. The Spanish term for bass drum. 2. The bass drum used in the Rumba and other folkloric styles. 3. Term used to describe the "and of beat 2" of the three side of the clave rhythm. This is the note emphasized by the bass drum.

Bolero—
An Afro-Latin ballad form usually with romantic lyric content.

Bongo(s)—
Small pair of single-headed drums tuned high in pitch and played while held between the players legs. They perform a combination of timekeeping pattern and improvised rhythmic variation or counterpoint within an ensemble.

Bongocero—
The bongo (and bell) player.

Botija—
A clay jug originally used to import Spanish olive oil into the New World regions, it became one of the first bass instruments of the Son style.

Buleador—
The basic rhythmic pattern of the Bomba style played on the Bomba drum.

Caballo ("A Caballo")—
1. Spanish term for horse. 2. In Afro-Latin music it is used to describe a rhythmic accompaniment that resembles in feel to the trotting of a horse. 3. Rhythmic accompaniment to the Pachanga style.

Cajón/Cajónes—
Resonant wooden crates of various sizes (originally crates to box and transport cod), used to play the early forms of Rumba. They are still used today by folkloric ensembles.

Campana—
1. Cowbell. 2. Term used specifically for the large hand-held bell played by the bongocero in a dance ensemble.

Campesinos—
(Cuban) peasant people. Sometimes referred to as Guajiros.

Canción—
Spanish songstyle focusing primarily on the lyrics/melody and a simple guitar accompaniment, it became one of the fundamental components in the development of the Son style.

Carabalí—
The people of the African Calabar region. They were the primary exponents of the Abacuá societies in Cuba.

Carnaval—(Carnival)
The Christian pre-Lent celebration usually lasting from three days to a week.

Cascara—
1. Shell. 2. Term used to describe the wooden shells

of the early timbales, still used today to describe the shells of any timbal. 3. Term used for the rhythmic pattern played on the sides (shells) of the timbales.

Cencerro—
Another term for the large cowbell (Campana).

Chachá—
The smaller of the two heads of the Batá drums.

Cha-Cha-Cha—
A dance and musical style emanating from the Nuevo Ritmo of the Danzón style.

Changuí—
1. The early predecessors to the Son groups using the original instrumentation of Guiro, Maracas, Bongo, Tres, and Marimbula. Some ensembles still performing today. 2. The early style of the Son performed by these groups.

Charanga—
1. Ensembles: Cuban groups that interpret the Danzón style. 2. Initially called Charanga Francesa, European influenced in their instrumentation of woodwinds, string section, and rhythm section of string bass, European tympani (which later became the timbales), and guiro. 2. General term for the music played by these ensembles.

Chekeré—
(Alternate spelling of shekeré) Calabash gourds of various sizes strung with beads.

Cierre—
A rhythmic break, either an arranged ensemble passage or only played by the percussion in either arranged or improvised fashion usually played as a transition to or from a section of a piece.

Cinquillo—
A five-note group of notes derived from the Son clave pattern that is both a part of the baqueteo—the timbale accompaniment to the Danzón—as well as a common rhythmic articulation in both arranged and improvised performance. The term also describes the interpretive performance (stretching) of the five notes of the clave pattern. This interpretation also applies to the Tresillo. See Tresillo.

Clave—
1. Instrument. Pair of polished sticks used to play the clave rhythm. 2. Rhythm. One of four two-bar rhythms serving as the key to Afro-Latin musical styles. Four types, two $\frac{6}{8}$ variations and the Rumba and Son.

Columbia—
One of the three Rumba styles, it is played in $\frac{6}{8}$, sung with a combination of Spanish and African lyrics, and traditionally danced only by men in a dance often depicting a challenge to each other. Played with the tumbadoras, guataca or cowbell, and clave and sometimes shekerés and bombo.

Combo—
Type of Latin ensemble developed in the 1950s through the influence of the jazz groups and big bands that employed the drum set, bass piano in the jazz rhythm section format, along with all of the standard Latin percussion of timbales (played by the drum set player, congas, and the like. They also employed saxophones and sometimes guitar.

Comparsa—
1. A musical gathering, dance, and parade taking place primarily during the Cuban Carnaval. 2. Term sometimes (incorrectly) used to describe the music that accompanies this dance and parade—the Conga.

Conga—
The musical instrumentation and style that accompanies the Comparsa, it is also a style developed, performed and integrated by ensembles separate form the Carnaval Comparsas. Sometimes the style is referred to by regional interpretation—as in Conga Habanera or Conga Santiaguera.

Congas—
Also called Tumbadoras, the single headed, hollowed Cuban drums derived from the Congolese Makuta drums. Initially made from hollowed logs with cowhides nailed or strung on, they are now made of wood and fiberglass with mass-produced hardware and heads.

Conguero—
A conga drummer.

Conjunto—
A style of Latin ensemble developed in the 1940s. It emanated from the Septeto instrumentation and was another interpreter of the Son styles. Originally consisting of the tres, contrabass, bongos, brass, and vocalists that played clave, maracas, and guiro. Later the guitar, piano, and congas were added.

Contradanza-
A European musical form and dance that was the predecessor to the Danza, Danza Habanera, and most significantly the Danzón style.

Corneta China/Trompeta China—
The Chinese trumpet used in the early Carnaval Comparsas and the first brass instrument to be added to the Sexteto ensembles, creating the Septeto.

Córo/Córo-Pregón—
Córo is chorus and the Córo Pregón is the call-and-response between the lead vocal, the Pregón—which is generally improvised—and the chorus, the Córo—which is generally arranged or a fixed part. It is a principal structural element of the Son and became a part of the traditional commercial Latin dance form via the Montuno section of an arrangement.

Conversación—
A conversation. In Batá performance, the conversation

and interaction that takes place between the Iyá (the lead or mother drum) and the Itótele (the middle drum).

Cuá—
The rhythmic stick pattern of the Puerto Rican Bomba style. It sometimes functions as a clave in this style.

Cuatro—
Guitar-like instrument derived from the Cuban Tres but containing four sets of two strings. Primarily associated with Puerto Rican styles.

Cucharas—
Spoons. Initially used to play the palitos accompaniment to the Cajones in the early Rumba styles. Still used today in folkloric ensemble presentations.

Danza—
Musical style and dance emanating from the Contradanza and a predecessor to the Danzón.

Danzón—
Songstyle and dance emanating from the Contradanza, Danza, and Danza Habanera and interpreted by the Charanga orchestras and instrumentation. Originally an ABAC form (A-Paseo [introduction], B-Flute melody, A-repeat of the Paseo, C-String Trio). Later a D section (the Nuevo Ritmo) was added creating an ABACD form. This D section integrated elements of the Cuban Son and spawned the Mambo as well as developments of the Montuno section of arrangements and later the Cha-Cha-Cha.

Décima—
The ten line verse structure common to the Spanish Cancion, it served as the traditional verse structure of the Cuban Son.

Descarga—
To unload. An instrumental improvisation or jam.

Diana—
A vocal introduction, (sometimes arranged, sometimes improvised) call-and-response style used in some Rumba styles.

El Barrio—
The name given to the East Harlem section of New York City in the 1920s and '30s after the migration and settlement of vast numbers of Puerto Rican and Cuban people in this area. Another term for Spanish Harlem.

Estribillo—
A vocal refrain or chorus, the term applies particularly to the vocal choruses of the Son style.

Gua-Gua—
1. Latin-American slang term used for a bus or a van. 2. The term used for the hollowed bamboo piece that is mounted and used to play the Palitos patterns. The Gua-Gua is said to "drive the ensemble."

Guaguancó—
One of the three Rumba styles, it is a medium to fast style played on the tumbadoras or cajones along with the clave, palitos, bombo and shekerés and danced traditionally by a male and a female depicting the sexual "capture" of the female by the male with a thrust called the Vacunáo.

Guajéo—
Originally the term used to describe the repeated rhythmic figure of the Tres in the Changui and Son styles, it was later also used to describe the same function by the string section in the Charangas and later the Moñas of the horn section.

Guajira—
1. A songstyle originating with the Campesinos (peasants) containing elements of the Spanish Cancion and the Cuban Son. It is societally somewhat of a parallel to the Blues of America. The lyric content is sometimes sad or longing, nostalgic or expressing the difficulties of an impoverished lifestyle. 2. Slang term for a Cuban peasant woman.

Guajiro—
A slang term for a (male) Cuban peasant and sometimes used as a term for a cowboy-type peasant farmer or rancher.

Guaracha—
1. Traditionally an early form of street or peasant music with satirical lyric content somewhat in the Son rhythm style. 2. Loose term for a general medium tempo Son Montuno or little brighter style tune or groove.

Guataca—
A hoe blade (played with a large nail or railroad spike) used to play what later became cowbell accompaniments to the Rumba Columbia and other folkloric Afro $\frac{6}{8}$ styles. Folkloric ensembles still use this instrument.

Guicharo—
Term used to describe guiros with finer ridges, particularly those found in some Puerto Rican styles.

Guira—
The term used to describe the metal scraper (guiro, scraped with a metal fork or Afro comb) used in the Dominican Merengue style.

Guiro—
1. (Instrument) Calabash gourd with ridges carved into the front and scraped with a stick. 2. (Rhythm) A $\frac{6}{8}$ rhythm acquiring this name because it is played with guiros—the initial name for what is now generally known as shekerés.

Habanera—
Style emanating from the Contradanza and Danza, it was the final precursor to the Danzón style.

Hierro—
Term used to describe the Guataca—the hoe blade—or other metal sound used as the cowbell

accompaniment to the Rumba Columbia and other folkloric Afro ⅜ styles.

Itótele—
The middle drum of the set of three Batá drums.

Iyá—
The lead drum (mother drum, Iyá Ilú) of the set of three Batá drums. Also the largest of the three.

Jaleo—
The second section of the merengue as well as the name of the tambora pattern played in this section of an arrangement.

Llame—
The call used in Batá performance to begin playing or to begin a conversation between the Iyá and the Itótele.

Lucumi—
The term used as the name of the Yoruban people in Cuba as well as their language and religion.

Mambo—
1. The musical section that evolved in the late 1930s and 1940s from the Nuevo Ritmo of the Danzón. 2. Up-tempo musical style that evolved in the 1940s and '50s as a blending of the mambo *section*, elements of the Son, and some influences of American Jazz orchestras. 3. A section of an arrangement usually following or developing from the Montuno section featuring newly arranged (or sometimes improvised) material such as Moñas in the horn section.

Maracas—
Canister rattles with handles originally made from gourds or rawhide and filled with beads, pebbles, seeds, or the like. Hand held and played in pairs.

Marimbula—
A large resonant wooden box with a (kalimba-like) thumb piano constructed over an opening in the box. It is of Congolese Bantú origin and was the original bass instrument in the Changui groups. The player sits on the box and plucks at the metal keys and strikes rhythmic figures on the box itself.

Martillo—
1. Hammer. 2. Name of the rhythm played on the Bongos. It is primarily a timekeeping pattern but the performance in an ensemble includes many improvised variations called repiques.

Merengue—
Songstyle of the Dominican Republic. Generally fast in tempo. Traditionally played on the Tambora, Guira, and Accordion; current ensembles feature a full rhythm section, alto saxophones and trumpets, congas and sometimes drum set.

Montuno—
1. Section of an arrangement featuring the Córo/ Pregón of the lead vocalist and chorus as well as instrumental solos. 2. Term used to describe the

repetitive rhythmic figure played by the piano.

Moña—
Layered parts played by the horn section featuring staggered entrances, layered and contrapuntal parts, and generally a building intensity. Usually introduced during the Mambo section of an arrangement or cued in during the Montuno section. They are generally written but sometimes improvised.

Mozambique—
Rhythm emanating from the Conga rhythm of the Cuban Carnaval Comparsas, created and developed in Cuba by Pello el Afrokan in the early 1960s. Originally a percussion rhythm, it later became a full ensemble style and was first popularized in the United States in the mid and late 1960s by Eddie Palmieri.

Nuevo Ritmo—
The D section added to the end of the Danzón in the late 1930s and early 1940s. Created by bassist/composer Israel "Cacháo" Lopez, it served as the takeoff point for the Mambo, montuno section, and later the Cha-Cha.

Okónkolo—
The smallest of the set of three Batá drums, it serves primarily as the timekeeper.

Orichas (Orishas)—
Deities of the pantheistic Santeria and other African, Afro-Latin, and Afro-Caribbean based religions.

Orquesta Típica—
Orchestras that were the traditional interpreters of the early forms of the various Danzas. Their instrumentation consisted of woodwinds, brass, strings, the guiro, and the traditional European tympani.

Pailas—
1. Another name for the timbales, sometimes used to describe a pair that is smaller than the larger orchestra timbales. 2. Paila is also a term used to describe the sides or shells of the timbales. "Play paila" means play the sides or play cascara.

Palito(s)—
1. Pair of sticks traditionally used to play the Gua-Gua that accompanies the Rumba styles. 2. The name of the patterns played on the Gua-Gua. In nontraditional settings the patterns can be played on any wood sound.

Pambiche—
Dominican rhythm that is a derivative of the Merengue and often written into Merengue arrangements.

Panderetas—
The name of the (jingle-less) tambourines used in the Puerto Rican Plena style.

Paseo—
1. The A section (introduction) to the Danzón form. 2. The short introduction to some Merengue arrangements.

Plena—

A folkloric Puerto Rican songstyle traditionally played on the Panderetas. The lyric content often deals with social or political statements, criticisms, or satire.

Ponche—
Term used to describe beat four of the three side of the clave or any of the rhythmic variations played off of this beat.

Pregón/Córo-Pregón)—
The lead part of the call-and-response between the lead vocalist and the chorus.

Quijada—
Instrument made from the jawbone of a donkey or mule and played by striking the lower jaw against the upper producing a sharp rattle effect. Today's Vibra-Slap was made to replicate the sound of the traditional Quijada.

Quinto—
The smallest, highest pitched and lead drum of the three tumbadoras used in the Rumba styles. Its role is an improvisational one in which it interacts with the vocals and dancers as well as plays solo features.

Rebajador—
The middle drum part in the Conga style (Conga, Rebajador, Salidor).

Requinto—
The lead drum in the Bomba style.

Rumba—
Three forms: Guaguancó, Yambú, and Columbia. An Afro-Cuban musical form comprised of drumming, call-and-response vocals, and dancing.

Rumba Flamenca—
A style of Rumba from southern Spain which greatly influenced the development of the Cuban Rumba styles.

Salidor—
1. In the Conga style, the high drum of the three basic tumbadora parts (Conga, Rebajador, Salidor).
2. In the Rumba Guaguancó, the low drum of the three parts (Salidor, Tres Golpes, Quinto).

Salsa—
1. Spanish term meaning sauce, usually a hot sauce.
2. Generic term developed in the early 1970s used to describe the blending of numerous specific styles into dance orchestra arrangements.

Santeria—
The pantheistic religion of the Yoruban/Nigerian people and the Yoruban/Lucumi culture of Cuba, as well as of Afro-Caribbean and others throughout the world. Marked by the multi-deity concept of various Orichas and the use of the Batá drums in the ritual ceremonies.

Sartenes—
Small frying pans welded together and used as bells for patterns in the Conga/Comparsa Carnaval styles. They originated as makeshift descendants of the African Agogo bell.

Segundo—
The name used to describe the second or middle drum (the tres golpes) in the set of three used in the Rumba styles. Also loosely used to describe the second drum in a pair or the middle drum in a set of three.

Septeto—
The Son ensemble that resulted from the addition of the Trompeta China (and later the trumpet) to the Sexteto ensemble. (Most prominent was the Septeto Nacional de Ignacio Piñeiro, founded in 1927).

Sexteto—
The initial form of Son group emanating from the Changui groups consisting of the tres, contrabass, guitar, bongos, maracas, and clave with vocals. (Most prominent was the Sexteto Habanero founded in 1920).

Shekeré—
(Alternate spelling of chekeré) Calabash gourds of various sizes strung with beads.

Son—
Most influential Cuban style initiating in the second half of the nineteenth century in the eastern province of Oriente. It combines Spanish elements of the Cancion style and instruments with African rhythm and percussion. Early forms were interpreted by the Campesinos and developed by the Changui groups.

Son Montuno—
Style emanating from the Son tradition.

Songo—
Contemporary Cuban rhythm which is a combination of Rumba, Son, and other folkloric styles. Its development has also been influenced by American Jazz and funk styles as well as American approaches to the rhythm section instruments in these styles.

Tambora—
Barrel-shaped double-headed drum from the Dominican Republic used in the Merengue style. The drum is played with a stick which strikes one head and the wooden shell of the drum, and the hand which plays the opposite head.

Timbales—
Pair of tunable drums mounted on a stand and played with sticks and some timekeeping strokes made directly with the hand on the lower drum. Measuring in sizes from 13" to 15" in diameter they are paired as 13" and 14" or 14" and 15". Initially used exclusively by the Charangas interpreting the Danzón, they became part of the Latin orchestra in the 1940s and are now a mainstay and signature sound of many Afro-Latin styles. The standard set now includes cowbells, woodblocks, and a cymbal. They descended from the European tympani.

Timbalitos—

Smaller and higher pitched versions of the standard timbales measuring in sizes from 9" to 12", they are usually added to the standard set for a setup of four drums and are mostly used in soloing.

Típico—
1. Spanish term for typical or traditional. 2. Term specifically used to describe the Orquesta Típica. 3. Term informally used to describe a traditional, folkloric or "old-style" sound or approach to playing an instrument or style.

Tres—
A smaller derivative of the Spanish guitar with either three sets of two strings or sometimes three sets of three strings. It is a key instrument and signature sound of the Changui and Son style.

Tres Golpes—
Term used to describe the middle drum (Salidor, Tres Golpes, Quinto) as well as the pattern played on this drum in the Rumba Guaguancó.

Tresillo—
Spanish term for triplet, it is used to describe the three-note group of the three side of the clave when the rhythmic interpretation is "in the cracks" between the duple and triple meter. In the Son parallel of the Afro $\frac{6}{8}$ clave, the rhythm is a literal triplet. In the Son clave it is an interpretive triplet. The tresillo functions the same as the cinquillo. See Cinquillo.

Trompeta China (Corneta China)—
See Corneta China.

Trova (Cancion)—
Another term used to describe a style of the Spanish Cancion form.

Tumbadora—
The single-headed, hollowed Cuban drums derived from the Congolese Makuta drums. Initially made from hollowed logs with cowhides nailed or strung on, they are now made of wood and fiberglass with mass-produced hardware and heads. Also generically called Conga drums.

Tumba Francesa—
1. Style of music of Dahomean roots originally developed in the eastern province of Oriente by the slaves who emigrated to Cuba after the Haitian revolution in 1791. 2. The drums used to play the style.

Tumbaó (bass, congas)—
The standard timekeeping patterns performed by the bass and congas in the popular dance styles such as the Son, Son Montuno, Guaracha, Mambo, and the like.

Yambú—
A form of Rumba traditionally performed on the Cajones. It is a slow to medium tempo duple meter style and is danced by male-female couples but does not include the Vacunáo of the Rumba Guaguancó.

Yoruba—
Term used to describe the Nigerian (Yoruba) people, their language, folklore, and musical styles. It is one of the most influential African populations in Cuba, the Caribbean and northern South America, particularly the northern regions of Brazil.

AUDIO INDEX AND GUIDE

Following is a table of contents of the recorded examples. Though not every example notated is recorded on the CD's, practically every example and style is represented in the audio even though it may not be recorded with the examples of that instrument or style. For example, the Rumba Guaguancó is not really played on timbales except for nontraditional settings. Nonetheless, there are parts included both for accompanying the Guaguancó as well as imitating it on the timbales. For more variations to play on the timbales you should also look to the palitos and bombo sections, as well as the tumbadora section, as these are the parts that are generally adapted to the timbales. This scenario applies to every instrument and songstyle presented and is particularly relevant to the drum set, since most of the things played on the set are percussion parts. In the drum set section priority was given to recording the patterns and styles

that are specific to the drum set. If you want more Cha-Cha or Bolero parts for the set then go to the percussion instruments of that style and apply those patterns to the set. If you aren't hearing a specific part or style at a given section, check the other sections. Also keep in mind that specific rhythms are traditionally played on certain instruments and not on others. For example, the Abakuá is not played on the drum set, but there are adaptations of it recorded for the drum set both as accompanying as well as solo parts. The accompanying parts are almost always combinations of the specific percussion instrument parts actually played in that style. These are the real thing. The drum set parts are hybrid parts consisting of some traditional percussion parts as well as some drum set colors and variations. Your specific musical situations will tell you which to use.

Compact Disc 1

Part 1~The Percussion Instruments

Compact Disc I (continued)

Compact Disc 2

Part 11 Section 1~The Rhythm Section

Bass Chapter

Prog.	Audio Ex.	Description	Page/Example	
1	154-155	Basic old style tumbaó	149	1&2
	156	Basic tumbaó	149	3
	157	Basic Cha-Cha/old style Mambo	149	4
	158-160	Tumbaó variations	149	6-8
2	161	Basic Guajira riff	149	9
3	162	Basic tumbaó over common progression 1	150	11
	163	Basic tumbaó over common progression 2	150	13
4	164	Freestyle tumbaó 1 over one chord vamp	151	14
	165	Freestyle tumbaó 2 over one chord vamp	151	15
5	166	Freestyle tumbaó over common changes	151	16
6	167	Cachaó Descarga riff	152	18
7	168	Los Van Van style lines	152	20-22
8	169	Afro $\frac{6}{8}$ style tumbaós	152	23&26
9	170	Tumbaó over F Blues progression	153	27
10	171	Tumbaó over Green Dolphin Street in 2-3	153	28

Part 11 Section 1~The Rhythm Section cont.

Piano Chapter

Prog.	Audio Ex.	Description	Page/Example	
11	172	Basic single line montuno in 2-3	155	1
	173	Basic single line montuno in 3-2	155	3
	174-175	Alternate starts to 3-2 montuno	156	4&5
12	176	Basic montuno w harmony added	156	6
	177	Basic montuno w harmony & octave 2-3	156	8
	178	Basic montuno w harmony & octave 3-2	157	9
	179	Basic two hand montuno	157	10
	180	Basic montuno variation	157	12
13	181	3 Montunos over G7 vamp	158	14-16
14	182	Montuno over common chord progression 1	158	17
	183	Montuno over common chord progression 2	159	18
15	184	Cha-Cha riff 1	159	20
	185	Cha-Cha riff 2	159	21
16	186	Guajira riff 1	160	22
	187	Guajira riff 2	160	23

Guitar & Tres Chapter

Prog.	Audio Ex.	Description	Page/Example	
17	188-190	3 Son style guajeos	161	1-3

Strings Chapter

Prog.	Audio Ex.	Description	Page/Example	
18	191-195	5 Charanga segments	162	1-3, 5&6

Horn Section Chapter

Prog.	Audio Ex.	Description	Page/Example	
19	196&197	2 Moñas	163	1&2

Part 11 Section 11~Arrangements, Charts...

Recording of the Arrangement

Prog.	Audio Ex.	Description	Page/Example
20	198	Recording of score	167-174

Part 11 Section III~The Songstyles & Scores

Songstyles Chapter

Prog.	Audio Ex.	Description	Page/Example	
21	199	Son	180	
22	200	Son Montuno	181	1
23	201	Mambo	184	2
24	202	Danzón/Paseo section	185	1
	203	Danzón/Nuevo Ritmo section	186	2
25	204	Cha-Cha 1	187	1
	205	Cha-Cha 2	188	2
26	206	Rumba Guaguancó	206	
27	207	Rumba Columbia	207	
28	208	Conga de Comparsa	208	
29	209	Mozambique 1	209	1
	210	Mozambique 2	210	3
30	211	Songo	211	
31	212	Abakuá	212	
32	213	Merengue	213	

Part 111~The Drum Set

Cha-Cha Section

Prog.	Audio Ex.	Description	Page/Example	
33	214	Cha-Cha comp variation	203	2
	215	Cha-Cha comp variation	206	1
	216	Cha-Cha solo drum set variation	207	4
	217	Cha-Cha-Funk pattern	208	11

Bolero Section

Prog.	Audio Ex.	Description	Page/Example	
34	218	Bolero	211	4

Son Montuno Section

Prog.	Audio Ex.	Description	Page/Example	
35	219	Son Montuno	216	2

Mambo Section

Prog.	Audio Ex.	Description	Page/Example	
36	220	Mambo/Cascara on HH	218	2
	221	Basic drum set pattern	219	1
	222	Paila variations on HH	220	3
	223	Basic drum set pattern	222	1
	224	Basic drum set pattern	222	2
37	225	Workout 1/Bell patterns & System 1	225/228	1-15/Sys 1
38	226	Workout 200/Campana & Bell patterns	225/235	1-15/Sys200

Rumba Guaguancó Section

Prog.	Audio Ex.	Description	Page/Example	
39	227	Rumba Guaguancó variation	244	39
40	228	RH bell w LH variations	245-247	1-24
41	229	RH bell w LH pattern	248	3
	230	RH bell w LH pattern & BD variation	249	3
42	231	Solo DS Combination & Improvisation	249	1

Rumba Columbia Section

Prog.	Audio Ex.	Description	Page/Example	
43	232	Rumba Columbia variation	251	2
44	233	Rumba Columbia variation	251	3

Compact Disc 2 (continued)

Charanga Section

Prog.	Audio Ex.	Description	Page/Example	
45	234	Charanga variation	253	1

Songo Section

Prog.	Audio Ex.	Description	Page/Example	
46	235	HH, Rim & BD	255	1
47	236	Bell, Snare, BD & HH	255	2
48	237	Improvisation based on previous example		
49	238	2 bell combination	255	3
50	239	Basic pattern w BD variations	257-258	1-19
51	240	2 bar variations around set	259-260	1-8
52	241	4 bar variations around set	260-261	9,11,12,13
53	242	Improvisation based on 4 bar pattern #9		
54	243	Combination w LH & BD variations	263	17

Pilón Section

Prog.	Audio Ex.	Description	Page/Example	
55	244	Basic Pilón combination	268	1
56	245	Pilón variation	269	7
57	246	Pilón variation	269	9
58	247	Pilón variation	269	12
59	248	Variation from conga drum parts	269	2

Conga de Comparsa Section

Prog.	Audio Ex.	Description	Page/Example	
60	249	Clave & Bell combination	270	2
61	250	Clave & Bell combination	271	4
62	251	Snare & Bombo combination	273	1
63	252	Snare, Bombo & Conga combination	274	5
64	253	Snare, Bombo & Conga combination	274	6
65	254	Clave & Bell on Toms combination	274	8
66	255	Clave & Conga on Toms combination	274	13
67	256	Clave & Conga on Toms combination	275	18

Mozambique Section

Prog.	Audio Ex.	Description	Page/Example	
68	257	Bell & Bombo on Toms combination	278	8
69	258	Bell & Bombo on Toms combination	278	9
70	259	4 bar combinations	282-283	2,3,6,7

Batá Section

Prog.	Audio Ex.	Description	Page/Example	
71	260	Batá ¢ variation	286	1
72	261	Batá § variation	286	2

Joropo Section

Prog.	Audio Ex.	Description	Page/Example	
73	262	Joropo 2 bar variation 1	286	1
74	263	Joropo 2 bar variation 2	286	2
75	264	Joropo 4 bar variation	286	3

Bomba Section

Prog.	Audio Ex.	Description	Page/Example	
76	265	Basic 2 bar combination	287	1
77	266	4 bar combination	288	8
78	267	4 bar combination	288	9

Merengue Section

Prog.	Audio Ex.	Description	Page/Example	
79	268	Verse combinations	290	1-3
80	269	Apanpichao combinations	290	4-7

Abakuá Section

Prog.	Audio Ex.	Description	Page/Example	
81	270	Bell & Congas on Toms combination	294	1
82	271	Congas on Toms combination	294	3
83	272	Snare & Toms combination	294	5

Guiro & Bembé Section

Prog.	Audio Ex.	Description	Page/Example	
84	273	Guiro/Bembé combination	295	1
85	274	Guiro/Bembé combination	295	2
86	275	Guiro/Bembé combination	295	3
87	276	Guiro/Bembé combination	295	5
88	277	Guiro/Bembé combination	296	7

Cha-Chá Lokua Fun Section

Prog.	Audio Ex.	Description	Page/Example	
89	278	Cha-Cha Lokua Fun variation	297	1

Guajira in § Section

Prog.	Audio Ex.	Description	Page/Example	
90	279	Guajira in §	297	1

Afro § with Backbeat Section

Prog.	Audio Ex.	Description	Page/Example	
91	280	§ with Backbeat	298	1-6, 7

Ending Segment

Prog.	Audio Ex.	Description	Page/Example
92	281	Outro Segment	